CATECHISM FOR YOUTH

CARLOS MIGUEL BUELA

CATECHISM
FOR YOUTH

Based on the Catechism of the Catholic Church

IVE Press

New York – 2008

Nihil obstat	Imprimatur
Rev. Luis Kukovica, SJ	Manuel Menéndez
Censor	Bishop of San Martín
Buenos Aires - November 23, 1975.	San Martín - January 2,1976.

C 1

TABLE OF CONTENTS

PART TWO WHAT WE MUST RECEIVE 143

TO THE READER

Dear Reader,

Embrace this Catechism lovingly and with care. In it, you are going to learn about, or recall, the most important things in life, those things which are the delights of the saints and are sweet as honey for the wise.

Is there anything more important than God and the things of God? By no means. And so, you are going to learn to know, to love and to serve God. This is something greater than going to some faraway planet on a spaceship, or reaching the depths of the sea in a submarine, or traveling the length and breadth of the entire world. In this Catechism, you are going to "have the power to comprehend with all the saints what is the breadth and length, and height and depth, and to know the love of Christ which surpasses knowledge" (Eph 3:18-19).

Since God is so great and we are so small, we must always ask him, with great humility, to give light to our intellect, ardor to our hearts, and generosity to our wills, so that, in this Catechism and throughout our entire lives, we can know him better, love him more each day, and serve him as only he deserves.

The Author

* The page numbers between parenthesis ( ) refer to the Catechism of the Catholic Church and the brackets [ ], refer to this Catechism.

13

THE FOUR PARTS OF CATHOLIC DOCTRINE

All God taught—that is, all Catholic doctrine contained in Tradition, Scripture, and taught by the Holy Father and the bishops in union with him—is a treasure so beautiful that if a person finds it, he will "sell all that he has" (*Mt* 13:44)[1] and buy it, that is, be prepared for the greatest sacrifices in order to possess it.

In the Catechism you are going to find this treasure and, in order to make it yours (or to possess it), you will have to make some kind of sacrifice. For example, you will have to study the lessons, memorize some things, etc.; but, this sacrifice is well worth it because what you are going to receive is worth much more.

This beautiful and rich treasure includes four parts:

1. WHAT ONE HAS TO BELIEVE OR THE PROFESSION OF FAITH;

2. WHAT ONE HAS TO RECEIVE OR THE CELEBRATION OF THE CHRISTIAN MYSTERY;

3. WHAT ONE HAS TO DO OR THE LIFE IN CHRIST;

4. WHAT ONE HAS TO PRAY OR CHRISTIAN PRAYER.

1. WHAT WE MUST BELIEVE

All we must believe is summarized in a profession of faith, which is called the "Creed" or "Article of Faith."

"Among all the creeds, two occupy a special place in the Church's life:

---

[1] All Scripture citations are taken from *The Holy Bible*. Revised Standard Edition, Second Catholic Edition. San Francisco: Ignatius Press, 1965.

-*The Apostles' Creed* is so called because it is rightly considered to be a faithful summary of the apostles' faith.

-*The Nicene-Constantinopolitan* or *Nicene Creed* draws its great authority from the fact that it stems from the first two ecumenical Councils (in 325 and 381)."[2]

THE APOSTLES' CREED	THE NICENE CREED
I believe in God, the Father almighty, creator of heaven and earth.	I believe in one God, the Father, the Almighty, maker of heaven and earth, of all that is, seen and unseen.
I believe in Jesus Christ, his only Son, our Lord.	I believe in one Lord, Jesus Christ, the only Son of God eternally begotten of the Father, God from God, Light from Light, true God from true God, begotten, not made, one in Being with the Father. Through him all hings were made. For us men and for our salvation, he came down from heaven:
He was conceived by the power of the Holy Spirit and born of the Virgin Mary.	by the power of the Holy Spirit he was born of the Virgin Mary, and became man.
He suffered under Pontius Pilate, was crucified, died, and was buried.	For our sake he was crucified under Pontius Pilate; he suffered, died, and was buried.

[2] *Catechism of the Catholic Church.* 2nd Edition. Washington, D.C.: Libreria Editrice Vaticana, 1994. 193-195.

He descended into hell.
On the third day he rose again.

He ascended into heaven
and is seated at the right
hand of the Father.

He will come again to judge
the living and the dead.

I believe in the Holy Spirit,

the holy catholic Church,
the communion of saints,
the forgiveness of sins,

the resurrection of the body,

and the life everlasting.

Amen.

On the third day he rose again
in fulfillment of the Scriptures;

he ascended into heaven
and is seated at the right
hand of the Father.

He will come again in glory
to judge the living and the
dead, and his kingdom will
have no end.

I believe in the Holy Spirit,
the Lord, the giver of life,
who proceeds from the
Father and the Son. With the
Father and the Son he is
worshiped and glorified. He has
spoken through the Prophets.

I believe in one holy catholic,
and apostolic Church.
We acknowledge one
baptism for the forgiveness
of sins.

I look for the resurrection of
the dead,

and the life of the world to
come.

Amen.

2. WHAT WE MUST RECEIVE

Salvation is something which is offered and thus, needs to be received. Normally, it is received through the Sacraments, which give us the grace of God. In the first Sacrament, Baptism, we receive this grace together with the theological and infused moral virtues and the gifts of the Holy Spirit.

Sacraments
1. Baptism
2. Confirmation
3. Eucharist (also called Communion)
4. Penance (also called Confession or Reconciliation)
5. Anointing of the Sick (previously called Extreme Unction)
6. Holy Orders
7. Matrimony

Theological Virtues
1. Faith
2. Hope
3. Charity

Infused Moral Virtues
1. Prudence
2. Justice
3. Fortitude
4. Temperance

Gifts of the Holy Spirit
1. Wisdom
2. Understanding (or intelligence)
3. Counsel
4. Fortitude
5. Knowledge
6. Piety
7. Fear of the Lord

Fruits of the Holy Spirit[3]
1. Charity
2. Joy
3. Peace
4. Patience
5. Kindness
6. Goodness
7. Generosity
8. Gentleness
9. Faithfulness
10. Modesty
11. Self-control
12. Chastity

3. WHAT WE MUST DO

What we must do is found in the Ten Commandments of the law of God, in the five precepts of the Church, and in the fourteen works of mercy, seven of which are corporal and seven of which are spiritual.

The Ten Commandments
1. I am the Lord your God: you shall not have strange gods before me.
2. You shall not take the name of the Lord your God in vain.
3. Remember to keep holy the Lord's Day.
4. Honor your father and mother.
5. You shall not kill.
6. You shall not commit adultery.
7. You shall not steal.
8. You shall not bear false witness against your neighbor.
9. You shall not covet your neighbor's wife.
10. You shall not covet your neighbor's goods.

---

[3] *Catechism of the Catholic Church.* 1832.

The Precepts or Commandments of the Church[4]

1. You shall attend Mass on Sundays and Holy Days of obligation and rest from servile labor.
2. You shall confess your sins at least once a year.
3. You shall receive the Sacrament of the Eucharist at least during the Easter season.
4. You shall observe the days of fasting and abstinence established by the Church.
5. You shall help to provide for the needs of the Church.

Works of Mercy[5]

Spiritual:

1. Counsel the doubtful.
2. Instruct the ignorant.
3. Admonish sinners.
4. Comfort the afflicted.
5. Forgive offenses.
6. Bear wrongs patiently.
7. Pray for the living and the dead.

Corporal:

1. Feed the hungry.
2. Give drink to the thirsty.
3. Clothe the naked.
4. Shelter the homeless.
5. Visit the sick.
6. Visit the imprisoned.
7. Bury the dead.

---

[4] *Catechism of the Catholic Church.* 2042-2043.
[5] *Compendium: Catechism of the Catholic Church.* United States Conference of Catholic Bishops. Washington, D.C.: Libreria Editrice Vaticana, 2006. Appendix B, p. 193.

4. WHAT WE MUST PRAY

It is impossible to be a Christian without prayer. Prayer can be mental or vocal. The two most important vocal prayers are the Our Father and the Hail Mary.

Our Father

Our Father, who art in heaven, hallowed be thy Name; thy kingdom come; thy will be done, on earth as it is in heaven. Give us this day our daily bread, and forgive us our trespasses as we forgive those who trespass against us; and lead us not into temptation but deliver us from evil. Amen.

Hail Mary

Hail Mary, full of grace, the Lord is with thee. Blessed art thou among women and blessed is the fruit of thy womb, Jesus. Holy Mary, Mother of God, pray for us sinners, now and at the hour of our death. Amen.

The Sign of the Cross

Before beginning prayer, it is suitable to make the Sign of the Cross. It is made upon oneself by bringing the fingers of your right hand toward your forehead, saying "In the name of the Father;" next bring them toward your chest, saying "and the Son" (which traces the vertical beam of the cross); next bring the same hand toward your left and then right shoulder, saying, "and the Holy Spirit" (which traces the horizontal beam of the cross); and, at the end, you say "Amen," which means: "So be it." To make the sign of the cross upon yourself is called **blessing oneself.**

"The Christian begins his day, his prayers, and his activities with the Sign of the Cross: 'in the name of the Father and of the Son and of the Holy Spirit. Amen.' The baptized person dedicates the day to the glory of God and calls on the Savior's grace which lets him act in the Spirit as a child of the Father. The sign of the cross strengthens us in temptations and difficulties."[6]

---

[6] *Catechism of the Catholic Church.* 2157.

"Because Christians realize that the Cross dominates history, they place the crucifix in their churches and along roadsides, or they wear it near their hearts. For the Cross is a genuine sign of the presence of the Son of God; by this sign he is revealed as the Redeemer of the world. *'In hoc signo vinces'* ("In this sign you will conquer")."[7]

The entire structure of a Christian's spiritual life is built upon these four foundations: the Faith, the Sacraments, the Commandments, and Prayer. Our spiritual life will grow in proportion to how well we know and live them.

> "I wish to tell you how important Jesus Christ is for you, and how important you are for him. Jesus is important for you because he is the Son of God who became man. He teaches you the deepest meaning of life: who you are and what life is all about. In knowing Jesus, in studying his teaching in the Gospels, you will also get to understand yourselves more fully. And you are important for Jesus because he loves you and died for you, so that you might live the fullness of life, both here on earth and later on in heaven. Yes, you are very important for Jesus. And you are very important for me and for the whole Church."
>
> *John Paul II*
> *to the youth of Papua New Guinea*
> *May 8, 1984*

---

[7] JOHN PAUL II. *Homily from the XII World Youth Day.* August 24, 1997.

PART ONE
WHAT WE MUST BELIEVE

THE PROFESSION OF FAITH

"To believe in Jesus is more than a matter of words. It is more than being attracted to Christ, as the rich young man was. Faith demands a generous response. It demands the commitment of your whole life to the person and message of Christ. But this must be done freely and deliberately, for you are able to accept or reject the gift Christ offers."

John Paul II
Farewell ceremony from Nadi to the youth of the Fiji Islands
November 22, 1986

23

SECTION ONE
"I BELIEVE" – "WE BELIEVE"

"You do not want your lives to be meaningless and of no importance, but that they be successful and happy... There can be only one answer for me and I hope for you too: Faith! For 'faith' means precisely this: to surrender ourselves, down to the very fibers of our being, into the hands of the living God, and to live our daily life from him, with him, and directed toward him."

John Paul II
to the youth of Einsiedeln, Switzerland
June 15, 1984
(Editorial translation)

CHAPTER ONE
MAN IS "CAPABLE OF GOD"

1. THE DESIRE FOR GOD

"The desire for God is written in the human heart, because man is created by God and for God; and God never ceases to draw man to himself. Only in God will he find the truth and happiness he never stops searching for."[8] Very beautifully Saint Augustine said: "Lord...you have made us for yourself, and our hearts are restless until they rest in you."[9]

"Man is by nature and vocation a religious being. Coming from God, going toward God, man lives a fully human life only if he freely lives by his bond with God.

Man is made to live in communion with God in whom he finds happiness: 'When I am completely united to you, there will be no more sorrow or trials; entirely full of you, my life will be complete' (Saint Augustine, *Conf.* 10, 28, 39: PL 32, 795).

When he listens to the message of creation and to the voice of conscience, man can arrive at certainty about the existence of God, the cause and the end of everything.

The Church teaches that the one true God, our Creator and Lord, can be known with certainty from his works, by the natural light of human reason (cf. Vatican Council I, can. 2, § 1: DS 3026).

We really can name God, starting from the manifold perfections of his creatures, which are likenesses of the infinitely perfect God, even if our limited language cannot exhaust the mystery.

'Without the Creator, the creature vanishes' (*GS* 36). This is the reason why believers know that the love of Christ urges them

---

[8] *Catechism of the Catholic Church.* 27.
[9] *Confessions.* Trans. John K. Ryan. New York: Doubleday, 1960. Book 1, 1, 1.

to bring the light of the living God to those who do not know him or who reject him."[10]

2. WAYS TO ARRIVE AT THE KNOWLEDGE OF GOD

How do we know God?

We arrive at the knowledge of God in two ways:

1. by the light of our intellect by means of created things;

2. by that same intellect—illumined by faith—by means of the teachings of the Church.

1. NATURAL KNOWLEDGE OF GOD

Just as upon seeing jewelry we use our intellect to think it must have been made by a jeweler; upon seeing a garden full of flowers we think of the gardener who carefully tends it; upon seeing a watch we think of the watchmaker who made it run with precision; moreover, upon seeing the immense clockwork of the universe, the stars and the planets which accurately run their courses, the beautiful garden full of flowers, the plants and trees that adorn the earth, and the precious jewels that children are, mothers, and men, we necessarily think of the Maker of it all. We think of the Supreme Artisan, of the Highest Intellect, who gave life and activity to everything; in one word, we think of God.

We necessarily think of God because it is impossible for things to make themselves. Who taught spiders how to spin their webs, bees how to make their hives, calves to nurse and stay near to their mothers? What school taught these wonders? They do not have intelligence. They do not know how to read, or write, or count, and yet, they do things that seem to require intelligence. Why? Because God, who is supremely intelligent, places instincts in these animals, in order that they—even though not intelligent—would do such marvelous things which in fact make us think of him. They make us think of him who is the cause of these marvels, "for from the greatness and beauty of created

---

[10] *Catechism of the Catholic Church.* 44-49.

things comes a corresponding perception of their Creator" (*Wis* 13:5). Artists are known from their works, "because ever since the creation of the world his invisible nature, namely his eternal power and divinity, has been clearly perceived in the things that have been made" (*Rom* 1:20). All of nature speaks to us of God, the flowers and the birds, the seas and the mountains, the stars and men, colors and snow, water and sun, earth, rivers, rain, everything, everything "tells of the glory of God" (*Ps* 19:1).

There is an inner voice which tells us "do not do that," and if we do it, we are saddened; or it tells us "do this," and if we do it, we become happy. It is the voice of conscience, which is the voice of God. All men have what God commands and prohibits written on their hearts and "their conscience also bears witness" (*Rom* 2:15) to this truth.

2. SUPERNATURAL KNOWLEDGE OF GOD

We can know God in a much deeper way by means of faith. In a much deeper way because in this instance it is God himself who tells us who he is, what he has done, what he has given us, what he promises, what he teaches, what pleases him, what he wants from us. In short, God teaches us the most intimate secrets of his heart, the greatest truths about himself, truths so great that no man could ever have imagined them. Through faith God reveals himself, allows himself to be known, and manifests himself. Furthermore, God does this because he wants to and because he loves us. God speaks to us in order to tell us what he is like and to tell us how we should be; and since he speaks to us, he tells us his Word, the Word of God.

> "Have the ideal alive in your heart and diffuse it to your surroundings. The flame of the high ideals in the hearts of youth today has not been put out, because no exterior force can suppress the profound desires of the soul. No evil exists that can hinder the force of goodness. There is no violence capable of extinguishing the force of love present in the hearts of youth."
>
> *John Paul II*
> *to the youth in the stadium in Foggia, Italy*
> *May 24, 1987*

CHAPTER TWO
MAN'S ENCOUNTER WITH GOD

1. THE REVELATION OF GOD

1. GOD REVEALS HIS LOVING PLAN

"By love, God has revealed himself and given himself to man. He has thus provided the definitive, superabundant answer to the questions that man asks himself about the meaning and purpose of his life.

God has revealed himself to man by gradually communicating his own mystery in deeds and in words."[11]

2. THE STAGES OF REVELATION

"Beyond the witness to himself that God gives in created things, he manifested himself to our first parents, spoke to them and, after the fall, promised them salvation (cf. *Gen* 3:15) and offered them his covenant.

God made an everlasting covenant with Noah and with all living beings (cf. *Gen* 9:16). It will remain in force as long as the world lasts.

God chose Abraham and made a covenant with him and his descendants. By the covenant God formed his people and revealed his law to them through Moses. Through the prophets, he prepared them to accept the salvation destined for all humanity.

God has revealed himself fully by sending his own Son, in whom he has established his covenant for ever. The Son is his Father's definitive Word; so there will be no further Revelation after him."[12]

---

[11] *Catechism of the Catholic Church*. 68-69.
[12] Ibid. 70-73.

2. THE TRANSMISSION OF DIVINE REVELATION

The Catholic faith is founded upon three pillars: Sacred Tradition, Sacred Scripture, and the Magisterium of the Church.

1. SACRED TRADITION

The first pillar: *Sacred Tradition*, also known as *Apostolic Tradition*. Jesus never wrote any book; rather, he orally taught a group of disciples called Apostles. Some of these Apostles wrote what Jesus taught; however, not all he taught, because as one of them says: "there are also many other things which Jesus did; were every one of them to be written, I suppose that the world itself could not contain the books that would be written" (*Jn* 21:25).

These unwritten teachings are known as Tradition, because they have been "transmitted" orally from one to another. God has revealed himself through these oral teachings. This revelation ended with the death of the last Apostle. After the Apostles, came the era of the Fathers and Doctors of the Church. They are the links that unite us with ancient Tradition; they are the living voice of Tradition. For this reason, we will cite them often, so that—from your youth—you can become acquainted with them.

2. SACRED SCRIPTURE

The second pillar: *the Bible*. It is the book of all books. "*Sacred Scripture* is the speech of God as it is put down in writing under the breath of the Holy Spirit."[13]

It consists of two large parts:

1. The Old Testament, which contains 46 books and covers the creation of the world until the arrival of Jesus. These books include:

---

[13] II VATICAN COUNCIL. *Dei Verbum.* 9; *Catechism of the Catholic Church.* 81.

a) Historical Books:

Genesis (Gen)	*2 Kings (2 Kings)*
Exodus (Ex)	*1 Chronicles (1 Chron)*
Leviticus (Lev)	*2 Chronicles (2 Chron)*
Numbers (Num)	*Ezra (Ezra)*
Deuteronomy (Deut)	*Nehemiah (Neh)*
Joshua (Josh)	*Tobit (Tob)*
Judges (Judg)	*Judith (Jud)*
Ruth (Ruth)	*Esther (Esther)*
1 Samuel (1 Sam)	*1 Maccabees (1 Mac)*
2 Samuel (2 Sam)	*2 Maccabees (2 Mac)*
1 Kings (1 Kings)	

b) Wisdom Books:

Job (Job)	*Song of Songs (Song)*
Psalms (Ps)	*Wisdom (Wis)*
Proverbs (Prov)	*Ecclesiasticus or Sirach (Sir)*
Ecclesiastes (Qoh)	

c) Prophetic Books:

Isaiah (Is)	*Obadiah (Obad)*
Jeremiah (Jer)	*Jonah (Jon)*
Lamentations (Lam)	*Micah (Mic)*
Baruch (Bar)	*Nahum (Nahum)*
Ezekiel (Ezek)	*Habakkuk (Hab)*
Daniel (Dan)	*Zephaniah (Zeph)*
Hosea (Hos)	*Haggai (Hag)*
Joel (Joel)	*Zechariah (Zech)*
Amos (Amos)	*Malachi (Mal)*

2. The New Testament, which is made up of 27 books and covers the birth of Jesus until the end of the world when Jesus will return at the Second Coming. They are:

a) The Four Gospels:

The Gospel according to Saint Matthew (Mt)
The Gospel according to Saint Mark (Mk)
The Gospel according to Saint Luke (Lk)
The Gospel according to Saint John (Jn)

b) What the Apostles did:

Acts of the Apostles (Acts)

c) The letters of Saint Paul:

They are fourteen letters sent by the Apostle Paul to different peoples or communities. For example, he sent two letters to the Christians in Thessalonica.

Romans (Rom)	*1 Thessalonians (1 Thess)*
1 Corinthians (1 Cor)	*2 Thessalonians (2 Thess)*
2 Corinthians (2 Cor)	*1 Timothy (1 Tim)*
Galatians (Gal)	*2 Timothy (2 Tim)*
Ephesians (Eph)	*Titus (Tit)*
Philippians (Phil)	*Philemon (Philem)*
Colossians (Col)	*Hebrews (Heb)*

d) Seven letters of other Apostles:

James (Jas)
1 Peter (1 Pet)
2 Peter (2 Pet)
1 John (1 Jn)
2 John (2 Jn)
3 John (3 Jn)
Jude (Jude)

e) The last book:

It is called *Revelation* (*Rev*), (or Apocalypse), and it was written by Saint John.

It is called Sacred Scripture because its principle author is God, and so it is truly the word of God. It is "profitable for teaching, for reproof, for correction, and for training in righteousness, that the man of God may be complete, equipped for every good work" (2 *Tim* 3:16-17).

The Apostolic Tradition helped the Church discern which writings constitute the list of the Holy Books.[14] All together this

---

[14] Cf. II VATICAN COUNCIL. Dei Verbum. 8.

list is called the "Canon" of Scripture. Since in the Catechism you will often come across quotes from Sacred Scripture, it would be convenient to familiarize yourself with the names of the 73 books inspired by the Holy Spirit in order to transmit to us the Word of God.

In order to make it easier to find a particular text, the books are divided into chapters, and every chapter is then divided into phrases or verses; these divisions are then numbered. For example, *Ephesians* 3:18-19 refers to the letter of Saint Paul to the Christians in Ephesus, chapter three, verses 18 to 19.

It is very important that you know the Sacred Scriptures, especially the New Testament.

It is said that just before his death Saint Louis, King of France, called his son, heir of the throne, and said to him as his last piece of advice: "Listen to the Word of God and guard it in your heart."[15] You must also put into practice this advice.

3. THE MAGISTERIUM OF THE CHURCH

The third pillar is the *Magisterium of the Church*, that is, what the Holy Catholic Church teaches through the Holy Father and the bishops in union with him.

Jesus himself taught us that the Pope would be *the Rock upon which he would build his Church*[16] and that this "rock" is so solid (especially on matters dealing with faith and morals), according to the promise of the Lord himself, that "the powers of death shall not prevail against it" (*Mt* 16:18).

The Church has had 265 popes, beginning with Saint Peter and presently led by Benedict XVI. Among them, the majority of them have been saints, a few of them have been sinners, but absolutely none of them have been heretics. In other words, no pope ever formally taught a lie or an error on the matters of faith or morals, that is to say, in what we must believe and what we must do. So, where the Holy Father is the Church is; where the

---

[15] *Spiritual Testament of his Son*, Acta Sanctorum, August 5, 1868 p. 546. (Editorial translation)
[16] Cf. *Mt* 16:18.

Church is Jesus is; and where our Lord Jesus Christ is there are torrents of Life, Truth, and the infinite Love of God.

Jesus promised that the popes would be infallible when he said to Saint Peter, and in him, to all of his successors: "I have prayed for you that your faith may not fail... strengthen your brethren" (*Lk* 22:32).

In extraordinary moments, the Holy Father calls together all bishops throughout the world in order that they work, under his direction, on issues pertaining to faith, morals, and discipline. These meetings are called Ecumenical Councils. The decisions of these councils must be approved by the Pope in order to be valid.

In summary, we can say that the truths of the faith which we must believe, the things we must do or not do, what we must receive and what we must pray for—if we want to reach eternal salvation—can all be found in Sacred Tradition, in Sacred Scripture and in the Magisterium of the Church, which comes through the Holy Father alone or in conjunction with an Ecumenical Council. If a person does not believe or refuses to accept what the Holy Father teaches on faith or morals, this person, regardless of how good he or she may seem, does not have the Catholic faith.

In order to know the treasure of the true doctrine of Christ, it is not enough to read Sacred Scripture or to know Tradition or to accept them both; but, it is also necessary to listen and embrace the interpretation made by the Pope, with the supreme authority he has received from Christ. If this were not so, we would "have as many schisms in the Churches as there are priests," as said by Saint Jerome.[17]

In summary:

"What Christ entrusted to the apostles, they in turn handed on by their preaching and writing, under the inspiration of the Holy Spirit, to all generations, until Christ returns in glory.

---

[17] *The Dialogue Against the Luciferians.* 9.

'Sacred Tradition and Sacred Scripture make up a single sacred deposit of the Word of God' (*DV* 10), in which, as in a mirror, the pilgrim Church contemplates God, the source of all her riches.

'The Church, in her doctrine, life and worship, perpetuates and transmits to every generation all that she herself is, all that she believes' (*DV* 8 § 1).

Thanks to its supernatural sense of faith, the People of God as a whole never ceases to welcome, to penetrate more deeply and to live more fully from the gift of divine Revelation.

The task of interpreting the Word of God authentically has been entrusted solely to the Magisterium of the Church, that is, to the Pope and to the bishops in communion with him.

'All Sacred Scripture is but one book, and this one book is Christ, because all divine Scripture speaks of Christ, and all divine Scripture is fulfilled in Christ' (Hugh of Saint Victor, *De arca Noe* 2, 8: PL 176, 642).

'The Sacred Scriptures contain the Word of God and, because they are inspired they are truly the Word of God' (*DV* 24).

God is the author of Sacred Scripture because he inspired its human authors; he acts in them and by means of them. He thus gives assurance that their writings teach without error his saving truth (cf. *DV* 11).

Interpretation of the inspired Scripture must be attentive above all to what God wants to reveal through the sacred authors for our salvation. What comes from the Spirit is not fully 'understood except by the Spirit's action' (cf. Origen, *Hom. In Ex.* 4, 5: PG 12, 320).

The Church accepts and venerates as inspired the 46 books of the Old Testament and the 27 books of the New.

The four Gospels occupy a central place because Christ Jesus is their center.

The unity of the two Testaments proceeds from the unity of God's plan and his Revelation. The Old Testament prepares for the New and the New Testament fulfills the Old; the two shed light on each other; both are true Word of God.

'The Church has always venerated the divine Scriptures as she venerated the Body of the Lord' (*DV* 21): both nourish and govern the whole Christian life. 'Your word is a lamp to my feet and a light to my path' (*Ps* 119:105; cf. *Is* 50:4)."[18]

---

[18] *Catechism of the Catholic Church.* 96-100; 134-141.

CHAPTER THREE
MAN'S RESPONSE TO GOD

1. I BELIEVE

"Faith is a personal adherence of the whole man to God who reveals himself. It involves an assent of the intellect and will to the self-revelation God has made through his deeds and words.

'To believe' has thus a twofold reference: to the person, and to the truth: to the truth, by trust in the person who bears witness to it.

We must believe in no one but God: the Father, the Son and the Holy Spirit.

Faith is a supernatural gift from God. In order to believe, man needs the interior helps of the Holy Spirit.

'Believing' is a human act, conscious and free, corresponding to the dignity of the human person.

'Believing' is an ecclesial act. The Church's faith precedes, engenders, supports and nourishes our faith. The Church is the mother of all believers. 'No one can have God as Father who does not have the Church as Mother' (Saint Cyprian, *De unit.* 6: PL 4, 519).

2. WE BELIEVE

We believe all 'that which is contained in the word of God, written or handed down, and which the Church proposes for belief as divinely revealed' (Paul VI, *CPG,* § 20).

Faith is necessary for salvation. The Lord himself affirms: 'He who believes and is baptized will be saved; but he who does not believe will be condemned' (*Mk* 16:16).

'Faith is a foretaste of the knowledge that will make us blessed in the life to come' (Saint Thomas Aquinas, *Comp. theol.* 1, 2)."[19]

3. YOUTH AND FAITH

"To search for the truth, discover it and rejoice in having found it, is one of the most exciting joys in life," Pope John Paul II said to youth. However, it happens that everyone who searches for the truth is searching for God, who is the eternal truth. This is why every youth who is searching for God has embarked on a thrilling adventure: "To discover God, to discover the Gospel and find the Savior is certainly—I assure you—a marvelous adventure."[20] It is the great adventure of knowing Jesus Christ!

An adventure without obstacles is not an adventure, so it is certain that those who embark upon this adventure will confront difficulties. One of these difficulties is the opposition their faith will encounter with atheism in all its dimensions, which without a doubt "is the most serious problem of our time."[21] This is likewise affirmed in the Second Vatican Council: "for without the Creator the creature would disappear."[22] In fact, never in the history of humanity has there been an atheism as militant as the one in our time. Not only did it dominate the minds of many modern philosophers, it also became an ideology and gained power in many nations, something that had never happened before on such a universal scale. Even though it is affirmed that theoretical atheism, one which openly denies and fights against the existence of God, is declining in the world; such is not the case with practical atheism, one which makes people "live as if God did not exist." Atheism with its negation of God does not affect God. It is similar to those who shoot at images of Jesus Christ; the bullets have no effect upon him. Actual atheism, even if it were increased to the nth power, does not take away a bit from God's intrinsic glory. Furthermore, far from destroying God, fierce and militant atheism works—against the wishes of its

---

[19] *Catechism of the Catholic Church.* 176-184.
[20] JOHN PAUL II. To the youth in the stadium of Kampala, 1993. (Editorial translation)
[21] PAUL VI. *Ecclesiam suam.* 100.
[22] *Gaudium et spes.* 36.

adherents—as a manifestation of the grandeur, the wisdom, the omnipotence, and above all the goodness and the mercy of God. The psalmist says: "Why do the nations conspire and the peoples plot in vain? …The rulers take counsel together against the Lord and his anointed …He who sits in the heavens laughs; the Lord has them in derision" (*Ps* 2:1-4). Saint Paul reminds us: "Do not be deceived; God is not mocked" (*Gal* 6:7); and to the Corinthians, Saint Paul recalls the words of Job: "For it is written, 'He takes the wise in their own craftiness'" (1 *Cor* 3:19 and *Job* 5:13). Atheism does not do anything to God; the one whom atheism destroys is man. In fact, atheism is an attack against man who "God created in his own image" (*Gen* 1:27). Atheism knows that it cannot affect God in his being, neither can blasphemy, sacrilege, hatred, or the negation of his existence (which is only a postulation, since it is affirmed without any proof). However, all of these can destroy the image of God in man; this is the greatest and only accomplishment of atheism: the destruction of man. Saint Irenaeus of Lyons, at the end of the second century, wrote that if man were to completely lack God, he would cease to exist. "For the glory of God is a living man; and the life of man consists in beholding God."[23]

---

[23] Cf. *Adversus haereses* IV, 20, 7.

SECTION TWO
THE PROFESSION OF THE
CHRISTIAN FAITH: THE CREED

"There are songs that are always beautiful, that never go out of fashion; there are songs whose echoes are never extinguished, our song, the song that resonates above the deafening noises of the history of the world, is the Creed, the song of our faith. In it, we profess our faith in the Father, who calls us to life; in our brother and Savior Jesus Christ; in the Holy Spirit, who continually creates life. Let us sing together this song of our faith."

John Paul II
to the Faithful in Münster, Germany
May 1, 1987
(Editorial translation)

INTRODUCTION

The Church has made a simple and concise summary of the principal truths of the faith in order that we may not forget the fundamental truths of faith we must believe in, in order that prayer may help us in telling God we believe everything he has taught us, and in order that we profess our Catholic faith before God and before man. This summary is called the Creed because it begins with the Latin word, *credo*, which means: I believe. It is always prayed while standing since it is a song of victory—it is the summary of our faith "that overcomes the world" (1 *Jn* 5:4). The holy martyrs gave their lives, covering the earth with their blood in order to defend and affirm the Catholic faith because they knew that "without faith it is impossible to please [God]" (*Heb* 11:6); and they wanted to please God. This is another reason why we stand when we pray the Creed: we want to demonstrate our disposition to defend and propagate the Catholic faith.

Furthermore, Jesus once said: "Every one who acknowledges me before men, I also will acknowledge before my Father who is in heaven" (*Mt* 10:32).

The great martyr Saint Peter of Verona, dipping his fingers in the blood of the mortal wound inflicted by his executioners, wrote the word Creed on the ground, making it known that he was dying for the Catholic faith summarized in the Creed, which is also called a "symbol."

The Creed—compendium of our faith—has twelve articles. The Catechism of the Catholic Church analyzes these twelve articles in three chapters:

-Chapter One: I believe in God the Father

-Chapter Two: I believe in Jesus Christ, the only Son of God

-Chapter Three: I believe in the Holy Spirit

As you come to know more deeply each of the articles of the Creed, you will become aware that: "The symbol is... with all certitude, the treasure of our soul."[24]

> "The intimate relationship Christ wants to establish with us is a singular friendship that can never fail. Jesus is faithful; he keeps what he promises. That is why, Christ is our true friend. You will not find a companion on the road more faithful than him. Thus, do not allow your response to him to be weak. Do not give him just the smallest finger of your hand! Open wide the gates of your friendship to him! Great things are not paid with little money. Give him your heart, your understanding, your hands! And if he personally calls you to follow him most intimately, do not deny him your company. With Christ there is no loss! He gives so abundantly that you will be able to enrich others and, with him, transform the world!"

> *John Paul II,*
> *To the youth in Gelsenkirchen (Germany),*
> *May 2, 1987*
> *(Editorial translation)*

---

[24] SAINT AMBROSE. *Explanatio Symboli.* 7: PL 17, 1196. (Editorial translation)

CHAPTER ONE
I BELIEVE IN GOD THE FATHER

ARTICLE 1
"I BELIEVE IN GOD THE FATHER ALMIGHTY, CREATOR OF HEAVEN AND EARTH"

We will now explain the three truths of fundamental importance in this first article of our faith:

1. God is One and Three;

2. God is Creator because he has made the world, the angels and men;

3. In the beginning of history, Adam and Eve, the first people God created, committed a sin which we call original sin.

1. GOD IS ONE AND THREE

1. THE NATURE OF GOD

a) The Greatness and Majesty of God

What is God? What is God like? God and his mysteries surpass knowledge (cf. *Eph* 3:19), and there is no created intellect which can know God completely, because God is too great for us. Let us make a comparison: suppose we could put together all the knowledge of God acquired by the saints, religious, nuns, priests, bishops, the Pope, all men and women who believe in God, those who have lived in the past and will live in the future, and even the angels and the Virgin Mary. All of this knowledge compared with the reality of God, is likened to all the animals, plants, oceans, the sun, the moon and the stars compared with less than a grain of sand. Why? Because God is infinite, he is not limited by anything or anyone. He is greater than all people and all things, since he is "above all" (*Eph* 4:6). He is like an ocean without limits. He is superior to all that we could say and think of him without comparison because all that is outside of God is limited and finite;

only God is unlimited and infinite. With our limited intelligence, we cannot come to completely know him who is infinite.

b) The Transcendence of God

Saint John of the Cross was a great saint who did not only know and love God, but also experienced God in a certain way. He said "all creatures of heaven and earth are nothing when compared to God. For example: all the beauty of creatures (minerals, plants, animals, man, angels) compared to the infinite beauty of God is the height of ugliness. As Solomon says in Proverbs: 'charm is deceitful and beauty is vain' (*Prov* 31:30)… All the grace and elegance of creatures compared to God's grace is utter coarseness and crudity… Compared to the infinite goodness of God, all the goodness of the creatures of the world can be called wickedness. 'No one is good but God alone' (*Lk* 18:19)… All the world's wisdom and human ability compared to the infinite wisdom of God is pure and utter ignorance, as Saint Paul writes to the Corinthians: 'The wisdom of this world is folly with God' (1 *Cor* 3:19)… All the sovereignty and freedom of the world compared to the freedom and sovereignty of the Spirit of God is utter slavery, anguish, and captivity… All the delights and satisfactions of the will in the things of the world compared to all the delight that is God are intense suffering, torment, and bitterness… All the wealth and glory of creation compared to the wealth that is God is utter poverty and misery in the Lord's sight."[25] Saint Teresa of Jesus also said: "whoever has God, wants for nothing. God alone is enough."[26] And Saint Paul, who on many occasions had marvelous visions of the things of God, teaches us that God is ineffable (cf. *2 Cor* 12:4), which is to say, that he is inexpressible in human language. All Saint Paul could say was: "no eye has seen, nor ear heard, nor the heart of man conceived, what God has prepared for those who love him" (*1 Cor* 2:9).

---

[25] "Ascent to Mount Carmel." *The Collected Works of St. John of the Cross.* Washington, D.C.: ICS Publications, 1991. I, 4.
[26] Found in the *Catechism of the Catholic Church*. 227.

God is infinite "in every perfection."[27] Thus, Jesus tells us that his heavenly Father is "perfect" (*Mt* 5:48) because God contains all the perfections of every creature in himself: "He is the all" (*Sir* 43:27).

c) The Unity of God

God is only one because if he were several gods they would have to distinguish themselves one from the other by some kind of imperfection. If this were so, they would not be God who is absolutely perfect.

Sacred Scripture teaches us: "God is one" (*Rom* 3:30).

d) The Truth of God

Is truth a perfection? Yes. Consequently, God is true. Furthermore, Christ has said: "I am… the truth" (*Jn* 14:6). God is absolutely true: "and this is eternal life, that they know you the only true God" (*Jn* 17:3). He has infinite understanding: "his understanding is beyond measure" (*Ps* 147:5). Consequently, God cannot be mistaken; he cannot deceive himself or be deceived. God always speaks the truth. He says what he thinks. He does not lie. He cannot mislead us. He is absolutely veracious: "it is impossible that God should prove false" (*Heb* 6:18). Lastly, God does what he says and fulfills what he promises because he is faithful: "Heaven and earth will pass away, but my words will not pass away" (*Mt* 24:35). "If we are faithless, he remains faithful—for he cannot deny himself" (*2 Tim* 2:13). God cannot disappoint us.

e) The Goodness of God

Is goodness a perfection? Yes. Consequently, God is good, infinitely good, for "no one is good but God alone" (*Lk* 18:19). Creatures are good because they participate in the goodness of God. God lacks sin, and so he is thrice holy: "Holy, holy, holy is the Lord" (*Is* 6:3). He is absolutely benevolent with us, his

---

[27] I VATICAN COUNCIL. *Dogmatic Constitution on the Catholic Faith.* Dz. 1782.

creatures: "For God so loved the world that he gave his only Son" (*Jn* 3:16).

f) The Immutability of God

To have the possibility to change is a sign of imperfection. Such imperfections are, for example, to know something and then later to forget it, to loose strength, or to say one thing and then later to deny it. This is why God does not change: he is "the Father of lights with whom there is no variation or shadow due to change" (*Jas* 1:17). God is not ignorant of anything he should know. He does not use up his strength. He does not contradict his judgments or change his decisions. He does not grow old because he is eternal, eternally young. He does not need to move himself because he is immense. He does not forget anything because everything is present at the same time for his intellect. He cannot be any better because he is absolutely and incomparably good, perfect and holy.

g) The Eternity of God

The angels have a beginning—God created them—and do not have an end because they cannot die. Other beings have a beginning and an end, either in part, like man, whose body decomposes into the earth while his soul stays intact; or completely, like plants and animals that do not have immortal souls like man. Only God does not have a beginning or an end, that is to say, he is eternal. "Before the mountains were brought forth, or ever you had formed the earth and the world, from everlasting to everlasting, you are God" (*Ps* 90:2). In God there is no before or after, past or future; he is a permanent now; he is a present that never dawns nor sets. I want to tell you also that only God is God. God is singular and ineffable; therefore, in God are singular and ineffable things. All that is not God has been made by another; only God was not made by anyone, because he is God. All the creatures known have a date of birth. There was a moment in which they stopped being nothing and began to exist. God is not a creature, he is the Creator. He never stopped being nothing in order to begin existing, because God always was and exists from all eternity, without beginning or end, without birth or death. He is the only one who does not have a part of being, because God is Being. He is the only one that does not have a part of goodness, because God is Goodness. He is the only one that does not have a part of truth, because God is Truth. He is the only one that does not exist by the work of another, because God is Existence itself. This pattern continues in all perfections because God possesses them all in an infinite degree. God is the Creator because he fully possesses everything he participates to his creatures, those which he draws out of nothing.

God neither made nor created himself—which would be an absurdity. If he had ever been nothing, he could not give himself being, because nobody gives what he does not have. In a word, God is God; or better yet, God Is. Just as we do not have any difficulty in thinking that God will never die—precisely because he is God—we should accustom ourselves to think that God was never born, created or made (even by himself), precisely because he is God.

h) The Immensity and Ubiquity

We are small; God is great. He is immense: "heaven and the highest heaven cannot contain you" (*1 Kings* 8:27). Therefore, God is present in the heavens, on the earth and everywhere. The psalmist exclaims: "Where shall I go from your Spirit? Or where shall I flee from your presence? If I ascend to heaven, you are there! If I make my bed in Sheol, you are there! If I take the wing of the morning and dwell in the uttermost parts of the sea, even there your hand shall lead me, and your right hand shall hold me...even the darkness is not dark to you..." (*Ps* 139:7-10, 12).

i) The Wisdom of God

God knows absolutely everything: "You have knowledge of all things" (*Esther* 14:15). He even knows "the number of drops of rain and the sands of the sea."[28] Furthermore, God knows our thoughts: "the Lord searches all hearts, and understands every plan and thought" (*1 Chron* 28:9), and even "all things before they come to be" (*Dan* 13:42).

---

[28] SAINT THOMAS AQUINAS. *Summa Theologica.* Trans. Fathers of the English Dominican Province. New York: Christian Classics, 1948. I, 23, 7.

j) The Freedom and Power of God

God is the Lord of everything. Thus, he is completely free to do that he wants, how he wants and when he wants.

God is not obliged by anything or anyone; he can neither become subordinate to anyone nor anything: "Whatever the Lord pleases he does, in heaven and on earth, in the seas and all deeps" (*Ps* 135:6).

He can do everything he wants to. He is omnipotent, all powerful: "with God all things are possible" (*Mt* 19:26). He can even make saints out of us!

k) The Power and Providence of God

God governs everything. He directs history and the actions of men. If what happens is good it is because God wants it to be; if what happens is bad, it is because God tolerates it. Evil does not come from God; but from man's misuse of his freedom. And why does God tolerate evil? For two reasons:

1. To respect our freedom: "It was he who created man in the beginning, and he left him in the power of his own inclination" (*Sir* 15:14). God wants us as sons, not as robots.

2. Because God is so wise and powerful, he knows how to bring about good from evil: "you meant evil against me; but God meant it for good" (*Gen* 50:20).

In his providence, God has everything arranged by "measure and number and weight" (*Wis* 11:20). He feeds the birds of the air and clothes the lilies of the field,[29] and even more he takes care of us. Therefore, we must always trust in him, placing ourselves in his hands, as the great friends of God have done. Servant of God Camila Rolón says: "Blindly I embark upon the vessel of Divine Providence and I do not fear the tempests that rise up from the tempestuous sea of this valley of miseries and I await with lively faith the end of this journey;"[30] "The Lord is faithful to his

---

[29] Cf. *Mt* 6:26, 28 ff.
[30] Letter from June 31, 1908. (Editorial translation)

promises and he will never abandon those who put their hope in him."[31]

l) The Justice and Mercy of God

God is infinitely just: "for he will render to every man according to his works" (*Rom* 2:6), rewarding the good and punishing the evil. "Those who by patience in well-doing seek for glory and honor and immortality, he will give eternal life; but for those who are factious and do not obey the truth, but obey wickedness, there will be wrath and fury" (*Rom* 2:7-8). "God is not mocked" (*Gal* 6:7).

God is infinitely merciful because "God is love" (*1 Jn* 4:8). Therefore, "there will be more joy in heaven over one sinner who repents than over ninety-nine righteous persons who need no repentance" (*Lk* 15:7).

m) The Simplicity of God

This is how God is: he is the most excellent and admirable being that you could describe or think of; infinitely perfect, true, good, immutable, eternal, immense, present everywhere, all-knowing, free, just, merciful, and governing everything with his providence.

But there is something else that you must know about how God is. Look at a dog; like you, he has a body; but he does not know how to add or subtract, he does not go to school or learn catechism, he does not know to pray like you do.

Why is there this difference? Because you have a spiritual soul that he does not have. We cannot touch this spiritual soul with our hands, or see it with our eyes, or weigh it in a scale, like we can do with bodies. This is so precisely because this soul is spiritual, immaterial, and incorporeal. Have you ever *seen* a thought with your eyes? Have you *seen* the love that you have for your mother? No. Why? Because love and thoughts are spiritual things. God is pure spirit, he does not have a body like ours

---

[31] Letter from March 7, 1911. (Editorial translation)

(Jesus has a body as far as he is man, not as far as he is God) and so we cannot see him with our eyes, nor touch him with our hands, nor weigh him; nevertheless, we can know him and love him with all the strength of our souls: "God is spirit, and those who worship him must worship in spirit and truth" (*Jn* 4:24).

"Nothing is divine and worthy of adoration outside of God. Man falls into slavery when he makes wealth, power, the state, sex, pleasure, or any other thing created by God divine or absolute—even his own being or human reason. God alone is the source of the radical liberation of all forms of idolatry, because the adoration of what is not worthy to be adored and making what is relative absolute, violates what is most intimate in the human person: his relationship with God and his realization as person (…) the fall of idols restores to man the essential domain of his liberty."[32]

2. THE HOLY TRINITY

We have seen what God is and how God is. But, who is God? When you make the Sign of the Cross upon your chest, you are expressing who God is. This is the central mystery of our faith. Let us see. When you make the Sign of the Cross, you say: "In the name of," singular; not "in the names of," plural. Why? Because there is only one true and living God. Yet, after saying "in the name of" you mention three names: "the Father, the Son and the Holy Spirit." Why? Because in the one true and living God there are three distinct Persons: the Father, the Son, and the Holy Spirit.

Therefore, God is not only one, but three. There are three Persons in him. This is the mystery of the Holy Trinity.

In reference to the Holy Trinity, the Catholic faith tells us to adore "three Persons equal in majesty, undivided in splendor."[33]

Therefore, we confess:

---

[32] III LATIN AMERICAN EPISCOPAL COUNCIL (CELAM). *Puebla Document.* 491. (Editorial translation)
[33] *Roman Missal.* Preface to the Mass of the Most Holy Trinity.

1. The distinction of the Persons. The Father is the Father, he is neither the Son nor the Holy Spirit; the Son is the Son, he is neither the Father nor the Holy Spirit; the Holy Spirit is the Holy Spirit, he is neither the Father nor the Son. In other words, they are three truly distinct Persons.

2. The unity in nature. They all have one and the same nature of God, because the Father is God, the Son is God, and the Holy Spirit is God; however, they are not three gods but only one, true God.

3. The equality in dignity. The Father is just as much God as the Son is and the Holy Spirit is; the Son is just as much God as the Father is and the Holy Spirit is; the Holy Spirit is just as much God as the Father is and the Son is. "The Father is immense, the Son is immense, and the Holy Spirit is immense; the Father is eternal, the Son is eternal, and the Holy Spirit is eternal... the Father is omnipotent, the Son is omnipotent, (and) the Holy Spirit is omnipotent."[34]

Saint Athanasius says that he who separates the Son from the Father (thinking that he is not as much God as the Father is) or reduces the Holy Spirit to the level of creatures, does not have either the Son or the Father, but is rather without God, worse than an infidel and is anything but a Christian. The heretics who, in order to affirm the unity of the nature of God, denied the Trinity of Persons erred in the mystery of the Trinity. On the other hand, those who, in order to affirm the Trinity of Persons, denied the unity of the nature of God, also erred in the mystery of the Trinity: "both unity in Trinity, and Trinity in unity must be venerated."[35]

Just as the color, the shape and the scent of a rose do not make three roses, but only one rose; just as one times one does not equal three, but one; just as the sun has shape, light and heat, yet it is not three suns, but one sun; just if we were to put three lighted matches together the three would form only one flame; in

---

[34] Cf. I COUNCIL OF NICEA. Dz. 54; I and II COUNCIL OF CONSTANTINOPLE. Dz. 86, 213.
[35] *Creed of Athanasius.* Dz 39.

a similar way—though on an infinitely superior level—God is Father, Son, and Holy Spirit. They are not three gods, but only one true God.

From all eternity, God the Father thinks a thought identical to himself in every way. As it is a thought of God, it is infinite like him. The Thought, or Word, by being infinite, constitutes a Person, the Second Person of the Holy Trinity: the Son. Now, the Father and the Son, who know each other, cannot do less than love each other. This love, as it proceeds from God, is infinite and, therefore, constitutes the Third Person of the Holy Trinity: The Holy Spirit.

Whenever you make the Sign of the Cross, think of this God who is all-powerful and eternal, immense and good, just and wise, Father, Son, Holy Spirit, infinitely happy, beautiful, free, transcendent, and pure and provident spirit. Think of this God who—not out of necessity but out of pure goodness—wants other beings to participate in his life, his truth, his love and his joy. God created you in order that you would be able to know him, love him and serve him, and in this way be very happy in this life, and happier still in the next life.

Saint Francis of Assisi, a great Saint, praised God in this way:

Thou art the Holy Lord, the only God, who works wonders.
Thou art strong, Thou art great, Thou art the Most High.
Thou art the Omnipotent King, Thou Holy Father,
King of Heaven and Earth.
Thou art Three and One Lord.
Thou art good, all good, the Highest Good, Lord God, living and true.
Thou art Charity and Love, Thou art Wisdom.
Thou art humility, Thou art patience, Thou art security.
Thou art quiet, Thou art joy and gladness.
Thou art justice and temperance.
Thou art riches unto sufficiency.
Thou art beauty, Thou art guard and our defender.
Thou art refreshment, Thou art fortitude.
Thou art our hope, Thou art our faith.
Thou art our entire sweetness.
Thou art our eternal life,

Great and admirable Lord,
God Omnipotent, Merciful Savior.[36]

2. CREATION

1. The Heavens and the Earth

God always existed, from all eternity. Outside of him absolutely nothing existed. He created everything that there is in the heavens and on earth, when he wanted to and how he wanted to: "You created all things, and by your will they existed and were created" (*Rev* 4:11).

Only God can create, that is to say, make something out of nothing. Everything depends on him, on his being and his work, because nothing exists for itself; rather everything exists for God. He gives everything being and the capacity to act, since "in him all things hold together" (*Col* 1:17) and he is the one who works in us "both to will and to work" (*Phil* 2:13). He made everything with his Word, which is to say, with his all-powerful will. And he made it because he wanted to.

Close your eyes—you do not see anything. Open them—you see everything. Likewise, in the beginning there was nothing outside of God, and God made everything. The most perfect beings that God created are the angels and man.

2. The Angels

The angels are a multitude, an army. The most well known among the angels are Saint Michael, chief of the angels; Saint Raphael, protector of travelers; Saint Gabriel, who appeared to the Holy Virgin; and the guardian angels who God gives to each one of us to protect us on earth and bring us to heaven. Jesus himself, referring to children, said: "See that you do not despise one of these little ones; for I tell you that in heaven their angels always behold the face of my Father who is in heaven" (*Mt* 18:10).

You should always pray:

---

[36] Saint Francis of Assisi. *The Praises of God Most High.*

Guardian angel, sweet companion, do not abandon me night or day. Do not leave me alone or I will lose my way.

Or also:

Angel of God, my guardian dear, to whom God's love entrusts me here, ever this day be at my side to light, to guard, to rule and to guide. Amen.

A group of the angels disobeyed God and became evil, by which they were condemned to hell: "God did not spare the angels when they sinned, but cast them into hell" (*2 Pet* 2:4, and *Jude* 1:6). They are demons or devils. They are envious over the fact that we do not want to be like them. They tempt us to evil in order to separate us from the path that leads us to heaven and in order to bring us to hell.

In order not to fall into temptation, we must pray to God, as Jesus taught us to say in the Our Father: "lead us not into temptation, but deliver us from evil" (*Mt* 6:13). We also must love the Holy Virgin Mary, who crushed the head of Satan,[37] she defeated him because she never knew even the shadow of sin. We must finally invoke Saint Michael, who also overthrew Satan, to whom you can pray this beautiful prayer:

Saint Michael the Archangel, defend us in battle. Be our protector against the wickedness and snares of the devil. Rebuke him, O God, we humbly beseech you. And you, O prince of the heavenly host, cast into hell Satan and all of the evil spirits who wander about the world seeking the ruin of souls.

The demons cannot do everything they want to. They are not all-powerful; only God is all-powerful. They can only do what God permits, and as Scripture says: "he will not let you be tempted beyond your strength, but with the temptation he will also provide a way of escape, that you may be able to endure it" (*1 Cor* 10:13). In other words, if a person falls into temptation and commits a sin, it is by his own fault and because he has rejected the help from God. "The devil fears fasting, prayer, humility,

---

[37] Cf. *Gen* 3:15.

good works, and is reduced to feebleness before the Sign of the Cross" (Saint Anthony Abbot).[38]

3. MAN

God also created man, Adam and Eve, our first parents. They were given immortal souls and elevated to divine life by grace.

We human beings are made of matter and spirit, of body and soul. God created the human creature "constituted as it were, alike of the spirit and the body"[39] and so unified that the soul is— in itself and essentially—the form of the human body.[40]

The body and the soul are so unified that they are separated only at death. The body, since it is composed of many parts, disintegrates into ashes. The soul, which is spiritual, is not composed of parts, and so it cannot die. For this reason, the soul is nobler than the body: "do not fear those who kill the body but cannot kill the soul" (Mt 10:28). Saint John Chrysostom said that "even if you were lord of the entire world, even if you were the king of the earth, and you were to purchase everything on earth, you would not be capable of buying one soul...the soul is more precious than the whole world."[41] Saint Mary Euphrasia Pelletier said: "One person is more precious than the whole world."[42] The most important thing that we have to do in the world, which constitutes the goal of our faith, is "the salvation of... souls" (1 Pet 1:9).

Our souls know by means of the intellect; and they love and choose by means of the will.

We should always use our intellect to know the truth because only "the truth will make you free" (Jn 8:32). We must always submit the will in service of the good, doing good always and to everyone, and doing evil never and to no one. "None of you

---

[38] SAINT ATHANASIUS. *Life of Saint Anthony Abbot.*
[39] IV LATERAN COUNCIL. Dz. 428.
[40] Cf. COUNCIL OF VIENNE. Dz. 481.
[41] *Homilies on the Gospel of Saint Matthew.* Homily 55, 3, Madrid: B.A.C., 1966. p. 164. (Editorial translation)
[42] Motto of the shield of the Congregation "Our Lady Charity of the Good Shepherd" and the "Daughters of the Cross," taken from St. John Eudes.

repay evil for evil, but always seek to do good to one another and to all" (*1 Thess* 5:15).

God makes us free in order that we may be able to love. If one "has had the power to transgress and did not transgress, and to do evil and did not do it" (*Sir* 31:10), he earns much merit for eternal life, and the reward will be greater.

Since our soul is spiritual, it is simple. Nevertheless, it lives, knows and loves. In spite of having many different operations, it is only one. It is the image of God, pure triune spirit, who is Life, Truth and Love; who is Father, Son, and Holy Spirit in one true God. Thus, our soul is more than an image; it is a likeness to God when it is in a state of grace.

Grace is a gift that God gives man because he wants to and because he loves them, in order that they be "children of God, and if children, then heirs" (*Rom* 8:16-17). Human beings are children of God since by grace they are "partakers of the divine nature" (*2 Pet* 1:4). By grace we participate in the Life, the Truth, and the Love of God.

3. ORIGINAL SIN

1. OUR FIRST PARENTS

We commit sin when we do something that God does not want. By not obeying him, we offend him. If it is a grave matter, it is called mortal sin because it brings death to the life of the soul, which is the grace of God.[43]

God gave Adam not only a body and a soul; but, more importantly, God gave him grace which made him a son and a friend of God. When Adam fell into mortal sin, he lost this grace for himself; and since he was the head of humanity, he lost it for all his descendants as well: "sin came into the world through one man, and death through sin, and so death spread to all men because all men sinned" (*Rom* 5:12).

---

[43] Cf. COUNCIL OF TRENT. Dz. 1512.

Consequently, we are all born in sin, "we were by nature children of wrath" (*Eph* 2:3). In other words, by being deprived of his grace, we are born enemies of God; we are creatures fallen in sin. Since the sin of Adam was committed at the origin of all things, it is called original sin. It can only be erased by Baptism.

When Adam and all of his descendants lost the grace of God, they fell out of the order; they disordered themselves with respect to God. As a consequence, man also became disordered in himself; in other words, he lost his internal order and complete dominion over his passions. He also became disordered in respect to inferior creatures, which—from then on—cause him pain and suffering. As men became disordered in their dealings with other men, rivalries, envies and jealousies appeared. Ultimately, the internal harmony between the soul and the body was broken, introducing death into history. "Therefore as sin came into the world through one man and death through sin, and so death spread to all men because all men sinned" (*Rom* 5:12).

All of these disorders are consequences of sin, or punishments from sin. The certain dominion the devil now has over humanity, for which he is called "ruler of this world," (*Jn* 12:31) is also a punishment for sin.

Without a doubt, these are terrible punishments. However, they are small punishments compared with the final punishment awaited humanity: hell. All men, due to Adam's original disobedience, were condemned to this terrible inheritance: to be born, suffer, die, and finally, fall into hell.

Why was the sin of our first parents so grave and have such terrible consequences? Let us look at an example: if one solider hits another solider, as a punishment he will get a couple of days of solitary confinement. If he hits a sergeant, there would be more days of solitary confinement; if a captain, even more days; and if a general, many more days. Why would they give the same solider more days of solitary confinement if the offense was always the same? This happens because the importance and dignity of the person offended is greater. Every mortal sin is, in a way, an infinite offense since the offense is not measured by the person who offends, but by the person who is offended. In the case of mortal sin, the person offended is the infinitely perfect

God. For this reason, only God could bring order back to what man had disordered by sin. Only the infinite God could settle the infinite offense caused by sin. Only God could liberate us from the slavery of sin, of death, of the devil and hell. Only God could lift us from our fallen state and return the grace once lost. Just as we cannot lift ourselves up by pulling on our own shoe laces, in the same way, once we had fallen into sin we could not have lifted ourselves up by our own strength. God had to extend a hand from above and from outside in order to lift us up. This hand is the grace of God.

2. CONSEQUENCES

Our first fathers and all of their descendants—all of us—due to original sin, should have been destined to suffer, die and go to hell forever. However, God had compassion on us and soon after he promised a Savior,[44] who would save us from our sins and give us the grace once lost. But this Savior would not come at once. God had to prepare men slowly in order that they would know how to recognize him.

So, God chose a People and made a covenant, or an alliance, with this People.

Several centuries after Adam and Eve, God chose a man named Abraham, who lived between 1,900 and 1,800 years before Christ, in order to make him the head of his People. God promised him that the Savior of the world would be born from his descendants: "By you all the families of the earth will shall bless themselves" (*Gen* 12:3). Abraham believed God and so he is called "our Father in Faith."[45]

Abraham had a son named Isaac. With Isaac, God renewed all the promises he had made with Abraham.

Isaac had two sons, Esau and Jacob. Jacob had twelve sons who later formed the twelve tribes of Israel. The chosen People

---

[44] Cf. *Gen* 3:15.
[45] *Roman Missal.* Eucharistic Prayer I.

grew and, due to a drought, had to take refuge in Egypt. The Egyptians enslaved them for 400 years.

Then, God chose Moses to liberate his People and bring them to the Promised Land. This happened about 1200 B.C. While on their journey, God made an alliance with this People on Mount Sinai: there he gave them the Ten Commandments.[46]

Joshua was the one who conquered the Promised Land and the Judges succeeded Moses in governing the people.

The people of God now had a law and a land. They lacked a political structure. So, God gave them a king. The first king was Saul (1035-1015 B.C.), then David (1015-975 B.C.), and finally Solomon (975-935 B.C.). Afterwards, there was a schism and the kingdom was divided into two: Israel and Judah.

Between 900 and 800 B.C., Elijah and Elisha appeared as great prophets to the people. The prophets Amos, Hosea, Isaiah, and Micah lived between 800 and 700 B.C. Finally, the prophets Jeremiah and Ezekiel lived around 600 B.C.

In this century, the Persians invaded the land and took the chosen people captive to Babylon. Then, in 538 B.C., the Jews returned to Palestine, but lived almost continually dominated by foreigners. First, the Jews were ruled by the Persians until 332 B.C.; then, by the Greeks until 143 B.C. Finally, the Jews lived under Roman power from 63 B.C. onward—except for a brief period of independence from 143 to 63 B.C.

And so, when the fullness of time arrived, Jesus Christ, the Son of God, our Lord and Messiah, Redeemer of the world, was born in Bethlehem. He was born from the seed of Abraham of the tribe of Judah and the family of David. He was born of the Most Pure Virgin Mary. In him, everything that was announced by the prophets was fulfilled. In him, the end times commenced. Thus, "Jesus Christ is the center of the universe and of history."[47]

---

[46] Refer to page 19 and 221.
[47] JOHN PAUL II. *Redemptor Hominum*. I, 1.

"Christ, the Redeemer of the world, is the one who penetrated in a unique unrepeatable way into the mystery of man and entered his 'heart.' Rightly therefore does the Second Vatican Council teach: 'The truth is that only in the mystery of the Incarnate Word does the mystery of man take on light.'"[48]

> "How can one dare to trust in an unstable and fragile world, one full of lies? Only, by having trust in the goodness of being created by God, who is love. How can we go to the extremes of trust? Walking behind Christ, him who, in the supreme hour of fidelity, was able to say: 'Father, into your hands, I commend my spirit.' (*Lk* 23:46). With Christ, trust in the Father. In faith, throw yourselves into the arms of God. He will not disappoint you. His fidelity never fails."

> *John Paul II*
> *to the youth of the Grand Duchy of Luxembourg*
> *May 16, 1985*
> *(Editorial translation)*

---

[48] JOHN PAUL II. *Redemptor Hominum.* II, 8.

CHAPTER TWO
I BELIEVE IN JESUS CHRIST

ARTICLE 2
"I BELIEVE IN JESUS CHRIST
HIS ONLY SON OUR LORD"

We often bless ourselves with the Sign of the Cross. What does this sign mean? It represents the second greatest mystery of our Catholic faith: that Jesus Christ, the Second Person of the Holy Trinity, who was made man, suffered and died on the cross in order to save us from our sins and bring us the grace of God that we had lost. He is the promised and awaited for Savior.

1. THE DIVINITY OF OUR LORD JESUS CHRIST

How do we know Jesus is God?

1. HE HIMSELF TAUGHT IT

"No one knows the Son except the Father and no one knows the Father except the Son" (*Mt* 11:27), which is to say, only the infinite intellect of God the Father can know the infinite being of God the Son, and vice versa. On another occasion, Jesus said: "I am in the Father and the Father in me" (*Jn* 14:10); and also: "that they may all be one; even as you, Father, are in me, and I in you" (*Jn* 17:21).

When Caiaphas asked Jesus: "I adjure you by the living God, tell us if you are the Christ, the Son of God," the Lord answered him: "You have said so" (cf. *Mt* 26:63-64; *Mk* 14:61).

2. HIS ENEMIES RECOGNIZED IT

They knew Jesus presented himself as the true Son of God: "He not only broke the Sabbath but also called God his Father, making himself equal with God" (*Jn* 5:18). Jesus' enemies also recognized him when he said: "I and the Father are one." On this occasion, the Jews wanted to stone Jesus for "blasphemy; because you, being a man, make yourself God" (*Jn* 10:30, 33).

Furthermore, they recognized Jesus when they asked Pilate to crucify him by saying: "He ought to die because he has made himself the Son of God" (*Jn* 19:7).

3. THE APOSTLES PREACHED IT

Saint Paul calls him: "our great God and Savior Jesus Christ" (*Tit* 2:13). He teaches that Jesus, "according to the flesh, is the Christ, who is God over all, blessed for ever" (*Rom* 9:5), etc. Saint Peter calls him "Lord and Christ" (*Acts* 2:36). After affirming that the Word was God, (the Word is the Second Person of the Holy Trinity), Saint John adds that "the Word became flesh and dwelt among us" (*Jn* 1:14). In this statement, he is affirming that "Jesus Christ...is the true God" (*1 Jn* 5:20).

4. HE DEMONSTRATED IT HIMSELF

1. Jesus demonstrated it by his own life, a true miracle of supernatural wisdom and holiness: "Which of you convicts me of sin?"(*Jn* 8:46).

For that reason, we say in the Liturgy: "You alone are Holy; You alone are the Lord; You alone are the most High."[49]

2. Jesus demonstrated it by numerous miracles. The miracles of Jesus are referred to without much detail in eighteen passages. Thirty-nine miracles are described in great detail in other passages.[50]

On page 315 you will find a complete list of the miracles of Jesus. You can entertain yourself by looking them up, learning something as well.

3. Jesus demonstrated it by multiple prophecies, which are intellectual miracles (see page 316).

4. Jesus demonstrated it by resurrecting from the dead by his own power. He affirms: "I lay down my life, that I may take it again. No one takes it from me, but I lay it down of my own

---

[49] *Roman Missal.* Gloria.
[50] Cf. *Mt* 4:23; 8:16; 9:35, etc.

accord. I have power to lay it down and I have power to take it again" (*Jn* 10:17-18).

5. Jesus demonstrated it by the moral miracle found in the continuity of the Catholic Church: Christ founded his Church, which has had a 2,000 year history filled with contradictory events; yet, in spite of all the time which has passed, it still has its original features. Furthermore, it does not stop communicating its salvific message to everyone who wants to see and hear it. The permanence of the Church is absolutely inexplicable by human and natural reasons.

2. THE HUMANITY OF OUR LORD JESUS CHRIST

Our Lord Jesus Christ is the Son of God made man: "He who is true God is also true man."[51] Jesus has a body and a soul like ours, he is the "one who in every respect has been tempted as we are, yet without sinning" (*Heb* 4:15). Jesus is born in Bethlehem.[52] He has a genealogy, or a family tree.[53] He summits himself to circumcision.[54] He has an infancy and a youth similar to his contemporaries.[55] He speaks, he experiences hunger[56] and thirst.[57] He eats and drinks.[58] He sleeps.[59] He sweats blood.[60] He is scourged and crucified, dies and is buried.[61] He has a human soul. He feels sadness,[62] fear,[63] anger,[64] love,[65] happiness,[66] and compassion.[67] He also cries.[68] He has a human

---

[51] SAINT LEO THE GREAT. *Tractatus septem et nonaginta:* PL 1657. (Editorial translation)
[52] Cf. *Mt* 2:1.
[53] Cf. *Mt* 1:1-17; *Lk* 3:23-38.
[54] Cf. *Lk* 2:21-22.
[55] Cf. *Lk* 4:22.
[56] Cf. *Mt* 4:2.
[57] Cf. *Jn* 19:28.
[58] Cf. *Mt* 11:19; *Lk* 5:34.
[59] Cf. *Jn* 4:6.
[60] Cf. *Lk* 22:44.
[61] Cf. *Mt* 26 and 27; *Mk* 14 and 15; *Lk* 22 and 23; *Jn* 18 and 19.
[62] Cf. *Mt* 26:37.
[63] Cf. *Mk* 14:33.
[64] Cf. *Mk* 3:5; *Jn* 2:15.
[65] Cf. *Mk* 10:21; *Jn* 19:26.
[66] Cf. *Jn* 11:15; *Lk* 10:21.
[67] Cf. *Heb* 2:17; 4:15; 5:2.
[68] Cf. *Lk* 19:41; *Jn* 11:35; *Heb* 5:7.

will and human desires as we see when, as a man,[69] he obeys his Father. In the Garden, he says to his Father: "Not what I will, but what thou wilt" (*Mk* 14:36).

The fact that God has made himself a man is one of the greatest mysteries of our faith. The Latin word for flesh is *caro, carnis.* Thus, the mystery by which God "became flesh" (*Jn* 1:14) is called the "Incarnation."

No possible comparison or example would make us completely understand this wonder. It surpasses the strength of our intellect and is superior to the entire created universe. However, in order to try to understand even a part of this mystery, we can imagine what it would be like for us if, offended by an ant that had bitten us, we made ourselves ants without ceasing to be people. How great our humility would be in taking on a nature so inferior to our own! What great love we would demonstrate for the ants! How many dangers we would have to endure for them! How many sufferings! However, in this example, our gesture of generosity would not imply a jump from the unlimited to the limited. Rather, it would remain always on the plane of the limited. We, who are already limited, would make ourselves even more limited. God, on the other hand, who is infinite and unlimited, "emptied himself" (*Phil* 2:7) and made himself man—finite and limited—without ceasing to be God.

It is unparalleled! What humility, what love, that God becomes man; that the Lord of all empties himself, becoming almost nothing! What generosity to willingly bear all the sufferings, such as those suffered by the Son of God in order to become man "so that men could become the sons of God!"[70]

3. ONE LORD JESUS CHRIST, TRUE GOD AND TRUE MAN

It is not enough, however, to confess that Jesus Christ has a human and a divine nature; that is to say, that Jesus is God and

---

[69] Cf. *Jn* 8:29; 5:30.
[70] SAINT AUGUSTINE. *Sermon 185:* PL 38, 997-999. (Editorial translation)

man at the same time. We must also affirm that what united both natures is the One Person of Christ, who is the Person of the Word, the Second Person of the Trinity. In Christ, there are not two persons, one divine and the other human; but, there is only One Person who is divine.

Saint Paul teaches us about Christ that: "He who descended is he who also ascended" (*Eph* 4:10). The unity of the Person of Jesus Christ is illustrated in that he descended, which is to say that the Son of God assumed a human nature; however, he also ascended, which is to say that the Son of Man, according to his human nature, was elevated to the sublimity of the immortal life. Thus, it is the same Son of God and Son of Man who ascends.[71]

Thus, the following expressions are true: "the Word became flesh" (*Jn* 1:14); the Virgin Mary is "Mother of God"[72]; they have crucified the Lord of glory (who is God) (cf. *1 Cor* 2:8), because actions belong to the Person. It is not my hand that writes, but rather I (my person). If I get into a car accident, the fault does not fall upon my foot for not breaking on time, but rather upon me.

In the same way, everything Jesus Christ did according to his human nature (to be born, speak, work, perform miracles, suffer, die) are actions that must be attributed to the Son of God, the Divine Person. Therefore, each of these actions, by being actions of the Word of God, possesses an infinite value; they are actions of God. If, in fact, there were two persons in Christ, you could not say that the Word became flesh. We would have to say that the Virgin is the Mother of the Christ-man, not the Mother of God. Furthermore, we could not write down that the Lord of Glory was crucified. Hence, our sins would remain in us because only God can save us from them.

Intending to emphasize the unity in Christ, some heretics denied the duality of the two natures found in Christ. Others, on the other hand, over-emphasized the duality in Christ and ended

---

[71] Cf. Saint Thomas Aquinas. *Summa Contra Gentiles*. Trans. Antón C. Pegis, F.R.S.C. Notre Dame: University of Notre Dame Press, 1975. IV, XXVIII.
[72] Council of Ephesus. Dz. 251.

up destroying the unity of the Person. All of these attempts "are not of God."[73]

Faith confesses that "with one accord we confess one and the same Son, our Lord Jesus Christ,... acknowledged in two natures,… not divided or separated into two persons, but one and the same Son only begotten God Word, Lord Jesus Christ."[74]

As a union of person, or hypostasis, the union of the two natures in Christ is called the **hypostatic union**.

ARTICLE 3
"I BELIEVE THAT HE WAS CONCEIVED BY THE POWER OF THE HOLY SPIRIT, AND WAS BORN OF THE VIRGIN MARY"

Our Lord Jesus Christ, as God, was begotten from all eternity by God the Father, without needing a mother. As man, he was born in time from a mother, without needing a father.

1. THE MOST HOLY VIRGIN MARY

1. HER INCOMPARABLE GREATNESS

"God the Father made an assemblage of all the waters, and he named it the sea. He made an assemblage of all his graces, and he called it Mary."[75] This is why the angel Gabriel called Mary "full of grace" (*Lk* 1:28). Mary is the most sublime creature that has ever existed and will ever exist. She is incomparably superior to all the angels and all the saints together. Why? Because she was the creature God chose to be the Mother of his only Son, the only creature who lovingly gave her flesh and her blood so that the Second Person of the Holy Trinity could become man in her womb. "When the Church 'enters more intimately into the

---

[73] Cf. *1 Jn* 4:3.
[74] COUNCIL OF CHALCEDON. Dz. 148.
[75] SAINT LOUIS MARIE DE MONTFORT. *True Devotion to Mary*. New York: Montfort Publications, 1980. 23.

72

supreme mystery of the Incarnation,' she thinks of the Mother of Christ with profound reverence and devotion. Mary belongs indissolubly to the mystery of Christ, and she belongs also to the mystery of the Church from the beginning, from the day of the Church's birth."[76]

For this reason, God showered Mary with remarkable privileges: being Immaculate from the very instant of her Conception in the womb of her mother, Saint Anne; being a perfect Virgin and Mother at the same time; being the Mother of God and the spiritual Mother of all men; being the Co-Redemptrix, Mediator and Dispenser of all graces; being assumed body and soul into heaven; being Queen and Lady of the Heavens and Earth; being Mother of the Church, etc.

2. THE NECESSITY OF PRAISING HER

Saint Augustine, who very much admired the glories of Mary, says: "all the tongues of men would not be enough to worthily praise her, not even when all their members would convert into tongues."[77]

We should often praise and implore her with these words:

With every breath of my life,	*Mientras mi vida alentare,*
All my love for you.	*Todo mi amor para ti.*
Dear Mother of mine, my Mother!	*¡Madre mía, Madre mía!*
Even though my love forget you	*Aunque mi amor te olvidare*
Never forget me!	*¡Tú no te olvides de mí!*

Do not think that the honor we pay to God diminishes because we give honor to his mother.

-"The glory of sons is their fathers" (*Prov* 17:6).

-"Who can pretend that the honor bestowed on a mother does not redound to the honor of the son?"[78]

---

[76] JOHN PAUL II. *Redemptoris Mater.* 27.
[77] *De Assumptione.* PL: 40, 1145. (Editorial translation)
[78] SAINT ALPHONSUS OF LIGUORI. *The Glories of Mary.* Illinois: Tan Books and Publishers, Inc., 1977. 5, I, p. 128.

-Saint Bernard says: "Let us not imagine that we obscure the glory of the Son by the great praise we lavish on the Mother."[79]

-"Without noticing, love for the Virgin led me to know and to love Jesus" (Blessed Ceferino Namuncurá).[80]

3. THE MOTHER OF GOD

When the Virgin went to visit her cousin Elizabeth, Elizabeth received her by calling her: "the mother of my Lord" (*Lk* 1:43). Hence, Mary is the true Mother of God, because she gave birth to God.

Saint Cyril of Alexandria, the main defender of the divine maternity of Mary, said: "If one does not recognize Mary as the Mother of God, it is due to a separation from God."[81] Consequently, the Council of Ephesus solemnly declared "the holy Virgin is the Mother of God (*Theotokos*)."[82] Why? Because the Most Holy Virgin conceived and gave birth to the Second Person of the Holy Trinity. In her holy womb, the Word assumed human nature. "In fact, the One whom she conceived as man by the Holy Spirit, who truly became her Son according to the flesh, was none other than the Father's eternal Son, the second person of the Holy Trinity."[83]

4. HER IMMACULATE VIRGINITY

The Holy Virgin was, then, the true Mother of God.

However, she remained "always virgin,"[84] that is to say, "before bringing forth, at bringing forth and always after bringing forth."[85]

---

[79] SAINT ALPHONSUS OF LIGUORI. *The Glories of Mary*. Illinois: Tan Books and Publishers, Inc., 1977. 5, I, p. 128.

[80] RAÚL ENTRAIGAS. *El Mancebo de la Tierra*. Ed. Inst. Salesiano de Artes Gráficas, Buenos Aires, 1970. p. 175. (Editorial translation)

[81] *Epistle* 101, 4. (Editorial translation)

[82] Dz. 111a.

[83] *Catechism of the Catholic Church*. 495.

[84] *Roman Missal*. Eucharistic Prayer I.

[85] PAUL IV, from August 7, 1555. Dz. 993.

Saint Basil said: "Those who are the friends of Christ cannot bear to hear that the Mother of God ceased to be a virgin at one point."[86]

It is true that the Gospels refer several times to the "brothers of Jesus," but in the language of the Jews "brother" means "close relative." Thus, these "brothers" are never called sons of Mary, because they are only close relatives of Jesus. Also, Saint Peter calls about three thousand people "brothers" (cf. *Acts* 2:29); and obviously Peter's mother did not have three thousand sons!

Pope Pius IX declared that the "most Blessed Virgin Mary, Mother of God…in the first instant of her creation and in the first instant of the soul's infusion into the body, was, by a special grace and privilege of God, in view of the merits of Jesus Christ, her Son and the Redeemer of the human race, preserved free from all stain of original sin."[87]

5. THE MOTHER OF ALL MEN

Jesus Christ is the one who brings the grace of God to all men: "I came that they may have life" (*Jn* 10:10). By bringing us to Jesus Christ, the Virgin offers us the supernatural life of grace, which is why she is the spiritual, supernatural Mother of all men.

"Wherefore in the same holy bosom of his most chaste Mother Christ took to Himself flesh, and united to Himself the spiritual body formed by those who were to believe in Him. Hence Mary, carrying the Savior within her, may be said to have also carried all those whose life was contained in the life of the Savior."[88]

At the foot of the cross, the Virgin was commissioned to be the Mother of all as Jesus said to her while pointing at Saint John: "Behold your son" (*Jn* 19:26). At that moment, Saint John represented all of mankind. The Virgin "now continues to fulfill from heaven her maternal function as the cooperator in the birth

---

[86] *Homilia in sanctam Christi generationem.* n. 5, PG: 31, 1468. (Editorial translation)
[87] *Ineffabilis Deus*, December 8, 1854: Dz. 2803.
[88] SAINT PIUS X. Encyclical letter *Ad diem illum.* 10.

and development of divine life in the individual souls of redeemed men."[89]

Mary is "our mother in the order of grace."[90] We must love her greatly, because "whoever loves Mary is blessed indeed (Saint Maria Mazzarello)."[91]

Since she is our Mother—our good Mother—and, in order that she may always nurture, educate, and protect us, we should consecrate ourselves to her every day with this beautiful and ancient prayer:

Blessed be your purity	*Bendita sea tu pureza*
And may it be so for eternity	*Y eternamente lo sea,*
For God recreates entirely	*Pues todo un Dios se recrea,*
In such gracious beauty.	*En tan graciosa belleza.*
To you celestial princess	*A Ti, celestial princesa,*
O Sacred Virgin Mary	*Virgen sagrada María*
I offer you today	*Yo te ofrezco en este día,*
My heart, my soul, my life;	*Alma, vida y corazón;*
Turn to me with compasssion	*Mírame con compasión;*
Never leave my side, dear Mother.	*No me dejes, Madre mía.*
Amen.	*Amén.*

You can also consecrate yourself to her with this prayer:

O my Lady, O my Mother	*¡Oh Señora mía! ¡Oh María mía…!*
I offer myself entirely to you,	*Yo me ofrezco todo a vos;*
and as assurance of my filial affection	*y en prueba de mi filial afecto*
I consecrate to you today,	*os consagro en este día*
my eyes, my ears,	*mis ojos, mis oídos,*
my lips and my heart—	*mi lengua y mi corazón,*
In a word, all my being.	*en una palabra, todo mi ser.*
Since I am all yours,	*Ya que soy todo vuestro,*
O Mother of Goodness,	*¡Oh Madre de bondad!,*

---

[89] PAUL VI. Apostolic exhortation *Signum magnum.* 21.
[90] VATICAN COUNCIL II. *Lumen Gentium,* 61.
[91] Cited in: ALBAN BUTLER. *Lives of the Saints.* t. II, 3rd ed. in Spanish, Mexico 1969, p. 298. (Editorial translation)

Keep me and defend me   *guárdame y defiéndeme*
as a possession belonging to you.   *como cosa y posesión vuestra.*
Amen.   *Amén.*

John Paul II took *Totus tuus* (All yours) from Saint Louis Marie Grignion de Montfort as the Episcopal motto of his papal shield.[92]

6. CO-REDEMPTRIX

"The sorrowful Virgin participated with Jesus Christ in the work of redemption, offering it in union with the cross as a Victim...as our Co-redemptrix associated to his sufferings."[93]

"At the foot of the cross, at each instant, she offered the sacrifice of the life of Jesus with the greatest pain and greatest love for us."[94]

Oh, how much the Virgin loved us! How much we should love her! Love is paid with love!

7. ASSUMED INTO HEAVEN

"The Immaculate Mother of God, the ever Virgin Mary, having completed the course of her earthly life, was assumed body and soul into heavenly glory."[95]

Since she is adorned with all virtues, being "full of grace" (*Lk* 1:28), she is an example of all the virtues for all men.

8. SUPPLICANT OMNIPOTENCE

At the wedding of Cana (*Jn* 2:1-11), upon the request of the Holy Virgin, Jesus anticipated his hour and performed his first miracle. From then on, the Holy Virgin has continued to intercede for us with her Son. The Holy Fathers and the Popes call her "Supplicant Omnipotence"[96] because she is capable of

---

[92] *True Devotion of Mary.* 233.
[93] PIUS XI. Epistle *Apostolica Explorata res.* February 2, 1923. (Editorial translation)
[94] SAINT ALPHONSUS OF LIGUORI. *The Glories of Mary.*
[95] PIUS XII. Apostolic Constitution *Munificentissimus Deus.* Nov. 1, 1950, 44.
[96] GREGORY ALASTRUEY. *Treatise on the Holy Virgin.* Madrid: BAC, 1945. p. 771 (Editorial translation)

obtaining from God everything that she asks him in prayer. We Catholics go to her with our supplications "not because we do not trust in the mercy of God, but rather because we do not trust our own dignity; and we entrust ourselves to Mary so that her dignity may supplement our misery."[97]

We must turn to the Holy Virgin every day, especially by praying the Holy Rosary.[98] In Lourdes and Fatima, the Virgin herself earnestly asked us to pray the Rosary every day.

Every Catholic should have a great devotion to the Virgin who is always before God praying for our salvation. "He who has assured the help of his Mother, will not perish before the eternal Judge."[99] "It is impossible for him, who directs himself with confidence to Mary and is embraced by her, to ever be lost."[100] Thus, as Pope John XXIII teaches: "he who refuses to grasp the helping hand of Mary, jeopardizes his salvation."[101]

With Saint Bernard, let us always ask her:

Remember, O most gracious Virgin Mary,
that never was it known
that anyone who fled to Thy protection,
implored Thy help,
or sought Thy intercession
was left unaided.
Inspired by this confidence,
I fly unto Thee,
O Virgin of virgins, my Mother!
To Thee do I come,
before Thee I stand, sinful and sorrowful.
O Mother of the Word Incarnate,
despise not my petitions,
but in Thy mercy, hear and answer me. Amen.

---

[97] SAINT ANSELM (Editorial translation)
[98] Cf. a practical method for praying the rosary is on page 325.
[99] SAINT PETER DAMIEN (Editorial translation)
[100] Cf. SAINT ANSLEM: PL 158, 956. (Editorial translation)
[101] Epistle, *Aetate hac nostra*. April 27, 1959.

9. MOTHER OF THE CHURCH

The Holy Virgin has been called Mother of the Church. As the Mother of the Head of the Church, Jesus Christ, she is also the Mother of the members that belong to the Head—that is to say—of all of us, Mother of all Christians. "Jesus Christ, the head of mankind, is born of her, the predestinate, who are the members of this head, must also to as a necessary consequence be born of her. One and the same Mother does not give birth to the head without the members nor to the members without the head... in the order of grace likewise the head and members are born of the same mother."[102] "At Calvary, Mary began to be, in a particular way, Mother of all the Church."[103]

It is normal for a son to honor his mother. Thus, the Church—the daughter of Mary—venerates her Mother under many titles and advocations. Some of them refer to the principle mysteries or virtues of her life: the Immaculate Conception, the Nativity, the Most Holy Name, the Presentation in the temple, the Purification, the Annunciation, the Visitation, Mother of God, Immaculate Heart, Our Lady of Sorrows, Mary Help of Christians, Mary Queen, the Assumption, of the Rosary, of Consolation, of Divine Providence, of Mercy, of Peace, of Piety, of Health, of Graces, of Succor, etc. Other advocations take the name of the places where she appeared or where there is devotion to her. For example: Our Lady of Lourdes, of Fatima, of Luján, of Itatí, of the Valley, of Montserrat, of Pompeya, of Carmel, of the Pillar, of the Snows, of Guadalupe, of the Garden, etc. These are all titles or advocations of the one and only Virgin Mary, Mother of God and our mother. We can call her by any name we like. She will always come to our help immediately, like a good mother who always longs for the best for her children.

And we should always say to each other: "Hail Mary, full of grace!"

---

[102] SAINT LOUIS MARIE DE MONTFORT. *True Devotion to Mary.* 32.
[103] SAINT ALPHONSUS OF LIGUORI. (Editorial translation)

2. THE MYSTERIES OF THE LIFE OF CHRIST

1. THE ENTIRE LIFE OF CHRIST IS A MYSTERY

We already know that Christ's eternal Father is God the Father; that Christ is the Second Person of the Holy Trinity, true God and true man united in one Person; and, that Christ's Mother is the Most Holy Virgin, as greeted by the angel Gabriel.[104]

"Many things about Jesus of interest to human curiosity do not figure in the Gospels. Almost nothing is said about his hidden life at Nazareth, and even a great part of his public life is not recounted. What is written in the Gospels was set down there 'so that you may believe that Jesus is the Christ, the Son of God, and that believing you may have life in his name.'

The Gospels were written by men who were among the first to have the faith and wanted to share it with others. Having known in faith who Jesus is, they could see and make others see the traces of his mystery in all his earthly life. From the swaddling clothes of his birth to the vinegar of his Passion and the shroud of his Resurrection, everything in Jesus' life was a sign of his mystery. His deeds, miracles, and words all revealed that 'in him the whole fullness of deity dwells bodily.'"[105]

The geographical location of the country of Jesus

The Annunciation took place in Nazareth, a village in Galilee, in the northern region of Palestine near the towns of Cana, Nain, (located around the Lake of Genesaret, also known as the Lake of Tiberias or of Galilee) Capernaum, Bethsaida, Magdala, Tiberias, etc. There were two other regions in Palestine: the central region, called Samaria, where the town of Sichar was; and the southern region, called Judea, where the city of Jerusalem and the towns of Bethlehem, Bethany, and Jericho were. Palestine is located in Asia Minor, on the eastern coast of the Mediterranean Sea. Currently, the territory is mostly occupied by the state of Israel.

---

[104] Cf. *Lk* 1:26-28.
[105] *Catechism of the Catholic Church*. 514-515.

2. THE MYSTERIES OF CHRIST'S INFANCY AND HIDDEN LIFE

a) The mystery of the Nativity

With a census decree ordered by the Roman Emperor (since at that time Palestine belonged politically to the Roman Empire), the Virgin Mary and Saint Joseph, her husband, had to go to the town of Bethlehem, which is approximately five miles south of Jerusalem. There, in a poor and humble stable, our Lord Jesus Christ, the Savior of the world, was born.[106]

We find an account of the birth of our Lord in the Gospel of Luke:

> In those days a decree went out from Caesar Augustus that all the world should be enrolled. This was the first enrollment, when Quirinius was governor of Syria. And all went to be enrolled, each to his own city. And Joseph also went up from Galilee, from the city of Nazareth, to Judea to the city of David, which is called Bethlehem, because he was of the house and lineage of David, to be enrolled with Mary his betrothed, who was with child. And while they were there, the time came for her to deliver the child. And she gave birth to her first born son and wrapped him in swaddling clothes, and laid him in a manger, because there was no place for them in the inn. And in that region there were shepherds out in the field, keeping watch over their flock by night. And an angel of the Lord appeared to them, and the glory of the Lord shone around them, and they were filled with fear. And the angel said to them, "Be not afraid; for behold, I bring you good news of great joy which will come to all the people; for to you is born this day in the city of David a Savior, who is Christ the Lord. And this will be a sign for you: you will find a babe wrapped in swaddling clothes and lying in a manger." And suddenly there was with the angel a multitude of the heavenly host praising God and saying, "Glory to God in the highest, and on earth peace among men with whom he is pleased!"
>
> When the angels went away from them into heaven, the shepherds said to one another, "Let us go over to Bethlehem and see this thing that has happened, which the Lord has made

---

[106] Cf. *Lk* 2:1-20.

known to us." And they went with haste, and found Mary and Joseph, and the babe lying in a manger. And when they saw him, they made known the saying which had been told them concerning this child; and all who heard it wondered at what the shepherds told them. But Mary kept all these things, pondering them in her heart.

And the shepherds returned, glorifying and praising God for all they had heard and seen, as it had been told them.

(Lk 2:1-20)

"The Church each year celebrates the mystery of this great love of God toward man (the 25th of December)."[107]

b) The mysteries of the infancy of Jesus

The Circumcision: Jesus was circumcised on the eighth day, according to the law. The Gospel narrates:

And at the end of eight days, when he was circumcised, he was called Jesus, the name given by the angel before he was conceived in the womb.

(Lk 2:21)

The Epiphany: Jesus was adored by three magi from the East, to whom he was revealed as the Messiah, as the Son of God and Savior of the world. This mystery is known as the Epiphany (which means manifestation), because it is the first manifestation of the Lord to the pagans or gentiles.

The Gospel according to Saint Matthew narrates:

Now when Jesus was born in Bethlehem of Judea in the days of Herod the king, behold, wise men from the East came to Jerusalem, saying. "Where is he who has been born king of the Jews? For we have seen his star in the East, and have come to worship him." When Herod the king heard this, he was troubled, and all Jerusalem with him; and assembling all the chief priests and scribes of the people, he inquired of them where the Christ was to be born. They told him, "In Bethlehem of Judea; for so it is written by the prophet: 'And you, O Bethlehem, in the land of

---

[107] SAINT CHARLES BORROMEO. *Cartas Pastorales, Acta Ecclesiae Mediolanensis.* t. II, Lyon 1683, 916-917. (Editorial translation)

Judah, are by no means least among the rulers of Judah; for from
you shall come a ruler who will govern my people Israel.'" Then
Herod summoned the wise men secretly and ascertained from
them what time the star appeared; and he sent them to
Bethlehem, saying, "Go and search diligently for the child, and
when you have found him bring me word, that I too may come
and worship him." When they had heard the king they went
their way; and lo, the star which they had seen in the East went
before them, till it came to rest over the place where the child
was. When they saw the star, they rejoiced exceedingly with great
joy; and going into the house they saw the child with Mary his
mother, and they fell down and worshiped him. Then, opening
their treasures, they offered him gifts, gold, frankincense, and
myrrh.

(Mt 2:1-11)

The Presentation of Jesus in the Temple: "Jesus is recognized as the
long-expected Messiah, the 'light to the nations' and the 'glory of
Israel', but also 'a sign that is spoken against.' The sword of
sorrow predicted for Mary announces Christ's perfect and unique
oblation on the cross that will impart the salvation God had
'prepared in the presence of all peoples.'"[108]

And when the time came for their purification according to
the law of Moses, they brought him up to Jerusalem to present
him to the Lord (as it is written in the law of the Lord, "Every
male that opens the womb shall be called holy to the Lord") and
to offer a sacrifice according to what is said in the law of the
Lord, "a pair of turtledoves, or two young pigeons."

Now there was a man in Jerusalem, whose name was Simeon,
and this man was righteous and devout, looking for the
consolation of Israel, and the Holy Spirit was upon him. It had
been revealed to him by the Holy Spirit that he should not see
death before he had seen the Lord's Christ. And inspired by the
Spirit he came into the temple; and when the parents brought in
the child Jesus, to do for him according to the custom of the law,
he took him up in his arms and blessed God and said, "Lord,
now lettest thou thy servant depart in peace, according to thy
word; for mine eyes have seen thy salvation which thou has

---

[108] *Catechism of the Catholic Church.* 529.

prepared in the presence of all peoples, a light for revelation to the Gentiles, and for glory to thy people Israel."

And his father and his mother marveled at what was said about him; and Simeon blessed them and said to Mary his mother, "Behold, this child is set for the fall and rising of many in Israel, and for a sign that is spoken against (and a sword will pierce through your own soul also), that thoughts out of many hearts may be revealed."

And there was a prophetess, Anna, the daughter of Phanuel, of the tribe of Asher; she was of a great age, having lived with her husband seven years from her virginity, and as a widow till she was eighty-four. She did not depart from the temple, worshipping with fasting and prayer night and day. And coming up at that very hour she gave thanks to God, and spoke of him to all who were looking for the redemption of Jerusalem.

(Lk 2:22-38)

The Escape to Egypt: "The **flight into Egypt** and the massacre of the innocents make manifest the opposition of darkness to the light: 'He came to his own home, and his own people received him not.' Christ's whole life was lived under the sign of persecution. His own share it with him. Jesus' departure from Egypt recalls the Exodus and presents him as the definitive liberator."[109]

This event is recounted by the apostle and evangelist Saint Matthew:

And being warned in a dream not to return to Herod, they departed to their own country by another way.

Now when they had departed, behold, an angel of the Lord appeared to Joseph in a dream and said, "Rise, take the child and his mother, and flee to Egypt, and remain there till I tell you; for Herod is about to search for the child, to destroy him."

And he rose and took the child and his mother by night, and departed to Egypt, and remained there until the death of Herod. This was to fulfill what the Lord had spoken by the prophet, "Out of Egypt have I called my son."

---

[109] *Catechism of the Catholic Church.* 530.

Then Herod, when he saw that he had been tricked by the wise men, was in a furious rage, and he sent and killed all the male children in Bethlehem and in all that region who were two years old or under, according to the time he had ascertained from the wise men.

Then was fulfilled what was spoken by the prophet Jeremiah: "A voice was heard in Ramah, wailing and loud lamentation, Rachel weeping for her children; she refused to be consoled, because they were no more."

But when Herod died, behold, an angel of the Lord appeared in a dream to Joseph in Egypt, saying, "Rise, take the child and his mother, and go to the land of Israel, for those who sought the child's life are dead." And he rose and took the child and his mother, and went to the land of Israel. But when he heard that Archelaus reigned over Judea in place of his father Herod, he was afraid to go there, and being warned in a dream he withdrew to the district of Galilee. And he went and dwelt in a city of Nazareth, that what was spoken by the prophets might be fulfilled. "He shall be called a Nazarene."

(Mt 2:12-23)

c) The mysteries of the hidden life of Jesus

After being presented in the Temple and adored by the magi, Jesus fled to Egypt. After two years, Jesus returned to Nazareth where, Joseph, his adoptive father, worked as a carpenter. When Jesus was twelve years old, he went to the Temple and conversed with the doctors of the Jewish law. Jesus remained in Nazareth until he was thirty years old, obeying, working alongside his fellow men, praying and growing "in wisdom and in stature and in favor with God and man" (*Lk* 2:52).

The finding of Jesus in the Temple is the only event in the Gospels that breaks the silence of the hidden years of Jesus. Saint Luke recounts this episode, which he probably heard from the lips of the Most Holy Virgin:

And the child grew and became strong, filled with wisdom; and the favor of God was upon him. Now his parents went to Jerusalem every year at the feast of the Passover. And when he was twelve years old, they went up according to the custom; and when the feast was ended, as they were returning, the boy Jesus stayed behind in Jerusalem. His parents did not know it, but supposing him to be in the company they went a day's journey,

85

and they sought him among their kinsfolk and acquaintances; and when they did not find him, they returned to Jerusalem, seeking him.

After three days they found him in the temple, sitting among the teachers, listening to them and asking them questions; and all who heard him were amazed at his understanding and his answers. And when they saw him they were astonished; and his mother said to him, "Son, why have you treated us so? Behold, your father and I have been looking for you anxiously." And he said them, "How is it that you sought me? Did you not know that I must be in my Father's house?" And they did not understand the saying which he spoke to them.

And he went down with them and came to Nazareth, and was obedient to them; and his mother kept all these things in her heart. And Jesus increased in wisdom and in stature, and in favor with God and men.

(Lk 2:40-52)

"During the greater part of his life Jesus shared the condition of the vast majority of human beings: a daily life spent without evident greatness, a life of manual labor. His religious life was that of a Jew obedient to the law of God, a life in the community. From this whole period it is revealed to us that Jesus was 'obedient' to his parents and that he 'increased in wisdom and in stature, and in favor with God and man.'

Jesus' obedience to his mother and legal father fulfills the fourth commandment perfectly and was the temporal image of his filial obedience to his Father in heaven. The everyday obedience of Jesus to Joseph and Mary both announced and anticipated the obedience of Holy Thursday: 'Not my will. . .' The obedience of Christ in the daily routine of his hidden life was already inaugurating his work of restoring what the disobedience of Adam had destroyed."[110]

---

[110] *Catechism of the Catholic Church.* 531-532.

3. The Mysteries of the Public Life of Jesus

a) The Baptism of Jesus

At about thirty years of age, Jesus began to manifest himself publicly and was baptized by Saint John the Baptist:

In those days came John the Baptist, preaching in the wilderness of Judea, "Repent, for the kingdom of heaven is at hand."

For this is he who was spoken of by the prophet Isaiah when he said, "The voice of one crying in the wilderness: Prepare the way of the Lord, make his paths straight."

Now John wore a garment of camel's hair, and a leather girdle around his waist; and his food was locusts and wild honey.

Then went out to him Jerusalem and all Judea and all the region about the Jordan, and they were baptized by him in the river Jordan, confessing their sins.

But when he saw many of the Pharisees and Sadducees coming for baptism, he said to them, "You brood of vipers! Who warned you to flee from the wrath to come? Bear fruit that befits repentance, and do no presume to say to yourselves, 'We have Abraham as our father'; for I tell you, God is able from these stones to raise up children to Abraham. Even now the axe is laid to the root of the tress; every tree therefore that does not bear good fruit is cut down and thrown into the fire. I baptize you with water for repentance, but he who is coming after me is mightier than I, whose sandals I am not worthy to carry; he will baptize you with the Holy Spirit and with fire. His winnowing fork is in his hand, and he will clear his threshing floor and gather his wheat into the granary, but the chaff he will burn with unquenchable fire."

Then Jesus came from Galilee to the Jordan to John, to be baptized by him. John would have prevented him, saying, "I need to be baptized by you, and do you come to me?" But Jesus answered him, "Let it be so now; for thus is it fitting for us to fulfill all righteousness." Then he consented.

And Jesus was baptized, he went up immediately from the water, and behold, the heavens were opened and he saw the Spirit of God descending like a dove, and alighting on him; and lo, a voice from heaven saying, "This is my beloved Son, with whom I am well pleased."

(Mt 3:1-17)

"From the beginning of his public life, at his baptism, Jesus is the 'Servant,' wholly consecrated to the redemptive work that he will accomplish by the 'baptism' of his Passion."[111]

b) The Temptations of Jesus

"The temptation in the desert shows Jesus, the humble Messiah, who triumphs over Satan by his total adherence to the plan of salvation willed by the Father."[112]

> Then Jesus was led up by the Spirit into the wilderness to be tempted by the devil. And he fasted forty days and forty nights, and afterward he was hungry. And the tempter came and said to him, "If you are the Son of God, command these stones to become loaves of bread." But he answered, "It is written, 'Man shall not live by bread alone, but by every word that proceeds from the mouth of God.'" Then the devil took him to the holy city, and set him on the pinnacle of the temple, and said to him, "If you are the Son of God, throw yourself down; for it is written, 'He will give his angels charge of you,' and 'on their hands they will bear you up, lest you strike your foot against a stone.'" Jesus said to him, "Again it is written, 'You shall not tempt the Lord your God.'" Again, the devil took him to a very high mountain, and showed him all the kingdoms of the world and the glory of them; and he said to him, "All this I will give you, if you will fall down and worship me." Then Jesus said to him, "Begone, Satan! For it is written, 'You shall worship the Lord your God and him only shall you serve.'" Then the devil left him, and behold, angels came and ministered to him.

(Mt 4:1-11)

The example of Jesus suffering the attacks of the devil in the desert should encourage us in the combat against sin. In order to give us strength against temptation, Jesus conquered "our temptations with his own:"[113]

-in order that nobody, no matter how holy they are, will believe themselves to be free from temptation: "My son, if you

---

[111] *Catechism of the Catholic Church.* 565.
[112] *Catechism of the Catholic Church.* 566.
[113] SAINT GREGORY THE GREAT. *Homilies about the Gospels.* XVI, 1. (Editorial translation)

come forward to serve the Lord...prepare yourself for temptation" (*Sir* 2:1);

-in order to teach us the promptitude, firmness, and justice needed in order to conquer the temptations of the devil: "the devil is conquered by Christ by righteousness, not by power;"[114]

-in order that we trust more in Christ's mercy; "For we have not a high priest who is unable to sympathize with our weaknesses, but one who in every respect has been tempted as we are, yet without sinning" (*Heb* 4:15).

You must not be afraid of having great temptations. Saint Augustine teaches: "Our advance is made through our temptation, nor does a man become known to himself unless tempted, nor can he be crowned except he shall have conquered, nor can he conquer except he shall have striven, nor can he strive except shall he have experienced an enemy, and temptations."[115]

c) The preaching of the Kingdom of God and the threefold mission of Jesus as Messiah

"Now after John was arrested, Jesus came into Galilee, preaching the gospel of God, and saying, 'The time is fulfilled, and the kingdom of God is at hand; repent, and believe in the gospel'" (*Mk* 1:14-15). From that moment on, Jesus gave himself completely to the fulfillment of his threefold messianic mission:

-to instruct as a Teacher;
-to legislate as a King;
-to sanctify as a Priest.

1. As Teacher Jesus taught the truth

Christ was able to say of himself "I am the Truth" (*Jn* 14:6). Christ is the "light of the world" (*Jn* 8:12) and those who heard him "were astonished at his teaching, for he taught as one who had authority" (*Mk* 1:22).

---

[114] SAINT AUGUSTINE *De Trinitate*. L. XIII, 14, 18.
[115] *Enarrations on the Psalms*. LXI, 2.

What did Jesus teach?

Above all, Jesus taught what must be believed: who God is and how God is (the Holy Trinity[116]); that he is the only Son of God;[117] that he came to save all men;[118] that salvation comes to us through the sacraments;[119] that he will judge all men;[120] and that he came to bring a kingdom that "is not of this world" (*Jn* 18:36).

Jesus taught what must be done: to obey the commandments,[121] especially the "new" commandment to love God and neighbor;[122] to live in purity;[123] and to know the laws of the Kingdom of God, etc. Similarly, Jesus taught what must be received: Baptism;[124] forgiveness of sins;[125] the Eucharist,[126] etc.

Finally, Jesus taught what must be prayed: the Our Father.[127]

How did Jesus teach?

Jesus taught in several ways:

-through parables: by making comparisons and similarities. There are 120 parables in the Gospels.[128]

-through great sermons: the Sermon on the Mount;[129] the Sermon of the Bread of Life or the Eucharistic Sermon;[130] the sermon at the Last Supper;[131] against the Pharisees;[132] about the vocation of the Apostles;[133] on the indissolubility of matrimony;[134]

---

[116] Cf. *Mt* 28:19.
[117] Cf. *Mk* 9:7.
[118] Cf. *Mt* 20:28.
[119] Cf. *Jn* 3:5.
[120] Cf. *Mt* 20:31-46.
[121] Cf. *Mt* 7:21.
[122] Cf. *Mt* 22:37 and *Jn* 13:34.
[123] Cf. *Mt* 5:28.
[124] Cf. *Mk* 16:16.
[125] Cf. *Jn* 20:22.
[126] Cf. *Jn* 6:51.
[127] Cf. *Mt* 6:9-13.
[128] Cf. page 319.
[129] Cf. *Mt* 5:7.
[130] Cf. *Jn* 6:25-71.
[131] Cf. *Jn* 13:31; 17:26.
[132] Cf. *Mt* 23.
[133] Cf. *Mt* 9:36; 10:42.
[134] Cf. *Mt* 19:3-12.

on the destruction of Jerusalem and the end of the world;[135] on the Father and the Son;[136] on the feast of Tabernacles;[137] and on the feast of the Dedication.[138]

-through conversations: with the Apostles, with Nicodemus,[139] with the Samaritan woman,[140] with the Jews, etc.

-through what he did: miracles, prayer, fasts, sufferings, giving us an example of all the virtues, etc.

2. As King Jesus gave laws

Jesus called himself the "Good Shepherd" (*Jn* 10:11) because he taught us the way to heaven. Among the Jews, a king was called "Shepherd of his people." Thus, Jesus, the Good Shepherd, is King. Before Pilate, Jesus said: "You say that I am a king" (*Jn* 18:37). As King, Jesus has dominion over everything: "All authority in heaven and on earth has been given to me" (*Mt* 28:18). He is truly "King of kings and Lord of Lords" (*Rev* 19:16).

In the Sermon on the Mount, Jesus proclaimed the fundamental law of the Kingdom. Jesus also organized the Kingdom on earth, which is the Church, by recruiting disciples, teaching them, instituting the sacraments, naming the leader over all, etc. Finally, as King, Jesus has "all judgment" (*Jn* 5:22) over humanity and his sentence is not able to be appealed. The condemned "will go into eternal punishment, but the righteous into eternal life" (*Mt* 25:46).

3. As Priest Jesus sanctified man

Our Lord Jesus Christ did not limit himself to bringing only new truths and new laws; but he also brought new life, which is the grace of God. He is "a great high priest who has passed through the heavens" (*Heb* 4:14), who "became the source of eternal salvation to all who obey him" (*Heb* 5:9) and who offered

---

[135] Cf. *Mt* 24.
[136] Cf. *Jn* 17:47.
[137] Cf. *Jn* 7:14; 10:21.
[138] Cf. *Jn* 10:22-42.
[139] Cf. *Jn* 3:1-21.
[140] Cf. *Jn* 4:4-26.

himself on the cross to "bear the sins of many" (*Heb* 9:28). The Lord "has laid on him the iniquity of us all" (*Is* 53:6). Jesus became "sin" for us (*2 Cor* 5:21), becoming accursed for us, since it is written: "Cursed be everyone who hangs on a tree" (*Gal* 3:13). Jesus is the "eternal and high priest."[141] On the cross, Jesus is not only the Victim offered—"Christ has been sacrificed" (*1 Cor* 5:7) —but also the Priest who makes the offering. Jesus saved us by the sacrifice of his death on the cross: he "gave himself as a ransom for all" (*1 Tim* 2:6), freeing us from a five-fold slavery:

1) **Sin:** "In him we have…the forgiveness of our trespasses" (*Eph* 1:7). He "gave himself for us to redeem us from all iniquity" (*Tit* 2:14);

2) **The evil world:** "In the world you have tribulation; but be of good cheer, I have overcome the world" (*Jn* 16:33);

3) **The devil:** "He has delivered us from the dominion of darkness" (*Col* 1:13) and "disarmed the principalities and powers and made a public example of them, triumphing over them in him" (*Col* 2:15). "The reason the Son of God appeared was to destroy the words of the devil" (*1 Jn* 3:8);

4) **Death:** Jesus "abolished death" (*2 Tim* 1:10);

5) **Hell:** When Jesus saved us from sin, he saved us from the eternal punishments we deserved for our sin. Thus, Jesus prepared for us a place in heaven so that "where I am you may be also" (*Jn* 14:3).

Jesus was "lifted up" (*Jn* 3:14) vertically between heaven and earth because he came to unite God with man and man with God. Jesus died with his arms extended horizontally to embrace in his charity all men of all times, thus uniting them with each other and with God.

And so, Jesus is King, Prophet and Priest:

-King who promulgates laws and governs: "I am the Way."

---

[141] SAINT POLYCARP. *Martyrdom of Polycarp.* XIV, 3. (Editorial translation)

-Prophet who teaches authentic doctrine: "I am the Truth."

-Priest who communicates sanctification: "I am the Life."

ARTICLE 4
"HE SUFFERED UNDER PONTIUS PILATE, WAS CRUCIFIED, DIED AND WAS BURIED"

1. THE PRELUDES TO THE PASSION

In the time of Christ, Palestine was a province of the Roman Empire, governed under Pontius Pilate.[142] Jesus had spent more than three years of public life performing miracles, enlightening the world with his doctrine, and "doing good" (*Acts* 10:38). However, "men loved darkness rather than light because their deeds were evil" (*Jn* 3:19). They called Jesus "mad" (*Jn* 10:20), "possessed" (*Mk* 3:22), "a glutton and a drunkard" (*Mt* 11:19), an "imposter" (*Mt* 27:63), a "sinner" (*Jn* 9:24), of "leading the people astray" (*Jn* 7:12) and of "blaspheming" (*Mt* 9:3). They hated Jesus, persecuted him and plotted his death since their deeds were evil while Jesus' were good: "he has done all things well" (*Mk* 7:37).

Christ simply preached the truth. Christ called each one by name, without any fear. To the Pharisees, Jesus said: "scribes and Pharisees, hypocrites...blind guides...serpents, brood of vipers" (*Mt* 23). Jesus continues: "If God were your Father, you would love me... you are of your father the devil" (*Jn* 8:42.44). However, instead of repenting and converting when they saw "the works which no one else did" (*Jn* 15:24), they hated Christ and his Father. Thus, they fulfilled the prophecy said about Christ: they "hate me without cause" (*Ps* 69:4). Consequently, "the chief priests and the Pharisees gathered the council, and said, 'what are we to do? For this man performs many signs. If we let him go on thus, everyone will believe in him'...So from that day on they took counsel how to put him to death" (*Jn* 11:47-48.53). Among

---

[142] Cf. *1 Tim* 6:13.

them, some who were not so evil, did not dare to confess Jesus as Lord and God "for fear of the Pharisees…lest they should be put out of the synagogue: for they loved the praise of men more than the praise of God" (*Jn* 12:42-43).

2. THE PASSION OF OUR LORD JESUS CHRIST

According to the Gospel, Jesus "having loved his own who were in the world, he loved them to the end" (*Jn* 13:1). In this, Jesus demonstrated his incomparably great love and the extremity of his unsurpassable charity. The passion of Jesus, "no matter how one looks at it, whether focusing on the person who did the suffering or on the reason why he suffered, the mystery is so great that to the end of the world nothing equal to it can ever happen."[143]

For Jesus, the cross "was the pulpit of the Preacher, the altar of the Sacrificing Priest, the arena of the Combatant, the workshop of the Wonder-worker."[144]

Holy Thursday

Between 6pm and 11pm, our Lord Jesus Christ ate for the last time with the Apostles in the Cenacle. There, Jesus washed their feet,[145] exposed the traitorous disciple,[146] instituted the Holy Eucharist and the Catholic Priesthood,[147] preached his last sermon,[148] predicted the denial of Peter,[149] and prayed for himself, for his disciples, and for all believers.[150]

Then, Jesus went to the Garden of Olives, approximately a mile from the Cenacle. He was there from about 11pm to 1am and it was there that he sweated blood.

---

[143] LUIS DE LA PALMA, S.J. *The Sacred Passion*. Trans. Mary Gottschalk. New York: Scepter Publishers, 2004. Introduction, p. 9.
[144] SAINT ROBERT BELLARMINE. *Book of the Seven Words*, Preamble.
[145] Cf. *Jn* 13:2-20.
[146] Cf. *Jn* 13:21-30.
[147] Cf. *Lk* 22:19-20.
[148] Cf. *Jn* 13:31-16:4.
[149] Cf. *Jn* 16:5-33.
[150] Cf. *Jn* 17:1-26.

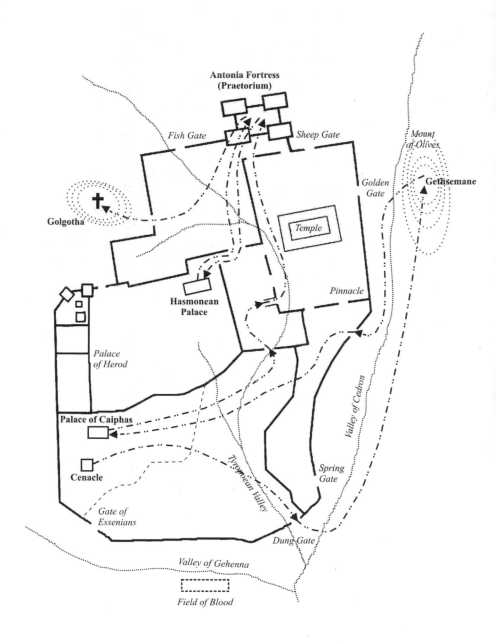

Antonia Fortress
(Praetorium)

Fish Gate

Sheep Gate

Mount
of Olives

Golden
Gate

Gethsemane

Golgotha

Temple

Hasmonean
Palace

Pinnacle

Palace
of Herod

Valley of Cedron

Palace of Caiphas

Cenacle

Tyropoean Valley

Spring
Gate

Gate of
Essenians

Dung Gate

Valley of Gehenna

Field of Blood

Good Friday

After Jesus was taken prisoner, he was brought to the house of Annas and Caiaphas where he was tried and condemned by the Sanhedrin (from about 1am to 6am).[151] Then, from 6am to 7am, Jesus was brought to the Antonia Fortress to appear before Pilate.[152] Between 7am and 8am, Pilate sent Jesus to Herod who was in the Hasmonean Palace.[153] After mocking Jesus and dressing him up like a fool, Herod sent him back to Pilate. From 8am to 10am, Pilate had Jesus scourged and crowned with thorns. Afterwards, Pilate attempted to free Jesus, but in the end he cowardly folded under the pressure of the Jews. Then, between 10:30am and 11:30am, Jesus, carrying the cross, began the *Via Crucis* (the way of the cross) from the Antonia Fortress to Calvary (about 7 or 8 blocks). Arriving at Calvary, or Golgotha, Jesus was crucified at noon. Hanging from the cross, Jesus preached his last sermon, which consisted of only seven words—seven phrases which are a summary of the Gospel. Seven claps of thunder that can still be heard echoing around the world. At 3pm, the Lord died. Between 4pm and 6pm, Jesus was buried.

Holy Saturday

The body of Jesus remained in the holy sepulcher watched over by the guards.

3. THE WORK OF OUR SALVATION

With his death on the cross, Jesus made reparation for the offenses men have committed and do commit against God. "The Lord has laid upon him the iniquity of us all" (*Is* 53:6) because he came "to give his life as a ransom for many" (*Mt* 20:28). "He made him to be sin who knew no sin" (*2 Cor* 5:21); which is to say that Jesus was made a "sacrifice for our sins."[154] Jesus died for all men without exception: "one has died for all" (*2 Cor* 5:14). Jesus

---

[151] Cf. *Mt* 26:50-66.
[152] Cf. *Jn* 18:23-28.
[153] Cf. *Lk* 23:6-12.
[154] XI COUNCIL OF TOLEDO. *Symbol of the Faith*. Dz. 286.

merited for all men the necessary graces for salvation, since "there is salvation in no one else" (*Acts* 4:12).

In her liturgies, the Church solemnly celebrates the mysteries of the Passion, Crucifixion, Death, and Burial of Jesus on the Thursday, Friday and Saturday of Holy Week. Likewise, these sacred mysteries are also commemorated and renewed in each Mass.

Whenever we look at the Crucifix, we must remember the great work Jesus accomplished for us, "who loved me and gave himself for me" (*Gal* 2:20). Kneeling in front of the Crucifix, we should pray:

Look upon me, good and gentle Jesus, kneeling before your holy presence. With great fervor, I pray that you may instill in my heart genuine convictions of faith, hope and charity, with a true sorrow for my sins and a firm resolve to amend them. As I, with all the love and compassion of my soul, contemplate your five wounds, I remember the words which long ago the prophet David spoke of you: "They have pierced my hands and my feet, I can count all my bones" (*Ps* 22:16-17). *Amen.*

"On this Cross is the 'Redeemer of man,' the Man of Sorrows, who has taken upon himself the physical and moral sufferings of the people of all times, so that *in love* they may find the salvific meaning of their sorrow and valid answers to all of their questions."[155]

4. LOVE FOR THE CROSS

The saints, who so loved our Lord Jesus Christ, also profoundly loved the cross. They knew that if the Master suffered the cross, his disciples would also have to suffer the cross because "a disciple is not above his teacher" (*Mt* 10:24).

Saint Paul said:

-"I decided to know nothing among you except Jesus Christ, and him Crucified" (*1 Cor* 2:2).

---

[155] JOHN PAUL II. Apostolic Letter *Salvifici Doloris*. 31.

-"If we endure with him, we shall also reign with him" (*2 Tim* 2:12).

-"I consider the sufferings of this present time are not worth comparing with the glory that is to be revealed to us" (*Rom* 8:18).

-"We rejoice in our sufferings, knowing…that hope does not disappoint us" (*Rom* 5:3ff).

-"For this slight momentary affliction is preparing us for an eternal weight of glory beyond all comparison" (*2 Cor* 4:17).

1. THE DESIRE OF THE SAINTS

The cross is the desire of the saints:

-"The hours that I spend without suffering seem to me to be lost hours, only pain makes my life more bearable" (Saint Margaret Mary Alacoque).[156]

- "Those who are captivated by the Passion of the honor of Christ, and who are hungry for the salvation of souls, hurry to take a seat at the table of the Holy Cross (Saint Catherine of Siena)."

-"O Lord, either to die or to suffer" (Saint Teresa of Avila).[157]

-"Not to die, but to suffer" (Saint Mary Magdalene de Pazzi).[158]

-"Lord, to suffer and be despised for You" (Saint John of the Cross).[159]

-"By the mercy of our beloved God, I do not desire to know anything else, nor enjoy any other consolation, apart from being crucified with Jesus" (Saint Paul of the Cross).[160]

---

[156] *Letter* 62 (March of 1687, to the Mother of Saumaise). (Editorial translation)
[157] *The Autobiography of St. Teresa of Avila.* Trans. David Lewis. Illinois: Tan Books and Publishers, Inc., 1997. XL, 27.
[158] FR. PÉREZ DE URBEL. *Año Cristiano.* t. II, ed. Poblet, Buenos Aires 1944, p. 408. (Editorial translation)
[159] *Spiritual Canticle of the Soul and the Bridegroom Christ.* Trans. David Lewis. London: Thomas Baker Publishing, 1919. Introduction.
[160] *Diario Espiritual.* 49 (November 23, 1720). (Editorial translation)

- "Those who truly love the cross of Christ our Lord find rest when they encounter these trials, and they die when they flee from them or are without them." (Saint Francis Xavier, Universal Patron of Catholic Missions).[161]

-"Never the Cross without Jesus. Or Jesus without the Cross" (Saint Louis Marie Grignion de Montfort).[162]

-"I desire and choose poverty with Christ poor, rather than riches; insults with Christ loaded with them, rather than honors; I desire to be accounted as worthless and a fool for Christ, rather than to be esteemed as wise and prudent in this world" (Saint Ignatius of Loyola).[163]

-"It is not good that the Head be crowned with thorns and the members live in comfort" (Saint Bernard).[164]

-"It is not good that Love be crucified" and "the loved one not crucify himself with love" (Saint Ignatius of Loyola).

-"There can be no redemption without Calvary" (Father Angel Buodo).[165]

-"Aside from the cross there is no other ladder to climb to heaven" (Saint Rose of Lima).[166]

-"What does anyone know who doesn't know how to suffer for Christ?" (Saint John of the Cross).[167]

2. THE LOVE AND THE JOY OF THE CROSS

The saints love suffering because it is the most exquisite way to follow Jesus and demonstrate how much they love him:

---

[161] SAINT FRANCIS XAVIER. *Letter of September 20th, 1542.*
[162] "Love of Eternal Wisdom." *God Alone.* New York: Montfort Publications, 1999. XIV, 172.
[163] LOUIS J. PUHL, S.J. *The Spiritual Exercises of St. Ignatius.* Chicago: LoyolaPress, 1951. 167.
[164] SAINT BERNARD. "Sermon II". *Obras Completas,* Ed. Cisterciences 5, p. 364-368. (Editorial translation).
[165] RAUL A. ENTRAIGAS. *El hornero de Dios.* Ed. Don Bosco, Buenos Aires 1961, p. 400. (Editorial translation).
[166] P. HANSEN. *Vida admirable de la hermana Rosa de Santa María de Lima.* Roma 1664, p. 137. (Editorial translation).
[167] "The Sayings of Light and Love." *The Collected Works of St. John of the Cross.* 175.

-"Lord, increase my sufferings, and with them increase thy love in my heart" (Saint Rose of Lima).[168]

-"The true earthly paradise is found in suffering for Christ" (Saint Louis Marie Grignion de Montfort)[169]

-"Christ is loved on the cross and crucified with Him. Not by any other way" (Blessed Luis Orione).[170]

-"Let us accept a tiny drop from his chalice for the love of him who, drank a bitter chalice for our love" (Servant of God Camila Rolón).[171]

The cross of Christ is joy. If it is not lived in joy, it may be a cross, but it will never be from Christ. This has been the constant teaching of the Apostles, the martyrs, the Doctors of the Church, and of all the saints:

-"I have great confidence in you; I have great pride in you; I am filled with comfort. With all our affliction, I am overjoyed" (*2 Cor* 7:4).

-"Count it all joy, my brethren, when you meet various trials" (*Jas* 1:2).

-"But rejoice in so far as you share Christ's sufferings, that you may also rejoice and be glad when his glory is revealed. If you are reproached for the name of Christ, you are blessed, because the spirit of glory and of God rests upon you" (*1 Pet* 4:13-14).

-"Blessed are you when men revile you and persecute you and utter all kinds of evil against you falsely on my account. Rejoice and be glad, for your reward is great in heaven, for so men persecuted the prophets who were before you" (*Mt* 5:11-12).

-"We must suffer with pleasure all the many tribulations that are presented to us in this world" (Servant of God Maria Antonia de la Paz y Figueroa).[172]

---

[168] ALAN BUTLER. *Butler's Lives of the Saints.* Vol. 8, Dublin, 1859. p. 509.
[169] "Friends of the Cross," *God Alone.* 34.
[170] Letter from June 24, 1937. (Editorial translation).
[171] Letter from April 16, 1911. (Editorial translation).

-"When you reach the time when patience makes tribulation seem sweet to you and even relished for Christ, you have found paradise on earth" (Thomas á Kempis).[173]

-"By the mercy of my beloved God, I do not desire to know anything, nor enjoy any consolation other than to be crucified with Jesus" (Saint Paul of the Cross).

-"Suffering is unknown to me. In it I find my joy, since Jesus is found on the cross. And what does suffering matter when one loves? ... What is sacrifice, what is the cross, but heaven, when Jesus Christ is on it?" (Saint Teresa of the Andes, Chilean Carmelite).[174]

- "I have arrived at not being able to suffer, because to me all suffering is sweet" (Saint Therese of the Child Jesus, Doctor of the Church and Universal Patron of Catholic Missions).[175]

-"The cross is the gift that God gives to his friends... I have suffered many more crosses than I seemed to be able to suffer. I disposed myself to ask for love of the cross and then I was happy. Truly, happiness is not found but there" (Saint John Marie Vianney).[176]

-"So great is the good that I wait for that all pain gives me comfort" (Saint John of the Cross).

-"Beloved Christ, crucified for love!... I desire to love you to the point of dying for love" (Blessed Elizabeth of the Trinity).[177]

Look often at Christ Crucified and tell him, together with Saint Ignatius of Loyola:

> *Soul of Christ, sanctify me*
> *Body of Christ, save me*
> *Blood of Christ, inebriate me*

---

[172] Letter from July 8, 1782. (Editorial translation).

[173] *The Imitation of Christ.* New York: Catholic Book Publishing Co., 1994. II, 12, 11.

[174] *Letter 14*: to Madre Angelica Teresa (September 5, 1917). (Editorial translation)

[175] *Story of a Soul.* Trans. John Clake, O.C.D. Washington, D.C.: ICS Publications, 1975. 12, 21.

[176] Cited in: ABBÉ MONNIN. *Esprit du Curé d'Ars,* Ed. P. Téqui, 1975, p. 141. (Editorial translation)

[177] Cited in: *Doctrina Espiritual de Sor Isabel,*. Ed. Desclée de Brower, Buenos Aires, 1948. (Editorial translation)

*Water from the side of Christ, wash me
Passion of Christ, strengthen me
O good Jesus, hear me
Within Thy wounds hide me
Permit me not to be separated from Thee
From the wicked foe defend me
At the hour of my death call me
And bid me come unto Thee
That with Thy saints I may praise Thee
For ever and ever. Amen.*[178]

Christ Crucified is the only path that leads to glory.

-"By means of suffering one moves toward glory, I want to go by this path" (Saint Vincenta María López y Vicuña).[179]

ARTICLE 5
"HE DESCENDED INTO HELL AND ON THE THIRD DAY HE ROSE FROM THE DEAD"

1. CHRIST DESCENDED INTO HELL[180]

Upon dying on the Cross, Jesus' soul separated from his body. However, Jesus' divinity did not separate either from the soul or the body. Jesus' body was brought to the tomb, where it remained all of Holy Saturday. Jesus' soul went to the dwelling of the just ones of the Old Testament. Jesus went there to retrieve them, to announce the redemption of man, and to console them. This is why Jesus could say to the good thief: "today you will be with me in Paradise" (*Lk* 23:43). Thus, we say that Jesus descended into hell.

"Hell" is understood as the place called the "bosom of Abraham" or "the limbo of the just." Here, "hell" does not refer to the hell of the condemned. "Scripture calls the abode of the

---

[178] Written by St. Ignatius of Loyola. Cited in: LOUIS J. PUHL, S.J. *The Spiritual Exercises of St. Ignatius.*
[179] From one of her letters. (Editorial translation)
[180] Cf. *Catechism of the Catholic Church.* 632-637.

dead, to which the dead Christ went down, 'hell'—*Sheol* in Hebrew or *Hades* in Greek—because those who are there are deprived of the vision of God. Such is the case for all the dead, whether evil or righteous, while they await the redeemer: which does not mean that their lot is identical, as Jesus shows through the parable of the poor man Lazarus who was received into 'Abraham's bosom': 'It is precisely these holy souls, who awaited their Savior in Abraham's bosom, whom Christ the Lord delivered when he descended into hell.' Jesus did not descend into hell to deliver the damned, nor to destroy the hell of damnation, but to free the just who had gone before him."[181]

There, Christ manifested his eternal power and glory as he had done before in heaven and on earth so that "at the name of Jesus every knee should bow, in heaven and on earth and under the earth" (*Phil* 2:10).

2. ON THE THIRD DAY HE ROSE FROM AMONG THE DEAD[182]

Then, "he was raised on the third day in accordance with the scriptures" (*1 Cor* 15:4). This refers to Easter Sunday when Jesus' soul reunited with his body, making his body a glorious body, one that would never die again. As God, Jesus rose by his own power, as once he prophesized to the Jews: "Destroy this temple, and in three days I will raise it up" (*Jn* 2:19).

As the power of the Father and the Son is one and the same, some scripture passages also affirm that Jesus was raised by God the Father.

"But God raised him up, having loosed the pangs of death, because it was not possible for him to be held by it" (*Acts* 2:24).

1. THE EMPTY TOMB

"'Why do you seek the living among the dead? He is not here, but has risen.' The first element we encounter in the framework

---

[181] Cf. *Catechism of the Catholic Church*. 633.
[182] Cf. Ibid. 638-658.

of the Easter events is the empty tomb. In itself it is not a direct proof of Resurrection; the absence of Christ's body from the tomb could be explained otherwise. Nonetheless the empty tomb was still an essential sign for all. Its discovery by the disciples was the first step toward recognizing the very fact of the Resurrection. This was the case, first with the holy women, and then with Peter. 'The disciple whom Jesus loved' affirmed that when he entered the empty tomb and discovered 'the linen cloths lying there,' 'he saw and believed.' This suggests that he realized from the empty tomb's condition that the absence of Jesus' body could not have been of human doing and that Jesus had not simply returned to earthly life as had been the case with Lazarus."[183]

2. THE APPEARANCES OF THE RISEN ONE

Once Jesus had risen, he appeared to others on several occasions. "To them he presented himself alive after his passion by many proofs, appearing to them during forty days, and speaking of the kingdom of God" (*Acts* 1:3). Furthermore, in order to demonstrate that he had truly risen, Jesus ate and drank,[184] walked,[185] and allowed himself to be touched: "they came up and took hold of his feet" (*Mt* 28:9). In order to demonstrate that he was the same one who had been crucified, Jesus showed them his hands, feet and side.[186] In order to teach them that he had risen to a glorious and immortal life, Jesus came in and out of the Cenacle while the doors were locked. Jesus also appeared and disappeared whenever he pleased, taking on different features, etc.

"The faith of the first community of believers is based on the witness of concrete men known to the Christians and for the most part still living among them. Peter and the Twelve are the primary 'witnesses to his Resurrection,' but they are not the only ones—Paul speaks clearly of more than five hundred persons to

---

[183] *Catechism of the Catholic Church.* 640.
[184] Cf. *Lk* 24:42; *Jn* 21:15.
[185] Cf. *Lk* 24:15.
[186] Cf. *Jn* 20:19-27 and *Lk* 24:40.

whom Jesus appeared on a single occasion and also of James and of all the apostles."[187]

This is he "who was put to death for our trespasses and raised for our justification" (*Rom* 4:25) in order to give us the life of sanctifying grace that we had lost when we sinned.

The mysteries of the Passion, Death and Resurrection of Jesus are called "the Paschal Mystery" and are solemnly commemorated in the Paschal Triduum. However, it is also commemorated every time the Holy Mass is celebrated when after the consecration the priest says: "Father, we celebrate the memory of Christ, your Son. We, your people and your ministers, recall his passion, his resurrection from the dead, and his ascension into glory...we offer to you...this holy and perfect sacrifice..."[188]

ARTICLE 6
"HE ASCENDED INTO HEAVEN AND IS SEATED AT THE RIGHT HAND OF GOD THE FATHER ALMIGHTY"

"So then the Lord Jesus, after he had spoken to them, was taken up into heaven, and sat down at the right hand of God" (*Mk* 16:19). Jesus "on the fortieth day after the resurrection with the flesh in which He arose and with His soul ascended into heaven."[189] He ascended "by his own power," power which Jesus possessed as God and power his glorified soul had over his glorified body. "He who had made all things was borne over all by His own power."[190]

"Is seated" is a way of saying that Jesus has reached the deserved repose due him as a victorious warrior. It is the position of King and Judge, full of power and majesty.

---

[187] *Catechism of the Catholic Church.* 642.
[188] *Roman Missal.* Eucharistic Prayer I.
[189] II COUNCIL OF LYONS. Dz. 462.
[190] GREGORY THE GREAT. Cited by SAINT THOMAS AQUINAS. *Catena Aurea.* Vol. II St. Mark. Oregon: Wipf & Stock Publishers, 2005. XVI v 19-20.

Among other things, the Ascension of Christ to heaven makes us always seek the essentials of life, those things invisible to the eyes of the body, and which do not fade or die. Saint Paul said to the first Christians: "If then you have been raised with Christ, seek the things that are above, where Christ is, seated at the right hand of God. Set your minds on things that are above, not on things that are on earth" (*Col* 3:1-2).

Moreover, the Ascension of our Lord should fill us with unwavering hope, since Jesus assures us: "In my Father's house are many rooms... I go and prepare a place for you...I will come again and will take you to myself, that where I am you may be also" (*Jn* 14:2-3). We are citizens of heaven! (cf. *Phil* 3:20). Just as the Apostles stood "looking into the sky" after the Ascension, we should have our eyes fixed on Jesus (cf. *Acts* 1:10).

3. AT THE RIGHT HAND OF THE FATHER

"He sat down at the right hand of the Majesty on high" (*Heb* 1:3) refers, according to Saint John Damascene, to "the glory and the honor of the divinity," which means that Christ reigns together with the Father. It also means that Christ has judicial power over the living and the dead. Knowing that the Lord is together with the Father must increase our trust in him immeasurably. We should say with Saint Paul: "I can do all things in him who strengthens me" (*Phil* 4:13). We should also pronounce with him another magnificent expression of total confidence: "for I know whom I have believed" (*2 Tim* 1:12).

ARTICLE 7
"FROM THENCE HE WILL COME AGAIN TO JUDGE THE LIVING AND THE DEAD"

Saint Peter said of Christ: "He is the one ordained by God to be the judge of the living and the dead" (*Acts* 10:42).

1. FINAL JUDGMENT AND PARTICULAR JUDGMENT

Christ will come into the world a second time, but different from the first coming: which was poor, humble and ignored in

Bethlehem. Rather, Christ will come in power and majesty. Everyone will be forced to acknowledge Christ as Judge, since he will come to pronounce the Final Judgment.

At his Second Coming, all of Christ's enemies will be completely defeated. Christ will then appoint all who have been faithful disciples to reign with him. However, even before the end of time, at the moment of our death, every one of us will be judged: "Each of us shall give account of himself to God" (*Rom* 14:12). "Just as it is appointed for men to die once, and after that comes judgment" (*Heb* 9:27). This is called **particular judgment**.

It is said that one day Saint Aloysius Gonzaga was gathered with some friends during recreation. A priest, in order to see what they thought, asked them what they would do if they knew they would die in just a few hours. One answered he would go to confession, another that he would go to pray, etc. The saint simply responded: "I would continue playing."[191] He was never afraid of death because he lived constantly in the grace of God. For him, as for Saint Paul, "to live is Christ, and to die is gain" (*Phil* 1:21) because he knew that the judgment of God is conformed to the truth (cf. *Rom* 2:2). Saint Rita of Cascia said that "death, for him who tries to serve God wholeheartedly, is nothing but a sweet dream."[192]

God will judge our hearts to see if we have believed the teachings transmitted by the Church. God will judge whether we have obeyed his commandments, if we have received the sacraments, and if we have prayed as we should have.

To the good, those who have died in the grace of God, Christ will say: "Come, O blessed of my Father, inherit the kingdom prepared for you from the foundation of the world" (*Mt* 25:34). To the evil, those who die in mortal sin without repenting, Christ will say: "Depart from me, you cursed, into the eternal fire prepared for the devil and his angels" (*Mt* 25:41).

---

[191] Cf. SAINT JOHN BOSCO. *La juventud instruida*. II, 1. (Editorial translation)
[192] From her life. (Editorial translation)

The vision of God is enjoyed in heaven. The absence of God is suffered in hell. In the former, creatures will be another motive of joy; in the latter, creatures will be another motive of torment. Happiness without end reigns in heaven. Sorrow without remedy reigns in hell. This is a resplendent felicity against a dark misery; a splendid love against a wicked hate.

The end of a man will be according to his life. Thus, it is fitting to "remember the end of your life, and then you will never sin" (*Sir* 7:36).

2. THE FINAL PURIFICATION OR PURGATORY

Jesus said: "Whoever speaks against the Holy Spirit will not be forgiven, either in this age or in the age to come" (*Mt* 12:32). Similarly, Pope Saint Gregory the Great, comments that "it is given to our understanding that some faults will be forgiven in this world and some in the future."[193]

This is to say that there is an intermediate place between heaven and hell, called purgatory. Souls, who have not died in mortal sin, but still need to be purified of their faults go to purgatory. All the souls in purgatory can be assisted by our prayers.[194]

An indulgence is the partial or total remission of temporal punishment due to sin whose guilt has already been forgiven. This punishment must be paid in this life by good works or in purgatory by a determined time of penalty.

> "There is no disappointment, dissipation or sin that cannot be overcome in Christ; just as there is no longing, necessity, or hope that, immersed in Christ, Lord and Redeemer, will not receive the hoped for benefits. (...) Christ is demanding. He asks for everything. He calls for unconditional generosity. But precisely by this totality, Christianity continues to be a religion always actual, and is destined to be in tune with youthful consciousness, which is prone to complete giving, foreign to only going halfway and hostile to formality and superficiality. Christ opens up an immense horizon to the youth. Christ reveals to him the relationship between eternity

---

[193] *Dialogues* 4, 39. (Editorial translation)
[194] Cf. *2 Mac* 12:43-46.

and time, between the future life and the present. He shows him that there is a profound connection between truth and goodness, and that, consequently, the moral level of an existence essentially depends on its own capacity for coherence, which has its roots in the intimate sphere of thought and the heart."

John Paul II,
Discourse to the youth of Bari (Italy)
March 11, 1984
(Editorial translation)

CHAPTER THREE
I BELIEVE IN THE HOLY SPIRIT

ARTICLE 8
"I BELIEVE IN THE HOLY SPIRIT"

1. WHO IS THE HOLY SPIRIT?

The Holy Spirit is the Third Person of the Holy Trinity who "proceeds from the Father and the Son" (from the Nicene-Constantinople Creed).

It is the Holy Spirit who bore fruit from the womb of Mary, bringing about the Incarnation.[195] It is the Holy Spirit who descended upon Jesus in the form of a dove at his Baptism.[196] It is the Holy Spirit who descended upon the Virgin Mary and the Apostles in the form of tongues of fire at Pentecost, fifty days after the Resurrection of Jesus.[197] The Holy Spirit is "Perfect Image of the Perfect Life, the Cause of living things, the Sacred Spring, the Sanctity that communicates sanctification."[198]

When Jesus announces and promises the coming of the Holy Spirit, he calls him the "Paraclete" (Jn 14:16), which is usually translated as "Consoler." Jesus also calls the Holy Spirit the "Spirit of Truth" (Jn 16:13). When speaking with Nicodemus, Jesus used the image of wind (the word 'spirit,' primarily means 'breath, air, wind') to help us understand that the Divine Spirit is the Breath of God. "The wind blows where it wills, and you hear the sound of it, but you do not know whence it comes or wither it goes; so it is with every one who is born of the Spirit" (Jn 3:8).

---

[195] Cf. Lk 1:35.
[196] Cf. Mk 1:10.
[197] Cf. Acts 2:3.
[198] SAINT GREGORY THAUMATURGUS. Ex. de la Fe E.P. 611. (Editorial translation)

Other beautiful symbols of the Holy Spirit are: water, anointing, a cloud, light, a seal, a hand, a finger, a dove and flames.[199]

Jesus said: "I came to cast fire upon the earth; and would that it were already kindled!" (*Lk* 12:49).

2. PENTECOST

"On the day of Pentecost when the seven weeks of Easter had come to an end, Christ's Passover is fulfilled in the outpouring of the Holy Spirit, manifested, given, and communicated as a divine person."[200]

Saint Luke in the *Acts of the Apostles* narrates the coming of the Holy Spirit upon the Apostles, who were gathered in the Cenacle "together with…Mary the Mother of Jesus" (*Acts* 1:14):

> When the day of Pentecost had come, they were all together in one place. And suddenly a sound came from heaven like the rush of a mighty wind, and it filled all the house where they were sitting. And there appeared to them tongues as of fire, distributed and resting on each one of them. And they were all filled with the Holy Spirit and began to speak in other tongues, as the Spirit gave them utterance.
>
> *(Acts 2:1-4)*

This event, which gave birth to the Church, was the fulfillment of the promise our Lord had made on several occasions to send the Holy Spirit. On one occasion, on the most solemn day of the Passover feast, Christ "proclaimed, 'If anyone thirst, let him come to me and drink. He who believes in me, as the Scripture has said, *Out of his heart shall flow rivers of living water.*' Now this he said about the Spirit, which those who believe in him were to receive" (*Jn* 7:37-39).

For this reason, we need to have a great desire to possess the Holy Spirit. He must be found in Jesus Christ, by believing in

---

[199] You can find a deeper explanation of their meaning in the *Catechism of the Catholic Church*. 694-701.
[200] *Catechism of the Catholic Church*. 731.

him. If you truly seek Christ, he will give you to drink from his Spirit. You will become so peaceful and content that inside of you "rivers of living water will flow," as Jesus says. You will not only have water in abundance for yourself, but you will also have it for many others.

3. THE HOLY SPIRIT, THE GIFT FROM GOD

"God is love" (*1 Jn* 4:8, 16) and love, which is the first gift, contains all the other gifts. "God's love has been poured into our hearts through the Holy Spirit who has been given to us" (*Rom* 5:5). He is the new law, the law of charity that "binds everything together in perfect harmony" (*Col* 3:14). He is the "principle of faith" (*Rom* 3:27), the "law of the Spirit" (*Rom* 8:2), "the Gospel of the grace of God" (*Acts* 20:24), and the "law of liberty" (*Jas* 2:12) because "where the Spirit of the Lord is, there is freedom" (*2 Cor* 3:17). He is "faith working though love" (*Gal* 5:6).

4. THE FRUITS OF THE HOLY SPIRIT

Those who are faithful to the inspirations of the Holy Spirit bear fruits of "love, joy, peace, patience, kindness, goodness, faithfulness, gentleness, self-control; against such there is no law" (*Gal* 5:22) because "the law is not laid down for the just" (*1 Tim* 1:9). That is to say, that those who are faithful to the Spirit are not content with merely observing the law, but they go beyond, living as Saint Augustine said: "Love and do what you will."[201] Since, he who truly loves will always do only what God wants.

There may be no harsher word in Sacred Scripture than those of Saint Paul: "anyone who does not have the Spirit of Christ does not belong to Him" (*Rom* 8:9). It is not enough to pray, give food to the poor, serve one's neighbor, sacrifice oneself or study, etc. if not done in the spirit. If there is not a spirit of prayer, a spirit of love for the poor, a spirit of study, of service, of sacrifice in the soul ... the mere external work is worth nothing.

---

[201] *Homilies on the First Epistle of John.* VII, 8.

It is also the Holy Spirit who prevents the Holy Mass from ever becoming something mechanical, routine and boring; but makes it something "unique." Every Mass validly celebrated is an imperceptible, but real manifestation of the Holy Spirit, since the Holy Spirit acts to manifest Christ. The presence of Jesus Christ is united with the action of the Holy Spirit: where Christ is, the Holy Spirit is. Saint Bernard states "the fact that Christ died for me would not benefit me if he had not vivified me with the Spirit."[202] You must frequently ask the Holy Spirit to teach you how to participate in the Holy Mass in an active, conscious and fruitful manner.

5. THE HOLY SPIRIT AND THE CHURCH

The Holy Spirit is the "soul of the Church": "What the soul is in our body, that is the Holy Ghost in Christ's body, the Church."[203] The Holy Spirit gathers us all in unity.

"The Church, a communion living in the faith of the apostles which she transmits, is the place where we know the Holy Spirit:

-in the Scriptures he inspired;

-in the Tradition, to which the Church Fathers are always timely witnesses;

-in the Church's Magisterium, which he assists;

-in the sacramental liturgy, through its words and symbols, in which the Holy Spirit puts us into communion with Christ;

-in prayer, wherein he intercedes for us;

-in the charisms and ministries by which the Church is built up;

-in the signs of apostolic and missionary life;

-in the witness of saints through whom he manifests his holiness and continues the work of salvation."[204]

---

[202] Letters. 107, 9:PL 182, 247 A. (Editorial translation)
[203] LEO XIII. Encyclical letter *Divinum illud munus*. 6.

Furthermore, "the Spirit helps us in our weakness; for we do not know how to pray as we ought, but the Spirit Himself intercedes for us with sighs too deep for words" (*Rom* 8:26). However, the Holy Spirit, Artisan of the works of God, is not only the Master of prayer, but also the gift given to us in prayer. The principal gift God gives to a man and a woman is God himself. There could be no greater gift than the infinite Being himself. The principal gift is the Holy Spirit and that which is given to us through him. We receive the gift of the Holy Spirit in a very special way in the Sacrament of Confirmation. However, whether we have already been confirmed or not, we must always ask God the Father for the gift of the Holy Spirit. We must also ask that he would help us to be attentive to the inspirations of the Holy Spirit, to discern the different movements and to carry out promptly the will of God. Our Lord taught us to make this petition with great trust: "What man among you, if his son asks for bread will instead of bread give him a stone?...If you then, who are evil, know how to give good gifts to your children, how much more will the heavenly Father give the Holy Spirit to those who ask Him!" (*Mt* 7:9, 11).

Let us often say:

Come, Holy Spirit, fill the hearts of Your faithful
and enkindle in them the fire of Your love.
V. Send forth Your Spirit and they shall be created.
R. And You shall renew the face of the earth.

We can also address the Holy Spirit with this beautiful prayer that is attributed to Saint Ferdinand, King of Castile:

Holy Spirit, Love of the Father and of the Son,
inspire me always with what I must think,
what I must say, and how I must say it,
what I must refrain from saying,
what I must write,
how I must work,

---

[204] *Catechism of the Catholic Church.* 688.

what I must do to obtain Your Glory,
the good of souls and my own sanctification. Amen.

John Paul II suggested to youth that they pray to the Virgin Mary, asking to receive the Holy Spirit with this prayer by Saint Idelfonsus:

I pray you, I pray you, O Blessed Virgin,
that I may receive Jesus from that Spirit
from whom you yourself begot Jesus.
May my soul receive Jesus through the power of
that Spirit through whom your flesh conceived
Jesus Himself.
May I love Jesus in that same Spirit
in whom you adore Him as Lord
and contemplate Him as Son.[205]

ARTICLE 9
"I BELIEVE IN THE HOLY CATHOLIC CHURCH, IN THE COMMUNION OF SAINTS"

INTRODUCTION

The Holy Cross is the symbol of a Catholic person because it symbolizes the three principle mysteries of our holy religion:

1. The mystery of the Holy Trinity: three Persons in one nature;

2. The mystery of Jesus Christ, our Lord, true God and true man, who dies on the cross to save us;

3. The mystery of the Holy Catholic Church, which is the Kingdom of salvation proceeding from and ending in the Trinity, continued, spread, and communicated by Jesus Christ throughout time and space; the supernatural ark of salvation by means of the sanctifying grace imparted in the sacraments.

---

[205] JOHN PAUL II. *Message to the XIII World Youth Day.* 9.

Four things express what the Church is:

1. Her nature;

2. Her attributes;

3. Her members;

4. Her states.

1. THE NATURE OF THE CHURCH

The Church essentially refers to the Holy Trinity: "a people made one with the unity of the Father, the Son and the Holy Spirit" (Saint Cyprian).[206] The Church is the People of God,[207] the Body of Christ,[208] and the Temple of the Holy Spirit.[209]

1. WE ARE THE PEOPLE BOUGHT WITH THE BLOOD OF CHRIST

Christ "died for all" (*2 Cor* 5:15). Christ wants "all men to be saved and to come to the knowledge of the truth" (*1 Tim* 2:4). This is why Christ founded the Church. He prepared her foundation during his public life: when he taught the doctrine which had to be preached; when he instituted the sacraments, which are the channels by which the grace of God comes to man; when he instituted the Holy Mass as a perpetual sacrifice for the expiation of sin; when he promulgated the laws which would govern the life of the faithful; when he established the Catholic priesthood; when he chose the authorities of his people, the Pope and the Bishops; and when Saint Peter confessed the faith in the divine and messianic nature of Jesus Christ: "You are the Christ, the Son of the living God" (*Mt* 16:16). This long preparation culminated in the sacrifice on the cross since the Church was brought forth from the pierced side of the Lord, just as Eve had come from the side of Adam. Christ is the new Adam; the Church is the new Eve: "the one and only immaculate virgin, holy

---

[206] *De orat. Dom.* 23; SAINT AUGUSTINE. *Sermon.* 73, 20, 33; SAINT JOHN DAMASCENE. *Adv. Iconoc.* 12; cf. II VATICAN COUNCIL. *Lumen Gentium,* 4.

[207] Cf. Ibid. 9-17.

[208] Ibid. 7.

[209] Ibid. 4; for these topics refer to JOHN PAUL II. *Christifideles laici.* 8, 11-13.

Mother Church."[210] This Church, born at the cross, "showed herself before the eyes of men on the great day of Pentecost."[211] There were, thus, three stages in the foundation of the Church by Christ: her preparation, her culmination and her presentation.

2. BAPTISM INCORPORATES US INTO THE CHURCH

We have been incorporated into the Catholic Church by Baptism. We have been made living members of Jesus Christ, in the name of the Holy Trinity. The Church is made up of men who have been saved by Christ. We call the buildings or temples where the members of the Church gather to worship and adore God, "churches." Jesus Christ dies for each and every one of us. He dies for the Church, which is to say, for all the men who make-up the Church—not for the bricks, the plaster, the doorknobs, the tiles, the pews, etc., of our temples.

3. THE SYMBOLS OR IMAGES OF THE CHURCH[212]

Sacred Scripture presents the Church to us through many images. The Church is:

a) Likened to a *sheep-fold* (*Jn* 10:1-10) whose door is Christ.

b) Likened to a *flock* (*Jn* 10:1-5) of sheep whose shepherd is Christ.

c) Likened to *God's field* (*1 Cor* 3:9) where the Lord planted the chosen vine[213] (*Mt* 21:33-43). The true vine is Christ and we are the branches who live because we are united to him who transmits the sap—that is to say, grace (*Jn* 15:1-5).

d) The *building of God* (*1 Cor* 3:9) where Jesus Christ is the corner stone (*Mt* 21:42).

e) The *house of God* (*1 Tim* 3:15) because, in her, all of God's true children live.

---

[210] COUNCIL OF VIENNA. Constitution *De Summa Trinitate et fide catholica.* Dz. 480.
[211] LEO XIII. Encyclical letter *Divinum illud munus.* 5: ASS 649.
[212] Cf. II VATICAN COUNCIL. *Lumen Gentium.* 6.
[213] Cf. *Is* 5:1-7.

f) The *family of God* (*Eph* 2:19-22) ·in which we are all children of the same Father and, consequently, all brothers and sisters.

g) The holy *temple* (*Eph* 2:21) of which we are living stones (*1 Pet* 2:5).

h) The *New Jerusalem* (*Rev* 3:12) or the *Heavenly Jerusalem* (*Heb* 12:22) because it is where God and man meet and where the glory of God is manifested.

i) The *spouse of Christ* (*Eph* 5:22-32) because Christ loved the Church and gave himself up for her, purifying us by Baptism and by the Word.

j) The *Kingdom of God* (*Mk* 1:15) or the *Kingdom of Heaven* (*Mt* 3:2) since, in the Church, God is the King and we are his subjects.

k) The *Body of Christ* (*1 Cor* 12:12-27). Everyone who is baptized is united to Christ, like the members of a body are united to the head. We are brothers and sisters, thus forming one family: the Church.

l) The *fullness of Christ* (*Eph* 1:23) because she is not only made of the Head, Christ, but also made of the members of the Head, other "Christs."[214]

m) *Our Mother* (*Gal* 4:26) since the Church, by means of the sacraments, engenders the supernatural life Christ came to bring.

n) The *People of God* (*Heb* 4:9) who continue the work of Jesus Christ.

2. ATTRIBUTES OR MARKS OF THE CHURCH OF JESUS CHRIST

These are the qualities or attributes of the Church of Jesus Christ. The Nicene-Constantinopolitan Creed points out four attributes: the Church Jesus founded is one, holy, catholic and apostolic.

---

[214] "In a certain way, then, it thus happens that with head and body the whole Christ is formed." JOHN PAUL II. *Christifideles Laici*. 14.

1. THE CHURCH IS ONE

It is one because there is "one Lord, one faith, one baptism" (*Eph* 4:5). The Church is one because there is one visible Head, the Pope, "perpetual principle and visible foundation of both unities."[215] The Church is one because it is the "one and the same Spirit, who apportions to each one individually as He wills" (*1 Cor* 12:11). The Church is one because "there is one body and one Spirit" (*Eph* 4:4). Furthermore, the Church is one because in every diocese there is only one bishop, who "united to the Pope," is the "visible principle and foundation of unity in their particular churches."[216]

"Only one Church exists, and only that one will arrive at port; all others will shipwreck…"[217] The other "churches" are not true because they have not been founded by Jesus Christ. The "ray of that Truth which enlightens all men"[218] present in the churches is the work of the Holy Spirit and a preparation for the Gospel.[219]

The unity of Christians: Ecumenism

Due to the promise-prophecy of Christ that "there shall be one flock, one shepherd" (*Jn* 10:16) and due to Christ's priestly prayer "that they may all be one" (*Jn* 17:21), the Catholic Church is committed to bring about the union of all Christians, that is to say, of all those "who invoke the Triune God and confess Jesus as Lord and Savior."[220] This task is called **ecumenism**. It is achieved by means of a permanent *renovation* of the Church toward a greater fidelity to her vocation, by the *conversion of heart* in order to lead a life more aligned with the Gospel, by *common prayer*, by a *reciprocal fraternal understanding* and by *dialogue* and collaboration.[221]

---

[215] I VATICAN COUNCIL. Dz. 1821.

[216] II VATICAN COUNCIL. *Lumen Gentium.* 23.

[217] SAINT FRANCIS DE SALES. *Meditaciones Sobre la Iglesia.* BAC, Madrid 1985, p. 46. (Editorial translation)

[218] VATICAN COUNCIL II. *Nostrae aetate.* 2.

[219] Cf. VATICAN COUNCIL II. *Lumen Gentium.* 16; cf. Eusebio de Cesarea. *Gospel Preparation.* 1, 1.

[220] VATICAN COUNCIL II. *Unitatis redintegratio.* 1.

[221] Cf. *Catechism of the Catholic Church.* 821.

2. THE CHURCH IS HOLY

The Church is holy because she is "devoted and consecrated to Jesus Christ;"[222] because "we are to grow up in every way into him who is the head, into Christ" (*Eph* 4:15). The Church is holy because the sacraments she distributes produce holiness, and because her end is holy: the glory of God and the salvation of men. The Church is holy because her members must be saints, that is to say, they must live in the grace of God (if there are members of the Church who are sinners, it is not the fault of the Church, but rather their own fault, as far as they do not want to be obedient members of the Church).

3. THE CHURCH IS CATHOLIC

The Church is catholic, which means "universal," according to totality and according to integrity. The Church is not confined within the borders of a single nation, epoch, race, civilization, social class, culture or language. "Greek and Jew...barbarian, Scyth'ian, slave, free man, but Christ is all, and in all" (*Col* 3:11). The Church is catholic because everyone who is saved is saved inasmuch as they adhere to the Church. Some are visibly united to her Body and invisibly united to her "soul"; while others, who are ignorant of the Gospel without fault and who obey the will of God, are saved because they belong to the "soul" of the Church. They are saved since they work under the influence of the grace[223] of the Holy Spirit, for "as Christ is the Head of the Church, so is the Holy Ghost her soul."[224]

a) The Mission

The whole Church has the mission of seeking the greater glory of God and the salvation of all men. Thus, "the pilgrim Church is missionary by her very nature."[225] The Church can

---

[222] *Roman Catechism*. I, IX.
[223] Cf. VATICAN COUNCIL II. *Lumen Gentium*. 16.
[224] LEO XII. Encyclical letter *Divinum illud munus*. 6.
[225] II VATICAN COUNCIL. *Ad gentes*. 2.

never stop listening to the command of her Lord: "Go into all the world and preach the gospel to the whole creation" (*Mk* 16:15).[226]

After 2,000 years, we can say that the missionary work is still in its beginning stages, since two thirds of humanity do not know Jesus Christ. "We cannot be content when we consider the millions of our brothers and sisters who, like us, have been redeemed by the blood of Christ, but who live in ignorance of the love of God. For each believer, as for the entire Church, the missionary task must remain foremost, for it concerns the eternal destiny of humanity and corresponds to God's mysterious and merciful plan."[227]

We must always pray for the missionaries who are spread out across the five continents; missionaries who many times crown their fidelity to Jesus Christ and to his Church with martyrdom.

We must ask for the increase of many missionary vocations from Christian families: "When parents are ready to allow one of their children to leave for the missions, when they have sought this grace from the Lord, he will repay them, in joy, on the day that their son or daughter hears his call."[228]

You must also never forget that you are called to be a missionary wherever you live, even in your own house: "There is a great need for youth to mission in their respective environments; joyful, strong, humble, courageous, tenacious youth who are willing to undertake challenges; youth that are capable of presenting Christ to the world with conviction, being his witnesses through their words and deeds, with their daily lives."[229]

b) Non-Christians: the inter-religious dialogue

"The missionary task implies a respectful dialogue with those who do not yet accept the Gospel. Believers can profit from this dialogue by learning to appreciate better 'those elements of truth

---

[226] Cf. JOHN PAUL II, Encyclical letter *Redemptoris Missio*, on the permanent validity of the missionary mandate, 2: "Missionary activity is a matter for all Christians, for all dioceses and parishes, Church institutions and associations."

[227] JOHN PAUL II. *Redemptoris Missio*. 86.

[228] Ibid. 80.

[229] JOHN PAUL II. To the youth of Treviso diocese (Italy). June 15, 1985. (Editorial translation)

and grace which are found among peoples, and which are, as it were, a secret presence of God.' They proclaim the Good News to those who do not know it, in order to consolidate, complete, and raise up the truth and the goodness that God has distributed among men and nations, and to purify them from error and evil 'for the glory of God, the confusion of the demon, and the happiness of man.'"[230]   This is called the **Inter-religious Dialogue**.

4. THE CHURCH IS APOSTOLIC

The Church is apostolic, that is to say, it is firm because it is founded on the Apostles. The Church is apostolic because the Apostles were the ones who propagated the Church throughout the world. The Church is apostolic because there is an uninterrupted line of pastors from the Apostles to the bishops of today and because their doctrine is identical to that of the doctrine of the Apostles. The Church continually repeats the same Creed. The Church is apostolic because it is hierarchical. Only the holy Catholic Church has these characteristics: she is "the mother and teacher of all the faithful"[231] and "the pillar and bulwark of the truth" (*1 Tim* 3:15). The Church is apostolic because the Church founded by Christ "subsists in the Catholic Church, which is governed by the successor of Peter and by the Bishops in communion with him."[232]

a) Roman

The Catholic Church is also called "Roman" because the Pope has his cathedra in Rome, founded upon the tomb of Saint Peter the Apostle, the first Pope. "Genuine faith which is ever preserved safe and whole in the Roman Church."[233]   Saint Vincent Ferrer teaches: "If the angels of God spoke against what was determined by the Roman Church we must not believe them, according to Saint Paul: 'But even if we or an angel from heaven,

---

[230] *Catechism of the Catholic Church.* 856.
[231] II COUNCIL OF LYONS. Dz. 460.
[232] II VATICAN COUNCIL. *Lumen Gentium.* 8.
[233] PIUS XI. Encyclical letter *Lux Veritatis.* 5.

should preach to you a Gospel contrary to that which we preached to you, let him be accursed'*(Gal* 1:8*)*."[234]

Therefore, according to the will of our Lord Jesus Christ, his Church has a determined structure. Unlike a mollusk, the Church has a skeleton; it is not purely spiritual, interior and invisible. The Church is rather human, social, exterior and visible. Its structure is hierarchical.

b) Vocations

Vocations to the consecrated life (priests, deacons, missionaries, religious, and consecrated laity) "affect the Church in one of its fundamental characteristics, in its apostolic dimension."[235] Vocations "are proofs of the vitality of the Church."[236] Vocations are the sign of the vitality and Christian maturity of the whole community. All Christians have the duty to pray to God for the increase, perseverance and sanctification of vocations, as the Lord taught us: "Pray therefore the Lord of the harvest to send out laborers into his harvest" (*Mt* 9:38).

c) Sects

The lack of true pastors causes many people to seek false pastors. The lack of priestly and religious vocations is one of the factors that has made us aware of what the Latin American bishops call the "invasion of sects."[237]

"The problem of the sects has reached dramatic proportions and has come to be a pressing concern, above all because of the growing proselytism,"[238] as pointed out by the bishops of our continent.

It must be clarified that protestant denominations who believe in the Trinity and the divinity of Jesus, those called national

---

[234] *Tratado del Cisma Moderno.* Ch. 5, Part 2; *Biografías y escritos.* Madrid: B.A.C., 1956. p. 447. (Editorial translation).

[235] JOHN PAUL II. Sunday Mediation. April 16, 1989.

[236] JOHN PAUL II. Homily in the Regional, Major Seminary of Seoul. May 3, 1984. 4.

[237] III GENERAL CONFERENCE OF THE LATIN AMERICAN EPISCOPATE. *Puebla Document.* 419. (Editorial translation)

[238] IV GENERAL CONFERENCE OF THE LATIN AMERICAN EPISCOPATE (October 12-28, 1992). *Santo Domingo Document.* 132. (Editorial translation)

Churches (such as the Lutheran Church, the reformed or Calvinist Church, or the Anglican Church) are not sects. In addition, those that are called free Churches (such as Presbyterians, Congregationalists, Baptists or Methodists) are not, properly speaking, sects either.

However, young people should be warned about those that are called "fundamentalist sects" and "new religious movements or free religious movements" like Jehovah's Witnesses, Mormons, or Pentecostals.

"Many pseudo-religious movements of an oriental character, occultism, fortune-telling and spiritism, disrupt the faith and cause uncertainty, giving false solutions to the greatest questions of man, his destiny, his liberty and the meaning of life."[239]

The youth of our time should be particularly warned about the Gnostic movement called "New Age" (or the Age of Aquarius). This movement calls for the end of Christianity, which they call the "Age of Pisces."

The youth should be apostles to the youth. Many youth are adrift, possibly due to our failure to give a clear testimony of Jesus Christ. They end up anchoring themselves in sects. The solution is to give an enthusiastic answer to their questions, specifically in three areas:

1. We need to know how to present a living liturgy: promoting a living liturgy in which the faithful are introduced to the mystery. This means that you must learn to "live the mass" and to enter into its mystery.

2. We must live in our community an authentic, heartfelt fraternity, one in which we treat each other as brothers and sisters.

3. Our community must be characterized by an active missionary participation.

---

[239] IV GENERAL CONFERENCE OF THE LATIN AMERICAN EPISCOPATE (October 12-28, 1992) 140-153. (Editorial translation)

In conclusion, the solution is in "a living liturgy, a heartfelt fraternity, and an active missionary participation."[240]

> "I ask young people themselves to listen to Christ's words as he says to them what he once said to Simon Peter and to Andrew at the lakeside: 'Follow me, and I will make you fishers of men' (*Mt* 4:19). May they have the courage to reply as Isaiah did: 'Here am I, Lord! I am ready! Send me!' (cf. *Is* 6:8) They will have a wonderful life ahead of them, and they will know the genuine joy of proclaiming the 'Good News' to brothers and sisters whom they will lead on the way of salvation.

> *John Paul II*
> *Encyclical letter Redemptoris Missio, 80*

3. THE MEMBERS OF THE CHURCH

1. THE POPE

The visible head of the Church is the Pope, the Vicar of Jesus Christ and Successor of Saint Peter, the "sweet Christ on earth" (Saint Catherine of Siena).[241] He is, as previously mentioned, infallible in the teachings of the truths of faith and morals. Everyone in the Church, even "these same Councils"[242] must submit themselves to him. He has the authority to promulgate laws for the entire Church.[243] He is the supreme judge on earth and he cannot be "judged by anyone" in this world.[244] Thus, "every human creature...by necessity for salvation are entirely subject to the Roman Pontiff."[245] He is the rock on which the Church is built.[246] For that reason, "wherever Peter is, the Church is there."[247] Therefore, "no other foundation can any one lay" (*1 Cor* 3:11).

---

[240] III GENERAL CONFERENCE OF THE LATIN AMERICAN EPISCOPATE. *Puebla Document.* 1122. (Editorial translation)
[241] *Letter 196 to Pope Gregory XI.*
[242] V LATERAN COUNCIL. Dz. 740.
[243] Cf. COUNCIL OF CONSTATINE. Dz. 588 and 589.
[244] Cf. ROMAN COUNCIL. Dz. 330.
[245] BONIFACE VIII. Bull *"Unam Sanctam."* Dz. 469.
[246] Cf. *Mt* 16:16-19.
[247] SAINT AMBROSE. *Writings about the Psalms.* 40, 30.

2. THE BISHOPS

The bishops are the successors of the Apostles.[248] They are the ones who manifest and preserve the apostolic tradition in the world.[249] Jesus said of them: "He who hears you hears me, and he who rejects you rejects me" (*Lk* 10:16). Saint Ignatius of Antioch taught: "Remain submitted to your bishop, just as Christ submitted himself to the Father... do not do anything against his will... united to the bishop, just as the Church is united to Christ and Christ to the Father, in order that, in all things, the harmony of unity may reign."[250] In addition, Saint Cyprian declared: "Whoever is not with the bishop is not with the Church."[251]

Together with the Pope as Head, the bishops are "formed after the manner of a college or a fixed group."[252] This college, or body of bishops, "has no authority unless it is simultaneously conceived of in terms of its head, the Roman Pontiff, Peter's successor."[253] The power of this college is solemnly expressed in the Ecumenical Councils. In addition, this college, as it is made up of many, expresses the variety and universality of the People of God. As it is gathered under one Head, it expresses the unity of the flock of Christ.[254]

3. THE PRIESTS[255]

Priests are the fathers and teachers of the People of God. They serve Christ Priest, Teacher and King in whose ministry they participate. They are instruments of God in bringing salvation to all men. In our communities, they represent Christ, Head and Pastor. They have the power to change bread and wine into the Body and Blood of the Lord, the power to forgive our sins and to preach the Word of God.

---

[248] Cf. II VATICAN COUNCIL. *Lumen Gentium.* 20-27; Decree *Christus Dominus.* 2.
[249] Cf. II VATICAN COUNCIL. *Lumen Gentium.* 20.
[250] *Letter to the Ephesians.* V, 1: II, 2: *Letter to the Smyraeans.* VIII, 1. (Editorial translation)
[251] *Letter 66.* VIII, 1. (Editorial translation)
[252] Cf. II VATICAN COUNCIL II. *Lumen Gentium.* 19.
[253] Ibid. 22.
[254] Cf. Ibid. 22.
[255] Cf. JOHN PAUL II. *Pastores Dabo Vobis.* 15.

4. THE LAITY[256]

The laity includes the vast majority of the People of God. They are fathers and mothers of families, workers, students, professionals, employees, politicians, businessmen, etc. Their specific vocation is to sanctify themselves living in the world, to do the will of God in the family, at work, at recreational activities, in athletics, etc. By obeying the commandments of the law of God in their places of work and rest, they allow God to reign in families, factories, unions, hospitals, courtrooms, the armed forces, schools, universities and sports leagues—in all of society. The laity must try to make God be "all in every one" (*1 Cor* 12:6) because there is nothing truly human that should not be put under the Royalty of Christ. Those who reject this, or who are opposed to or fight against Christ reigning in society, or even those who do not care whether or not he reigns, are actually working for the devil, since individuals and nations must serve someone. They will either serve God or the devil. There is no room for any type of neutrality. "To serve God is to reign."[257]

5. RELIGIOUS OR CONSECRATED[258]

The religious or consecrated members of the Church remind us of the importance of the treasures of heaven. They follow Jesus very closely in the fulfillment of the evangelical counsels of chastity, poverty and obedience, trying to live the beatitudes.

This state of life belongs undoubtedly to the life and holiness of the Church.[259]

"By their state in life, religious give splendid and striking testimony that the world cannot be transformed and offered to God without the spirit of the beatitudes."[260]

---

[256] Cf. JOHN PAUL II. *Christifideles Laici.* 1, 8, 11-14.
[257] *Roman Missal.* Mass for Peace.
[258] Cf. JOHN PAUL II. *Vita Consecrata.* 21, 33, 35.
[259] Cf. II VATICAN COUNCIL. *Lumen Gentium.* 44.
[260] II VATICAN COUNCIL. *Lumen Gentium,* 31.

4. THE THREE STATES OF THE CHURCH

The Church has three states: militant, suffering and triumphant.

The Church is not only constituted of the living who are on the road to heaven, which is to say, those on pilgrimage and fighting for Christ (the Church Militant). The militant church includes the wheat (the good, "the children of the kingdom") and the weeds (the evil, "the children of the evil one") according to the parable in *Matthew* 13:38. However, the Church is also constituted of those, who, having died in the grace of God, still have to be purified from the temporal punishments incurred by their sins. These souls are now in purgatory (the Church Suffering). Finally, the Church is principally made up of our brothers and sisters who are already enjoying the Triune God in heaven, (the Church Triumphant), together with the Virgin, the good angels and all the saints who have triumphed over their enemies.

In these three states, **the Communion of Saints** is formed. Together with the Church Triumphant (those reigning triumphantly in heaven) and the Church Suffering (those patiently paying their debts in purgatory), we, the Church Militant (those pilgrims who fight for Christ on earth), belong to this one and only Church of Christ by: adoring the "unity in Trinity, and Trinity in unity";[261] confessing faith in Jesus in declaring "you are the Christ, the Son of the living God" (*Mt* 16:16), the "true God of true God... who for our salvation... was made man";[262] and grafting ourselves to him by means of Baptism, participating in the divine life brought to us by means of sanctifying grace. This is the Communion of Saints. This communion, or "common union," is fruit of the same divine life, of the same grace of God that runs like sap along the entire length of that Vine, the Church, uniting all of its members in God who is three times holy.

---

[261] The *Creed* which is called Athanasian. Dz. 39.
[262] COUNCIL OF NICEA I. Dz. 54

The Mystic Body of Christ, made up of the faithful in heaven, in purgatory and on the earth, has a type of circulatory system that distributes heavenly goods. This is why we can pray and intercede for each other. This is why a Catholic who lives in the United States is united by grace with all the Catholics in any part of the world. Furthermore, this union is stronger, deeper and more solid than the union of my hand with my brain, because a supernatural union brought about by grace is, without a doubt, superior to any union of the natural order. This is why we must have an intense love for all the saints: our most beloved brothers and sisters who, like us, once had to fight and suffer in order to finally triumph with the help of the grace of God. This is why we also have the duty to pray for the dead, to alleviate what they have left to suffer. They will return all we have done for them in abundance.

CONCLUSION

In the Church, mystery, communion and mission are always interwoven. None of these aspects of the one reality founded by Jesus Christ should ever be obscured. Three dimensions are essential for this Church: the Eucharistic dimension, since "the Eucharist makes the Church and the Church makes the Eucharist";[263] the Marian dimension, since Jesus entrusted us to Mary, "Behold, your mother" (*Jn* 19:27); and the Petrine dimension, since Jesus said "on this rock I will build my church" (*Mt* 16:18).

Let us love our holy Mother Church who has begotten, is begetting and will beget sons and daughters "of whom the world is not worthy" (*Heb* 11:38): colossal vessels of sanctity, titans of virtue, champions of faith and giants of charity. With their example, let us persevere to the end. "By the grace of God, I have always professed the Roman Catholic religion and, by that same grace, I hope to die in her" (Saint Thomas More, martyr).[264]

---

[263] Cf. SAINT AUGUSTINE. *Contra Faustum*. 12, 20: PL 432, 265. (Editorial translation)

[264] On his way to martyrdom, Saint Thomas More asked for those present to "pray for him and give witness with him that there he was suffering death, in faith and for the faith of the holy Catholic Church." This is a testimony taken from Margaret Roper in *CHAMBERS*. "Tomás Moro." Ed. Juventud Argentina, Buenos Aires 1964. p. 352. (Editorial translation)

Let us say time and again:

Lord, I deeply love your Church,
One, Holy, Catholic, Apostolic and Roman,
Because Her invisible head is Jesus Christ, our Lord,
Because the Holy Virgin Mary is Her most splendid fruit,
Because the saints of all times adorn Her,
Because She shines resplendently throughout the ages;
By the courage of the Patriarchs,
By the fidelity of the Prophets,
By the faith of the Apostles,
By the sufferings of the Martyrs,
By the firmness of the Pontiffs,
By the prudence of the Bishops,
By the wisdom of the Doctors,
By the fortitude of the Confessors,
By the total surrender of the Priests,
By the purity of Virgins,
By the temperance of the Penitents,
By the audacity of the Founders,
By the testimony of the Holy Laity,
By the sweetness of the contemplative monks,
By the silence of the hermits,
By the splendor of the Holy Kings,
By the vehemence of the preachers,
By the apostolic zeal of the missionaries,
By the sacrifice of those who show hospitality,
By the nobility of the mendicants,
By the brightness of the educators and catechists,
By the patience of those persecuted,
By the humility of those who obey,
By the fervor of the converts,
By the abnegation of the militants,
By the innocence of those that live without mortal sin,
By the contrition of sinners,
By the simplicity of those who live like children,
By the confidence of those who abandon themselves in your hands,
By the constancy of those who persevere to the end,
By the generosity of those who give,
By the joy and the love of the saints of all times.

Because of this and much more, I love, Lord, your Church,
One, Holy, Catholic, Apostolic and Roman. Amen.

> "The Church has so much to talk about with youth, and youth
> have so much to share with the Church. This mutual dialogue, by
> taking place with great cordiality, clarity and courage, will provide a
> favorable setting for the meeting and exchange between generations,
> and will be a source of richness and youthfulness for the Church and
> civil society. In its message to young people the Council said: 'The
> Church looks to you with confidence and with love... She is the real
> youthfulness of the world... Look upon the Church and you will find
> in her the face of Christ'."

> *John Paul II*
> *Christifideles Laici, 46*

ARTICLE 10:
"I BELIEVE IN THE FORGIVENESS OF SINS"

Our Savior is so merciful that he particularly wanted that "repentance and forgiveness of sins should be preached in his name to all nations" (*Lk* 24:47).

Since sin is an offense against God, it is, in a certain sense, infinite. Thus, only God can forgive sins: "Who can forgive sins but God alone?" (*Mk* 2:7). The Lord says: "I am He who blots out your transgressions for my own sake, and I will not remember your sins" (*Is* 43:25). We always ask him to "forgive us our trespasses" (our sins) (*Mt* 6:12).

In Baptism, God forgives us of the original sin we are all born with. If the baptized person has reached the age of reason, he is also forgiven of any other sin committed as long as he has sincere contrition. In Baptism, God also gives us sanctifying grace, a gift by which we live "in newness of life" (*Rom* 6:4).

The same Christ who "has authority on earth to forgive sins" (*Mk* 2:10), was the one who, before leaving this world, transmitted this tremendous power to the Apostles and priests: "If you forgive the sins of any, they are forgiven; if you retain the sins of any, they are retained" (*Jn* 20:23).

"In the forgiveness of sins, both priests and sacraments are instruments which our Lord Jesus Christ, the only author and liberal giver of salvation, wills to use in order to efface our sins and give us the grace of justification."[265]

Priests have the authority to forgive all sins, in the name and with the power of Christ, as long as the penitent has repented of his sins. If he has not repented, he cannot be forgiven by even God himself, because God never acts against the freedom of man. Saint Augustine teaches: "He who created you without you, will not save you without you."[266] God did not need our collaboration in order to create us. However, in order to save us, God has desired our collaboration, placing no obstacles to his saving grace.

If we have seriously repented of our sins, however grave they may be, when the priest absolves us, we are truly forgiven by God: "Though your sins are like scarlet, they shall be as white as snow" (*Is* 1:18). "There will be more joy in heaven over one sinner who repents than over ninety-nine righteous persons who need no repentance" (*Lk* 15:7).

"There is no offense, however serious, that the Church cannot forgive. 'There is no one, however wicked and guilty, who may not confidently hope for forgiveness, provided his repentance is honest.' Christ who died for all men desires that in his Church the gates of forgiveness should always be open to anyone who turns away from sin."[267]

It is always good to meditate on "the incomparable greatness of the risen Christ's gift to his Church: the mission and the power to forgive sins through the ministry of the apostles and their successors: 'The Lord wills that his disciples possess a tremendous power: that his lowly servants accomplish in his name all that he did when he was on earth.' 'Priests have received from God a power that he has given neither to angels nor to archangels…God above confirms what priests do here below.' 'Were there no forgiveness of sins in the Church, there would be no hope of life

---

[265] *Roman Catechism*. 1, 11, 6; cited by the *Catechism of the Catholic Church*. 987.
[266] *Sermon* 169. XI, 13; PL: 38, 923. (Editorial translation)
[267] *Catechism of the Catholic Church*. 982.

to come or eternal liberation. Let us thank God who has given his Church such a gift."'[268]

ARTICLE 11:
"I BELIEVE IN THE RESURRECTION OF THE BODY"

There is a "spiritual resurrection," which is the step from the death of sin into the life of grace. There will also be a bodily resurrection, when the "souls will be reunited with their bodies,"[269] and this is the truth of faith expressed in the Creed. This is why, to avoid mistakes, we say resurrection "of the body" in order to make it understood that a body of human nature, the same body that died, will rise.

God "will give life to your mortal bodies" (*Rom* 8:11) and this risen body will be "of the same nature but of a distinct glory."[270] This body will be of a distinct glory because the risen body "cannot die" (*Lk* 20:36) or suffer. The risen body will be completely obedient to the spirit: "it is raised a spiritual body" (*1 Cor* 15:44). This body will be of a distinct glory because it will never oppose any motion of the soul.

The same material world will also be transformed because "we wait for new heavens and a new earth" (*2 Pet* 3:13).

"Belief in the resurrection of the dead has been an essential element of the Christian faith from its beginnings. 'The confidence of Christians is the resurrection of the dead; believing this we live.'"[271]

"How can some of you say that there is no resurrection of the dead? But if there is no resurrection of the dead, then Christ has not been raised; if Christ has not been raised, then our preaching is in vain and your faith is in vain... But in fact Christ has been

---

[268] *Catechism of the Catholic Church.* 983.
[269] PAUL VI. *Creed of the People of God.* 28.
[270] SAINT GREGORY THE GREAT. *The Morals.* 1, 14. (Editorial translation)
[271] *Catechism of the Catholic Church.* 991.

raised from the dead, the first fruits of those who have fallen asleep" (*1 Cor* 15:12-14, 20).

1. CHRIST'S RESURRECTION AND OUR RESURRECTION[272]

God progressively revealed the resurrection of the dead to his People. In the Old Testament, we have an example in the Maccabean martyrs of faith in the resurrection. When King Antiochus was about to put to death the fourth of the seven brothers, he said to the King: "One cannot but choose to die at the hands of men and to cherish the hope that God gives of being raised again by him. But for you there will be no resurrection to life!" (*2 Mac* 7:14). The book of the prophet Daniel also states: "And many of those who sleep in the dust of the earth shall awake, some to everlasting life, and some to shame and everlasting contempt. And those who are wise shall shine like the brightness of the firmament; and those who turn many to righteousness, like the stars for ever and ever" (*Dan* 12:2-3).

"The Pharisees and many of the Lord's contemporaries hoped for the resurrection. Jesus teaches it firmly. To the Sadducees who deny it he answers, 'Is not this why you are wrong, that you know neither the scriptures nor the power of God?' Faith in the resurrection rests on faith in God who 'is not God of the dead, but of the living.'

But there is more. Jesus links faith in the resurrection to his own person: 'I am the Resurrection and the life.' It is Jesus himself who on the last day will raise up those who have believed in him, who have eaten his body and drunk his blood."[273] "For this is the will of my Father, that every one who sees the Son and believes in him should have eternal life; and I will raise him up at the last day" (*Jn* 6:40). "He who eats my flesh and drinks my blood has eternal life, and I will raise him up at the last day" (*Jn* 6:54).

---

[272] Cf. *Catechism of the Catholic Church*. 997-1001.
[273] *Catechism of the Catholic Church*. 993-994.

In his public life, our Lord already offers a sign and pledge of the resurrection by restoring life to some of the dead. For example, Jesus raises his friend Lazarus who had been dead for four days. "Your brother will rise again," Jesus said to Martha, who in turn responded, "I know that he will rise again in the resurrection at the last day." Then Jesus announced the great promise: "I am the resurrection and the life; he who believes in me, though he die, yet shall he live, and whoever lives and believes in me shall never die" (*Jn* 11:25-26).

"To be a witness to Christ is to be a 'witness to his Resurrection,' to '[have eaten and drunk] with him after he rose from the dead.' Encounters with the risen Christ characterize the Christian hope of resurrection. We shall rise like Christ, with him, and through him. From the beginning, Christian faith in the resurrection has met with incomprehension and opposition. 'On no point does the Christian faith encounter more opposition than on the resurrection of the body.' It is very commonly accepted that the life of the human person continues in a spiritual fashion after death. But how can we believe that this body, so clearly mortal, could rise to everlasting life?"[274]

HOW ARE THE DEAD RESURRECTED?

What does resurrection mean? At death—the moment the soul separates from the body,—the body of man corrupts, while his soul encounters God, in the hopes of reuniting with his glorified body. God, in his omnipotence, will truly give our bodies an incorruptible life, uniting them to our souls by virtue of the resurrection of Jesus.

Who will be raised? All men who have died: "those who have done good, to the resurrection of life, and those who have done evil, to the resurrection of judgment" (*Jn* 5:29, cf. *Dan* 12:2).

How? Christ rose with his own body: "See my hands and my feet, that it is I myself" (*Lk* 24:39). Yet, Christ did not come back to an earthly life. In the same way, in Christ all will rise with their

---

[274] *Catechism of the Catholic Church.* 995-996.

own body, the one they have now. However, this body will be "like his glorious body" (*Phil* 3:21), the "spiritual body" (*1 Cor* 15:44).

This "how" surpasses our imagination and our understanding. It is only accessible through faith. Nevertheless, our participation in the Eucharist already gives us an anticipation of the transfiguration of our bodies by Christ "...our bodies, when they receive the Eucharist, are no longer corruptible, having the hope of the resurrection to eternity."[275]

When? Undoubtedly, our bodies will be raised on the "last day" (*Jn* 6:39-40, 44, 54; 11:24), at the end of the world. In fact, the resurrection of the dead is intimately related with the Second Coming of Christ: "For the Lord himself will descend from heaven with a cry of command, with the archangel's call, and with the sound of the trumpet of God. And the dead in Christ will rise first" (*1 Thess* 4:16).

2. DYING IN CHRIST JESUS

"To rise with Christ, we must die with Christ: we must 'be away from the body and at home with the Lord.' In that 'departure' which is death the soul is separated from the body. It will be reunited with the body on the day of resurrection of the dead.

Death is the end of earthly life. Our lives are measured by time, in the course of which we change, grow old and, as with all living beings on earth, death seems like the normal end of life. That aspect of death lends urgency to our lives: remembering our mortality helps us realize that we have only a limited time in which to bring our lives to fulfillment: 'Remember also your Creator in the days of your youth, . . . before the dust returns to the earth as it was, and the spirit returns to God who gave it.'"[276]

[275] SAINT IRENAUS. *Adversus haereses.* 4, 18, 5.
[276] *Catechism of the Catholic Church.* 1005, 1007.

The Meaning of Christian Death

"Because of Christ, Christian death has a positive meaning: 'For to me to live is Christ, and to die is gain.'...'It is better for me to die in Christ Jesus than to reign over the ends of the earth. Him it is I seek—who died for us. Him it is I desire—who rose for us. I am on the point of giving birth...Let me receive pure light; when I shall have arrived there, then shall I be a man.'

In death, God calls man to himself. Therefore the Christian can experience a desire for death like Saint Paul's: 'My desire is to depart and be with Christ.' (*Phil* 1:23). He can transform his own death into an act of obedience and love towards the Father, after the example of Christ (*Lk* 23:46) and the saints:

- 'My earthly desire has been crucified; . . . there is living water in me, water that murmurs and says within me: Come to the Father.'

- 'I want to see God and, in order to see him, I must die.'

- 'I am not dying; I am entering life.'

The Christian vision of death receives privileged expression in the liturgy of the Church: 'Lord, for your faithful people life is changed, not ended. When the body of our earthly dwelling lies in death we gain an everlasting dwelling place in heaven.'

Death is the end of man's earthly pilgrimage, of the time of grace and mercy which God offers him so as to work out his earthly life in keeping with the divine plan, and to decide his ultimate destiny. When 'the single course of our earthly life' is completed, we shall not return to other earthly lives: 'It is appointed for men to die once.' There is no 'reincarnation' after death.

The Church encourages us to prepare ourselves for the hour of our death. In the litany of the saints, for instance, she has us pray: 'From a sudden and unforeseen death, deliver us, O Lord;' to ask the Mother of God to intercede for us 'at the hour of our death' in the *Hail Mary*; and to entrust ourselves to Saint Joseph, the patron of a happy death.

'Every action of yours, every thought, should be those of one who expects to die before the day is out. Death would have no great terrors for you if you had a quiet conscience...Then why not keep clear of sin instead of running away from death? If you aren't fit to face death today, it's very unlikely you will be tomorrow.'"[277]

Saint John Bosco, the patron of youth, advised his youth to meditate frequently on death: "Now the devil, in order to seduce you to sin, tries to distract you from thinking that a thought is sinful, persuading you to cover up and excuse the fault, telling you that there is no great evil in such a pleasure, in such a disobedience, in not going to Mass on solemnities. However, at the moment of death, he will make you aware of the gravity of the faults and he will show them all to you vividly. How will you respond to him at such a terrible moment? Woe to him who finds himself not in the grace of God!... You will see all this when the road to eternity is opened before you. Eternity in glory or eternity in torment is determined at that moment. Do you understand what I am telling you?"[278]

The saints give us examples of how we should live prepared to die at the least expected moment. Saint Francis of Assisi, right before his death, sang:

Praised be You, my Lord through Sister Death,
from whom no-one living can escape.
Woe to those who die in mortal sin!
Blessed are they She finds doing Your Will.[279]

"Let us consider the essential problems: life and death, mortality and immortality. In the history of humanity, Jesus has inverted the meaning of human life. If daily experience shows existence as a passage towards death, the Paschal Mystery opens up the perspective to a new life beyond death. Thus, the Church, that professes in the *Creed*, the death and resurrection of Jesus, has every reason to

---

[277] *Catechism of the Catholic Church.* 1010-1014.
[278] *La Juventud Instruida*, IV, III. (Editorial translation)
[279] *Lessons from the Life of St. Francis of Assisi.* Part 9.

pronounce these words: 'I believe in the resurrection of the body and life everlasting.'"

John Paul II
to youth gathered in Rome
March 20, 1997
(Editorial translation)

ARTICLE 12:
"I BELIEVE IN LIFE EVERLASTING"

"Everlasting" means that it will never pass away and never end. It is like saying "eternal life" or eternal glory.

The grace of God is likened to the living water brought by Christ, creating us to be "a spring of water welling up to eternal life" (*Jn* 4:14). This grace is likened to the sap that gives life to the branches, uniting them to the trunk. This grace, which is the beginning of eternal life on earth, which unites us to Jesus and to our brothers, and which is a prelude and anticipation of heaven, is the one thing needful (cf. *Lk* 10:42). This grace is "God's seed" (*1 Jn* 3:9), which springs from the earth, grows, develops, and will bear splendid fruit in glory.

By the grace of God we have within us the gift of faith. By virtue of this gift we believe in God and in our Redeemer. Thus, by this faith we begin to have eternal life. "This is eternal life, that they know you the only true God, and Jesus Christ whom you have sent" (*Jn* 17:3). Eternal life, which is begun on earth, is nourished by the Eucharist: "he who eats my flesh and drinks my blood has eternal life" (*Jn* 6:54). For our life to develop fully, we must obey the commandments of God, as Jesus taught the doctor of the law who asked him: "Teacher, what shall I do to inherit eternal life?" (*Lk* 10:25). If someone sins gravely, he loses the grace of God and is separated from him. Just as branches, when separated from the tree, lose life, do not bear fruit and are only used to be gathered and "thrown into the fire and burned" (*Jn* 15:6), so is the end of a soul who sins gravely.

On the other hand, he who remains united to Christ by grace "bears much fruit" (*Jn* 15:5) and will enjoy God for all eternity.

The hope that God will give us eternal life in heaven encourages us throughout our earthly life, considering that "the sufferings of this present time are not worth comparing with the glory that is to be revealed to us" (*Rom* 8:18). Not even the prospect of death will afflict us excessively, because "we have a building from God, a house not made with hands, eternal in the heavens" (*2 Cor* 5:1).

Eternal life in heaven is the greatest happiness. It is without the pollution of any evil and it is without end. This happiness is so great that it is inexpressible.

Let us make a comparison in order to obtain some idea of this happiness. We know that a magnifying glass placed at a certain angle produces fire from the rays gathered from the sun. Let us imagine three huge magnifying glasses with diameters as big as the earth. Let us gather under the first magnifying glass all the life that has existed, exists now and will exist; all the life of plants, flowers, animals, men, angels, saints; the valiant life of heroes; the life expressed in great acts of humanity; the life of the wise, the great artists; the life that kings and emperors have lived; that country and townspeople have lived; the life expressed in feasts, in reunions, in conversations; and all the life of thoughts and actions purified from all evil and sin. Under the second magnifying glass, let us gather together the truth of all the sciences and technology; all the natural and supernatural truths men have ever known; and the truths all the saints and angels have known. Finally, under the third magnifying glass, let us gather all the love that men and angels have had, have and will have; the love of mothers for their sons; the love between spouses and lovers; the love of the saints for God, of all heroes for their countries, of knights for their ladies; the love of missionaries for pagans, of nurses for the sick, of teachers for their students; the love of the Holy Virgin for her Son, etc. Then, let us angle these three magnifying glasses into one point and put it on our heart and our minds. What happiness, what joy, what peace, what satisfaction, what blessedness!

The happiness, joy, peace, and blessedness of heaven are without comparison infinitely greater than this. This is because heaven will consist in enjoying not only the sum of all temporal life, truth and love, but in the infinite Life, Truth and Love of God, in enjoying God himself. In heaven, God is for his saints "true light, complete satisfaction, everlasting joy, complete blessedness and perfect happiness."[280] There "we shall be like him, for we shall see him as he is" (*1 Jn* 3:2), "face to face" (*1 Cor* 13:12). "For with you is the fountain of life; in your light do we see light" (*Ps* 36:9). "My soul thirsts for God…when shall I come and behold the face of God?" (*Ps* 42:2). Such is the exclamation of the one who contemplates the heaven promised and awaited.

> "The encounter with Jesus surpasses life. Apart from Jesus, there is nothing more than darkness and death. You are thirsty for life. For eternal life! For eternal life! Search for it and find it in him, who not only gives life, but is life itself."

John Paul II
Santiago, Chile
April 2, 1987
(Editorial translation)

---

[280] SAINT AUGUSTINE. *Pies Preces.* Homily 3.

PART TWO
WHAT WE MUST RECEIVE

THE CELEBRATION OF THE CHRISTIAN MYSTERY

"Through Baptism, Confirmation, the Sacrament of Reconciliation, the Eucharist, and other communitarian signs of the Church, Christ has already come to us, without any merit on our part, and often without our recognizing him immediately. May Mary help us to receive with simplicity of heart the message of the love of God, to believe in him despite the doubts our society and our own spirit plant in our hearts."

John Paul II
Papal Meditation with the youth
August 15, 1983
(Editorial translation)

SECTION ONE
THE SACRAMENTAL ECONOMY

"Christ now lives and acts in and with his Church... He acts through the sacraments in what the common Tradition of the East and the West calls 'the sacramental economy'; this is the communication (or 'dispensation') of the fruits of Christ's Paschal mystery in the celebration of the Church's 'sacramental' liturgy."

Catechism of the Catholic Church, 1076

CHAPTER ONE
THE PASCHAL MYSTERY
IN THE AGE OF THE CHURCH

1. THE LITURGY,
WORK OF THE MOST HOLY TRINITY

"In the liturgy of the Church, God the Father is blessed and adored as the source of all the blessings of creation and salvation with which he has blessed us in his Son, in order to give us the Spirit of filial adoption.

Christ's work in the liturgy is sacramental: because his mystery of salvation is made present there by the power of his Holy Spirit; because his Body, which is the Church, is like a sacrament (sign and instrument) in which the Holy Spirit dispenses the mystery of salvation; and because through her liturgical actions the pilgrim Church already participates, as by a foretaste, in the heavenly liturgy.

The mission of the Holy Spirit in the liturgy of the Church is to prepare the assembly to encounter Christ; to recall and manifest Christ to the faith of the assembly; to make the saving work of Christ present and active by his transforming power; and to make the gift of communion bear fruit in the Church."[281]

2. THE PASCHAL MYSTERY
IN THE CHURCH'S SACRAMENTS

John Paul II once said: "I address you all and I tell you: let yourselves be embraced by the mystery of the Son of Man, by the mystery of the death and resurrection of Christ. Let yourselves be embraced by the Paschal mystery!

---

[281] *Catechism of the Catholic Church.* 1110-1112.

Let this mystery penetrate the depths of your lives, your conscience, your sensibility, and your hearts, in such a way that it gives true meaning to everything that you do."[282]

1. SUPERNATURAL LIFE

Grace

Our Lord Jesus Christ came to earth to bring us "life, and have it abundantly" (*Jn* 10:10). "The Son of God became man to make men sons of God."[283] Already from his Incarnation, but above all on the cross, Jesus won that "life" which makes us children of God. This life is the grace of God which brings us salvation. Grace reaches us through the seven sacraments. They descend from Mount Calvary, where our Lord died on the cross, like seven rivers that water the earth; and the plants that spring up on their banks will thus grow strong, lush and fruitful. The sacraments are these rivers which bring the "living water" (*Jn* 4:10) of the grace of God to us. The sacraments reach us by means of the salvation Jesus worked once and for all on the altar of the cross. If we receive the sacraments frequently, we will grow to be spiritually strong, lush and fruitful.

The grace of God, which is the supernatural life that Christ communicates, makes us a "new man" (*Eph* 4:24), a "new creation" (*2 Cor* 5:17; Gal 6:15), "a holy nation" (*1 Pet* 2:9), "friends" of God (*Lk* 12:4; *Jn* 15:14), "children…heirs of God" (*Rom* 8:17), "God's offspring" (*Acts* 17:29) and "partakers of the divine nature" (*2 Pet* 1:4). This grace creates in us "a new heart...a new spirit" (*Ezek* 36:26), a "spirit of sonship" (*Rom* 8:15). This grace receives different names: "seal" of God (*2 Cor* 1:22), spiritual unction (cf. *2 Cor* 1:21), "God's seed" (*1 Jn* 3:9), "imperishable seed" (*1 Pet* 1:23), "a spring of water welling up to eternal life" (*Jn* 4:14), "light" (*Eph* 5:8) and "breastplate" (*1 Thess* 5:8).

---

[282] Homily given during the II World Youth Day in Buenos Aires, Argentina on April 12, 1987. (Editorial translation)
[283] SAINT AUGUSTINE. *Homily 194*. III, 4. (Editorial translation)

The infused virtues

The grace of God, or sanctifying grace, is accompanied by the infused virtues and the gifts of the Holy Spirit.

Infused virtue is a firm disposition of the soul given by God in order that it be able to accomplish supernatural and meritorious acts.

These virtues are like the motors of the ship of our soul on its journey toward eternal life. If these supernatural acts tend directly to God, knowing him, waiting for him, or loving him, then we have the infused theological virtues, which are: faith, hope and charity (cf. *1 Cor* 13:13). If these supernatural acts deal with the necessary means to reach God, our ultimate end, then we have the infused moral virtues, which are many. The four principal infused moral virtues are called **cardinal** (from the Latin word *cardo* which means hinge, because the moral life turns on and is sustained by these virtues). These are: prudence, justice, fortitude and temperance (cf. *Wis* 8:7). The gifts of the Holy Spirit are gifts from God that give wings to our desire for holiness. They are like the unfurled sails of the ship of the soul which make it ready and docile to the impulse of the Holy Spirit who "blows where it wills" (*Jn* 3:8). There are seven of these gifts: wisdom, understanding, counsel, fortitude, knowledge, piety, and fear of God (cf. *Is* 11:2).

Grace, which is a free gift of God, is the root of these virtues and gifts.

a) The Theological Virtues

1-Faith

Faith is the first theological virtue, without which "it is impossible to please him" (*Heb* 11:6). Without it, nobody can have either hope or charity. "Faith is the assurance of things hoped for, the conviction of things not seen" (*Heb* 11:1).

By faith, we believe in God and in all that God has revealed and proposed, by means of the Church, in order that we may believe.

2-Hope

Hope is the second theological virtue by which we hope to reach the reward of heaven. "For in this hope we were saved...we wait for it with patience" (*Rom* 8:24-25). "If for this life only we have hoped in Christ, we are of all men most to be pitied" (*1 Cor* 15:19).

By hope we are confident that we will arrive at the glory of heaven by means of grace and our good works.

3-Charity

Charity is the third theological virtue by which we love God above all things and we love our neighbor as ourselves for love of God. It is the only theological virtue that will remain in heaven. In heaven, we will not need faith because we will see what we believe in; and we will not need hope because we will possess what we hope for here below. However, we will never be without charity because the love of God does not end. Charity is the queen of all virtues since without her no other virtue is perfect. If charity is not present, then neither faith, nor generosity, nor prophecy, not even the ability to work miracles will help us reach eternal life.[284]

b) The Moral Virtues

These virtues involve the means which bring us to God. Their immediate object is not God himself—like the theological virtues—but rather created goods insofar as they are ordered to the ultimate, supernatural end.

1-Prudence

Prudence is the virtue that makes possible the right governing of our actions insofar as they are ordered to the supernatural end.

2-Justice

By the virtue of justice, we give to God or to our neighbor what belongs to him, respectively.

---

[284] Cf. *1 Cor* 13:1-13.

3-Fortitude

Fortitude is the virtue that gives us the strength we need in order to not renounce what is good, however difficult it may be, even at the cost of life itself.

4-Temperance

Temperance is the virtue that regulates the sensible pleasures within the right boundaries.

Each one of these moral virtues—called cardinal—brings with it a whole court of subordinate virtues which depend on it. Some examples are magnanimity, humility, and gratitude. All together there are more than fifty.

The gifts of the Holy Spirit

These gifts dispose the intelligence and the will to receive the impulse of the Holy Spirit. Due to them all virtues collaborate in a divine way, that is to say, with increasing perfection. There are seven:

a) Wisdom: by this gift we are made capable of correctly and wisely judging the things of God.

b) Understanding: this gift gives our intellect the sight of an eagle, which allows us to penetrate the truths of faith and the truths of the natural order in relation to the supernatural end.

c) Counsel: this gift allows us to make right judgments in particular cases, suggesting to us what is useful for the supernatural end.

d) Fortitude: this gift gives us strength to practice every kind of heroic virtue with invincible confidence and great security so that we will triumph over the greatest obstacles or dangers that could emerge.

e) Knowledge: by this gift we rightly judge created things in relation to God.

f) Piety: by this gift we filially love God and fraternally love our neighbor who is a son of the same Father.

g) Fear of God: this gift communicates a special docility in order to do the will of God in everything.

2. THE SACRAMENTS OF SALVATION

We were all born deprived of the grace of God, the infused virtues and the gifts of the Holy Spirit. We are children of wrath by nature (cf. *Eph* 2:3) and we can all say: "I was brought forth in iniquity, and in sin did my mother conceive me" (*Ps* 51:5). We are all born with original sin.

Hence, to lift us out of sin and bring us to holiness, our Lord instituted the seven sacraments. We call a sacrament something that is sacred and sanctifying, that gives us, returns to us when lost, or increases our sanctifying grace.

"The sacraments are efficacious signs of grace, instituted by Christ and entrusted to the Church, by which divine life is dispensed to us. The visible rites by which the sacraments are celebrated signify and make present the graces proper to each sacrament. They bear fruit in those who receive them with the required dispositions.

The Church celebrates the sacraments as a priestly community structured by the baptismal priesthood and the priesthood of ordained ministers.

The Holy Spirit prepares the faithful for the sacraments by the Word of God and the faith which welcomes that word in well-disposed hearts. Thus the sacraments strengthen faith and express it.

The fruit of sacramental life is both personal and ecclesial. For every one of the faithful on the one hand, this fruit is life for God in Christ Jesus; for the Church, on the other, it is an increase in charity and in her mission of witness."[285]

> "In the Paschal mystery the limits of the many sided evil in which man becomes a sharer during his earthly existence are surpassed: the cross of Christ, in fact, makes us understand the

---

[285] *Catechism of the Catholic Church.* 1131-1134.

deepest roots of evil, which are fixed in sin and death; thus the cross becomes an eschatological sign."

John Paul II
Encyclical letter Dives in Misericordia, V, 8

CHAPTER TWO
THE SACRAMENTAL CELEBRATION OF THE PASCHAL MYSTERY

1. CELEBRATING THE CHURCH'S LITURGY

"The liturgy is the work of the whole Christ, head and body. Our high priest celebrates it unceasingly in the heavenly liturgy, with the holy Mother of God, the apostles, all the saints, and the multitude of those who have already entered the kingdom.

In a liturgical celebration, the whole assembly is *leitourgos*, each member according to his own function. The baptismal priesthood is that of the whole Body of Christ. But some of the faithful are ordained through the sacrament of Holy Orders to represent Christ as head of the Body.

The liturgical celebration involves signs and symbols relating to creation (candles, water, fire), human life (washing, anointing, breaking bread) and the history of salvation (the rites of the Passover). Integrated into the world of faith and taken up by the power of the Holy Spirit, these cosmic elements, human rituals, and gestures of remembrance of God become bearers of the saving and sanctifying action of Christ.

The Liturgy of the Word is an integral part of the celebration. The meaning of the celebration is expressed by the Word of God which is proclaimed and by the response of faith to it.

Song and music are closely connected with the liturgical action. The criteria for their proper use are the beauty expressive of prayer, the unanimous participation of the assembly, and the sacred character of the celebration.

Sacred images in our churches and homes are intended to awaken and nourish our faith in the mystery of Christ. Through the icon of Christ and his works of salvation, it is he whom we adore. Through sacred images of the holy Mother of God, of the angels and of the saints, we venerate the persons represented.

Sunday, the 'Lord's Day,' is the principal day for the celebration of the Eucharist because it is the day of the

Resurrection. It is the pre-eminent day of the liturgical assembly, the day of the Christian family, and the day of joy and rest from work. Sunday is 'the foundation and kernel of the whole liturgical year' (*SC* 106).

The Church, 'in the course of the year, …unfolds the whole mystery of Christ from his Incarnation and Nativity through his Ascension, to Pentecost and the expectation of the blessed hope of the coming of the Lord' (*SC* 102 § 2).

By keeping the memorials of the saints—first of all the holy Mother of God, then the apostles, the martyrs, and other saints— on fixed days of the liturgical year, the Church on earth shows that she is united with the liturgy of heaven. She gives glory to Christ for having accomplished his salvation in his glorified members; their example encourages her on her way to the Father.

The faithful who celebrate the Liturgy of the Hours are united to Christ our high priest, by the prayer of the Psalms, meditation on the Word of God, and canticles and blessings, in order to be joined with his unceasing and universal prayer that gives glory to the Father and implores the gift of the Holy Spirit on the whole world.

Christ is the true temple of God, 'the place where his glory dwells;' by the grace of God, Christians also become the temples of the Holy Spirit, living stones out of which the Church is built.

In its earthly state the Church needs places where the community can gather together. Our visible churches, holy places, are images of the holy city, the heavenly Jerusalem, toward which we are making our way on pilgrimage.

It is in these churches that the Church celebrates public worship to the glory of the Holy Trinity, hears the word of God and sings his praise, lifts up her prayer, and offers the sacrifice of Christ sacramentally present in the midst of the assembly. These churches are also places of recollection and personal prayer."[286]

---

[286] *Catechism of the Catholic Church.* 1187-1199.

2. LITURGICAL DIVERSITY
AND UNITY OF THE MYSTERY

"It is fitting that liturgical celebration tends to express itself in the culture of the people where the Church finds herself, though without being submissive to it. Moreover, the liturgy itself generates cultures and shapes them.

The diverse liturgical traditions or rites, legitimately recognized, manifest the catholicity of the Church, because they signify and communicate the same mystery of Christ.

The criterion that assures unity amid the diversity of liturgical traditions is fidelity to apostolic Tradition, i.e., the communion in the faith and the sacraments received from the apostles, a communion that is both signified and guaranteed by apostolic succession."[287]

In the Catholic Church there are two large groups of liturgical traditions. Both are fully Catholic and neither is superior to the other. They are the eastern rite and the western rite. The eastern rite is composed of six families:

1. Byzantine
2. Alexandrian or Coptic
3. Syriac
4. Armenian
5. Maronite
6. Chaldean

The western, or Latin, rite is composed of four families:
1. Roman (our rite)
2. Ambrosian
3. Mozarabe o Hispano-visgothian
4. The rites of different religious orders

The Catholic Church breathes with two lungs: "One cannot breathe as a Christian, moreover, as a Catholic, with only one

---

[287] *Catechism of the Catholic Church.* 1207-1209.

lung; there must be two lungs, that is to say, the eastern and the western."[288]

> "Each day between Easter Sunday and the second Sunday of Easter, *in albis*, essentially make up one day. The liturgy focuses on one event, on one sole mystery. 'He has risen, he is not here' (*Mk* 16:6). Easter has been fulfilled. He has revealed the past. He has confirmed the truth of his words. He has said the last words of his message: the message of Good News, the Gospel message. God himself who is Father—the Giver of Life,—who does not want death (cf. *Ezek* 18:23-32) and who has 'created all things that they might exist' (*Wis* 1:14), has manifested the depths of his love, in him and for Him. Love means life. The resurrection is the definite testimony of Life, of Love."

John Paul II
Wednesday audience
April 18, 1979
(Editorial translation)

---

[288] JOHN PAUL II. *To the representatives of other Christian Confessions.* Paris, France, May 31, 1980.

SECTION TWO
THE SEVEN SACRAMENTS
OF THE CHURCH

"Jesus has also provided for your needs through the Sacraments of the Church, particularly the Eucharist and the Sacrament of Penance. The conversion of your hearts is brought about by Christ's action and Christ reaches out to you in his Sacraments, which will always be for you an expression and celebration of your faith and your life in Christ."

John Paul II
To the youth of Newfoundland (Canada)
September 12, 1984

CHAPTER ONE
THE SACRAMENTS OF CHRISTIAN INITIATION

The Sacraments are sensible and efficacious signs of grace—producing what they signify—instituted by Jesus Christ in order to sanctify us. United with grace, they bestow the accompanying gifts and virtues.

"Christ instituted the sacraments of the new law. There are seven: Baptism, Confirmation (or Chrismation), the Eucharist, Penance, the Anointing of the Sick, Holy Orders and Matrimony. The seven sacraments touch all the stages and all the important moments of Christian life: they give birth and increase, healing and mission to the Christian's life of faith. There is thus a certain resemblance between the stages of natural life and the stages of the spiritual life."[289]

Four of the seven Sacraments can be received numerous times: Communion, Penance, Anointing of the Sick, and Matrimony (in the case of the death of a spouse). Three of them can only be received once: Baptism, Confirmation, and Holy Orders.

These three are only received once because they leave an indelible mark, a permanent seal which nothing or no one can ever remove. In heaven, this mark will be a cause of greater glory. In hell, it will be a cause of greater confusion since it will remind us that, while we could have been faithful, we betrayed Christ through sin. Consequently, it will remind us that instead of an eternity of glory, we must suffer an eternity of condemnation due to our own fault.

1. THE SACRAMENT OF BAPTISM

Baptism is the first and most necessary of the sacraments. It makes us children of God, living temples of the Holy Spirit, and heirs of heaven. Baptism erases original sin and, if the baptized is an adult, erases all of his mortal and venial sins as long as he has

---

[289] *Catechism of the Catholic Church.* 1210; cf. SAINT THOMAS AQUINAS. *Summa Theologica.* III, 65, 1.

repented. Baptism infuses the grace of God in our souls, along with its virtues and gifts.

Baptism is a birth to the supernatural life. This is why Jesus teaches: "Unless one is born of water and the Spirit, he cannot enter the kingdom of God" (*Jn* 3:5). In Baptism, the water touches our body and the Holy Spirit transforms our soul.

By Baptism, we are grafted into Christ like branches on a vine and participate in his own Divine Life.

Baptism is so important and necessary that without it, there is usually no salvation. This is why, in the case of the danger of death, anyone can and must baptize. In cases of emergency, baptism is done by pouring natural water over the head of the person being baptized while saying: "(Name), I baptize you in the name of the Father, the Son and the Holy Spirit," with the intention of doing what the Church does.

By Baptism, we commit to live in a way that is worthy of Christ. We do this since, in a certain sense, we are "other christs" by grace; and since we are members of Christ's Body, demonstrating, by our way of life, that Christ lives in us.

2. THE SACRAMENT OF CONFIRMATION

At Confirmation, the Holy Spirit is given for the intrepid testimony of the faith, as it "was thus given to the Apostles on the day of Pentecost, so that the Christian might boldly confess the name of Christ."[290]

The Apostles were not content by the simple reception of the Holy Spirit. At the commandment of Christ, they communicated the Spirit to others by the laying on of hands. For example, we read in *Acts of the Apostles* that when the Apostles found out that some disciples had only been baptized, they "prayed for them that they might receive the Holy Spirit…Then they laid their hands on them and they received the Holy Spirit" (*Acts* 8:15, 17); in other words, they confirmed them.

---

[290] COUNCIL OF FLORENCE. Dz. 697.

On the day of Pentecost, the Apostles received the Holy Spirit and then immediately endeavored to preach the Gospel with all their strength.

Before receiving the Spirit, on the other hand, they were cowards, hiding themselves for fear of the Jews.

We also are made valiant soldiers of Jesus Christ thanks to the Holy Spirit we receive in the Sacrament of Confirmation.

3. THE SACRAMENT OF THE EUCHARIST

1. INTRODUCTION

Aware of our weakness, our Lord Jesus Christ wanted to institute a sacrament that, as spiritual nourishment, would give us strength and vigor. His heart overflowed with love, "having loved his own who were in the world, he loved them to the end" (*Jn* 13:1). He wanted to remain present in this sacrament in order to be with us "to the close of the age" (*Mt* 28:20). Furthermore, Jesus wanted to leave us this sacrament as a perpetual sacrifice offered to God in reparation for our sins.

The Eucharist is carried out in the Holy Sacrifice of the Mass. The formula of the consecration, which is the most important and solemn moment of the Mass, expresses the three fundamental truths of the Catholic faith in regards to the Eucharist. The Eucharist is: Sacrament, Real Presence, and Sacrifice. Let us analyze this formula:

-"Take this, all of you, and eat it"..."Take this, all of you, and drink"...: The Eucharist is Sacrament; it is spiritual nourishment; a renewal of the Last Supper; and, the heavenly banquet for our sanctification. "For my flesh is food indeed, and my blood is drink indeed" (*Jn* 6:55).

-"This is my body"..."this is my blood"...: The Eucharist is the Real Presence of Christ. Christ himself, in his Body and Blood, with his soul and divinity, is present in this sacrament. This sacrament not only gives us grace, but it also gives us the Author of Grace: "He who eats my flesh and drinks my blood has eternal life" (*Jn* 6:54).

-"That will be given up"..."that will be shed"...: The expressions "body given up" and "blood shed" express the sacrificial character of the Eucharist. In the Eucharist, Christ sacrifices himself in expiation for our sins. Thus, Christ appeases the just anger of God, making him favorable and clement, making satisfaction even for the souls in Purgatory. "The bread which I shall give for the life of the world is my flesh" (*Jn* 6:51). The Eucharist is the renewal of the Sacrifice on the Cross. Its end, similar to the end of the cross itself, is the glorification of God and the sanctification of men.

The words "Do this in memory of me" remind us that only those who have received the apostolic powers by ordination to the priesthood can celebrate the Eucharist.

2. THE INSTITUTION OF THE EUCHARIST

During his public life, Jesus prepared the Apostles so that they would be able to understand this sacrament, which is the heart and center of the Catholic Church. In order for the Apostles to understand that he had the power to turn wine into his Blood and make his Body present under the appearance of bread in the thousands and thousands of places around the world where Holy Mass is celebrated, Jesus prepared them by the miracle of the water turned into wine[291] and the miracle of the multiplication of the bread.[292] He also prepared them through his word, especially in the Sermon on the Eucharist.[293] After this long preparation, Jesus solemnly instituted the Eucharist at the Last Supper. He consummated it in the Sacrifice on the Cross, and ordained it be perpetuated on our altars "until he comes" (*1 Cor* 11:26).

3. THE HOLY SACRIFICE OF THE MASS

a) Parts of the Mass

The Holy Mass is one single act of worship consisting in two parts. The first part is centered on the Word of God because

---

[291] Cf. *Jn* 2:1-11.
[292] Cf. *Mt* 14:13-21; 15:32-39.
[293] Cf. *Jn* 6:25-71.

different texts of the Holy Scriptures are read and explained here. The second part is the principal one; it is centered on the Eucharist and the Sacrifice. It consists of three important moments:

1. The presentation of the gifts, or the Offertory. This is when the wine and the bread that will become the Body and the Blood of Jesus are offered to God.

2. The consecration. This is when, by the words of the priest, Christ renews his immolation for man, and the bread and wine become the Body and the Blood of Jesus. At this moment, Christ descends upon the altar.

3. Communion. This is when we receive the Body and the Blood of Jesus truly present under the appearance of bread and wine. At this moment, Christ descends into our hearts.

b) The same Sacrifice of the Cross

The Holy Sacrifice of the Mass is the same Sacrifice of the Cross, yet without the shedding of blood. The victim sacrificed and offered is one and the same; the Priest who offers it is one and the same; and the act of oblation is one and the same. On the Cross, the victim is Christ; and in the Mass, the victim sacrificed is also Christ. On the Cross, Christ is the Eternal High Priest who offers himself; and in the Mass Christ is also the main Priest. The same act that was offered on the Cross is perpetuated in the Mass.

What is, then, the role of the priest who celebrates the Mass? His role is to represent Christ. This is why when he consecrates the bread he does not say: "This is the body of Christ;" but, "This is my Body." This is clearly not because the bread turns into the priest's own body, but because the priest is acting in the person of Christ. The priest is taking the place of Christ, representing Christ, acting in the name and with the power of Christ. Christ is the main priest who acts, in such a way, that the essential effect of the Mass does not depend on the greater or lesser virtue of the visible priest. "Nothing more by a good nor less by a bad priest is accomplished,"[294] since the Sacrifice of the Mass does not depend on the merits or sanctity of the secondary priests; but rather, on the virtue, merits, sanctity and power of Christ our Lord, Eternal High Priest.

The supreme and infinite value of the Holy Mass comes from the fact that it is the Sacrifice of God made man. If we were to sum up all the sacrifices of men, great as they may be, they are nothing in comparison with the Mass. "Oh! If you only knew the value of a Holy Mass" (Blessed Luis Guanella).[295] When we go to Holy Mass, we must bring and offer our own sacrifices. We must do this in order that, united with the Sacrifice of Christ, they acquire merit for eternal life and complete in us "what is lacking in Christ's afflictions" (*Col* 1:24).

c) Differences between the Mass and the Cross

The differences between the Sacrifice of the Cross and the Sacrifice of the Mass are secondary.

1. On the Cross, Christ suffers, dies, and sheds blood: it is a bloody sacrifice. In the Mass, the risen Christ "will never die again" (*Rom* 6:9); Christ does not suffer or shed blood: it is an unbloody sacrifice.

2. On the Cross, Christ offers himself alone. He did not need anyone else to fulfill his priestly act. In the Mass, Christ has desired to need the heart, the voice, and the hands of a visible minister.

3. Christ on the Cross—suspended between heaven and earth—unites God to man and man to God by acquiring all the graces necessary for salvation. Christ in the Mass, once again suspended between heaven and earth—this time in the hands of the priest—continues working for the salvation of men by uniting them to God, applying and distributing the graces won "for ever" (*Heb* 7:17) on the altar of the Cross in every Mass.

---

[294] INNOCENT III, *Letter "Eius Exemplus."* Dz. 424.
[295] *El siervo de la caridad.* Ed. Tamborini, Madrid, 1980. p. 201. (Editorial translation)

d) The Essence of the Sacrifice of the Mass

The sacrificial action takes place at the moment of consecration: when the separation of the Body and Blood of Christ, which actually took place in the Sacrifice on the Cross, is mystically represented in the Mass. This is represented by the act in which the priest consecrates the bread and the wine separately. At the consecration of the bread, the Body of Christ is made directly present by the actual words of consecration themselves. At the consecration of the wine, the Blood of Christ is made directly present by these same words. Body on one side and blood on the other means the shedding of blood, or sacrifice, in all the languages of the world. The priest, when consecrating the species of bread and wine, separates, "with an unbloody incision, the Body and Blood of the Lord, using his voice as a sword."[296]

We say "unbloody incision" and that it is "mystically represented" because, by reason of the words, the Body of Christ is present under the species of bread and the Blood of Christ is present under the species of wine. However, by reason of concomitance and because the Body of Christ is a living body,[297] the Blood, Soul and Divinity of Christ are also present under the species of bread, and the Body, Soul and Divinity of Christ are also present under the species of wine. In such a way, the whole of Christ is entirely present in each of the two species.

Not all bread, or any type of bread, is the Body of Christ. Not all wine, or any type of wine, is the Blood of Christ. Only and uniquely, by means of the consecration in the Holy Mass, are bread and wine transformed into the Body, Blood, Soul and Divinity of our Lord Jesus Christ.

e) The Presence of Christ in the Eucharist

Jesus is present under the accidents of bread and wine. However, Christ is not present in just any way. Christ in the Eucharist is "truly, really, and substantially contained."[298]

---

[296] SAINT GREGORY OF NAZIANZUS. *Enchiridium Patristicum.* 171. (Editorial translation)
[297] Cf. *Rom* 6:9.
[298] COUNCIL OF TRENT. *Decree On the Most Holy Eucharist.* Dz. 874.

1-True Presence

We sometimes kiss a photo of an absent or deceased family member because, somehow, they are present to us in the image. Likewise, we salute our flag because it symbolizes our country, which is, somehow, made present in its colors.

Jesus is not present in this way in the sacrament of the altar. Rather, Jesus is present in a true way. When you get home from school you do not kiss a picture of your mother on the wall; rather, you kiss her. Why is that? It is because the photo is just an image of her. She is truly present, on the other hand, only in the place where she is situated. This is why when you enter a church the first thing you do is adore Jesus truly present in the tabernacle. In images of him only his figure is found, for example, in the crucifix. For this reason, when you enter a church, after making the sign of the cross, the first thing you must do is to look for the tabernacle. Beside the tabernacle, there is a lamp, called the sanctuary lamp, which is permanently lit. This lamp indicates to us that "Here is the Most Holy Sacrament; here is our Lord Jesus Christ." Furthermore, since we cannot remain with Jesus the whole day long—we must sleep, eat, work, etc.— this lamp represents us and expresses our desire to never separate ourselves from the good Jesus. Once you have found the tabernacle, you should genuflect, which consists in bending the right knee until it touches the ground, acknowledging your lowliness and adoring God's greatness. This is the greeting we must always give Jesus truly present in the tabernacle. We must do it when we come in, when we leave, and every time we pass in front of him.

2-Real Presence

Thus, Christ is truly present. However, there is more. With the Church, we acknowledge Christ is really present. What does it mean to be "really" present? Let us present an example. I can imagine that right now a robber has entered into my house. This robber is, somehow, present in my house, at least in my imagination. In fact, I begin to be afraid, to sweat, my legs tremble, my heartbeat quickens, but this is only happening in my imagination. In reality, there is no robber in my house. Christ is not present in the Eucharist in this way, present only in the imagination. He is not present because I think or imagine him to be, but because he really is present. Regardless of my faith or what I understand, apart from my spirit and all of my thoughts, Christ is found really present under the appearance of bread and wine. Christ has said it so and this is what the Catholic Church teaches.

3-Substantial Presence

Therefore, Christ is truly and really present. However, this is not all. He is also present in a substantial way. In order to understand this, let us look at another example. Since a power plant produces the electricity which lights up a lamp in my room, somehow, we can say the power plant is present in my room. It is present in its effects since because of it I have light. Some heretics have said that Christ is present only in this way in the Eucharistic Sacrament: by the good effects the soul receives. When we receive communion, we are made better, more loving, and our soul is strengthened. It is as if we only receive a force or power proceeding from the glorified body of Christ (which is in heaven) not the same substance of the glorified body of Christ present in the Eucharist. However, our faith teaches us that Christ is present not only by the good effects he produces in our souls, like the power plant in the lamp; but that Christ is substantially present. He is present not only illuminating, but as the source of all light: "I am the light of the world" (*Jn* 8:12).

4-The way Christ makes himself present

Our Lord Jesus Christ is truly, really and substantially present under the appearance of bread and wine when the bread and wine are transformed into Christ's Body and Blood. This transition, or change, of the substance of the bread and wine which completely disappear in order to be transformed into the Body, Blood, Soul and Divinity of our Lord Jesus Christ is called: **Transubstantiation** (which means the transition or change from one substance to another).

The appearances of the bread and wine (also called accidents or species), such as scent, color, flavor, taste, size, weight, measure and shape, remain the same. The substance is the only thing that changes. This means that we experience the same thing with our senses: sight, smell, touch and taste. Since the species do not change, we continue to see, smell, touch and taste the same accidents after the consecration as before. What changes is the substance.

f) The Eucharist as Sacrament

When we receive Jesus Christ under the appearance of bread and wine we say that we are receiving communion because when we receive Jesus we are intimately united to him. We are also united more than before with all the Catholic men and women who are in the grace of God. Communion means "common union:" union between ourselves and Christ, and union between ourselves and our brothers and sisters.

1-Dispositions needed in order to receive the Eucharist

In order to receive Jesus in communion, our soul must be free of all mortal sin. If we have committed a grave or mortal sin, we must go to confession before receiving communion. It is not enough to have just repented. Whoever comes forward to take communion in a state of mortal sin commits a horrible sacrilege. Consequently: "Whoever, therefore, eats the bread or drinks the cup of the Lord in an unworthy manner will be guilty of profaning the body and blood of the Lord. Let a man examine himself, and so eat of the bread and drink of the cup. For any one who eats and drinks without discerning the body eats and drinks judgment upon himself. That is why many of you are weak and ill, and some have died" (*1 Cor* 11:27-30).

It is not necessary to always go to confession before receiving communion. It is only an obligation if we have sinned gravely. Venial sins (sins of a lesser degree) are forgiven with repentance, good works, the use of holy water, with the prayers of the Mass itself, etc.

We should not eat or drink anything except water an hour before receiving communion. This is to show respect for the Lord. We must be aware of who we are going to receive and so approach communion with devotion.

2-Frequent Communion

It is convenient to receive Holy Communion often because we need the spiritual nourishment in order to be able to conquer temptations, not fall away from the path toward heaven, practice all the virtues and increase the grace in our soul. In fact, even the smallest increase of grace in one person "is greater than the good of nature in the whole universe."[299] We unite ourselves to Christ and live for him due to the Eucharist: "he who eats me will live because of me" (*Jn* 6:57). Let us imitate what the saints have done and "receive frequent communion."[300] Saint Cajetan said: "I will not be satisfied until I see Christians approach the Celestial Banquet with the simplicity of hungry and joyful children, and not filled with fears and false shame."[301] Thus, Saint John Bosco, apostle of the youth, insisted: "Some say that in order to receive communion frequently it is necessary to be a saint. This is not true! It is a lie. Communion is for the one who wants to become a saint, not for the saints; remedies are given to the sick, and nourishment is given to those who are weak. How happy would I be if I could see enflamed in you that fire which the Lord came to bring on earth!"[302]

"Communion is necessary to us just as breathing is necessary to the lungs" (Saint Peter Julian Eymard).[303]

Every time we participate in the Holy Sacrifice of the Mass we should receive communion! If it is not possible to receive communion sacramentally because we lack the required dispositions of the soul, we should at least partake of a spiritual communion, saying:

My Jesus, I believe that You are present in the Most Blessed Sacrament. I love You above all things, and I desire to receive You into my soul. Since I cannot now receive You sacramentally, come at least spiritually into my heart.

[299] SAINT THOMAS AQUINAS. *Summa Theologica.* I-II, 113, 9, ad. 2.
[300] SAINT JOHN BOSCO. *Reglamento* 98. (Editorial translation)
[301] Cited in: ALAN BUTLER. *Vidas de los Santos* [Lives of the Saints]. Vol. III, op. cit. p.277. (Editorial translation)
[302] LEMOYNE. *Memorias Biográficas de Don Bosco.* VII, 678-679. (Editorial translation)
[303] *Obras Eucarísticas.* Ed. Eucaristía, Madrid, 1963. p. 567. (Editorial translation)

I embrace You as You were already come, and I unite myself wholly to You. Never permit me to be separated from You.[304]

With this or another similar formula, we can make a spiritual communion several times a day, when we pass in front of a Catholic Church, in moments of temptation, when we wake up, when we go to sleep, in any time or place.

3-Visits to the Most Holy Sacrament

Just as we visit our family and friends, we must visit Jesus who awaits us in the tabernacle. We should speak to him about our lives, ask him for the things we need, and adore him as the Blessed Virgin, Saint Joseph, the shepherds, the three magi, the angels and men did at the manger in Bethlehem.

Saint John Bosco advised the youth: "Visits to Jesus in the Most Holy Sacrament are extremely necessary means in order to conquer the devil. Go and visit Jesus frequently and the devil will not be able to conquer you."[305]

The number of visits we make to Jesus will be proportional to our love for him. Even if they only last a minute, they have the flavor of eternity. From your youth, you should become accustomed to make many visits to Jesus in the Most Holy Sacrament. In this way, you will be preparing yourself for the immense blessing and the enormous happiness of adoring Jesus for an entire night, in what is called **Nocturnal Adoration**.

---

[304] SAINT ALPHONSUS LIGUORI. "Spiritual Communion." *Visits to the Most Blessed Sacrament and to the Blessed Virgin Mary.* Illinois: Tan Books and Publishers, Inc., 2000. p. 2.
[305] *Memorias Biográficas.* VIII, 49. (Editorial translation)

CHAPTER TWO
THE SACRAMENTS OF HEALING

4. THE SACRAMENT OF PENANCE OR CONFESSION

Jesus could have decided that angels be priests instead of men. However, Christ chose men so that they could have compassion on the ignorant and the lost since he too "is beset with weakness" (*Heb* 5:2). From among men, Christ "chose the most miserable and rejected in order to confuse the strong; in order that the divine hand shine brighter than the evil of the instrument which serves him."[306] Christ chose men in order that "no flesh might boast in the presence of God" (*1 Cor* 1:29). Christ gave them tremendous powers: not only the power to transform bread and wine into the Body and Blood of Jesus, as we have seen, but also the power to forgive sins. "If you forgive the sins of any, they are forgiven; if you retain the sins of any, they are retained" (*Jn* 20:23).

Jesus knew that many of his children, due to the weakness of human nature and wounded by original sin, would lose the sanctifying grace received at Baptism by committing mortal sin. He knew that many of them, having repented like the prodigal son, would want to return to friendship with God, to live united to him by grace.

To make this possible, Christ instituted the Sacrament of Penance, also called Confession or Reconciliation. By this Sacrament, when we repent and confess our sins to a priest, Christ restores the sanctifying grace once lost by mortal sin.

Just as only priests can celebrate the Holy Mass, only priests can forgive grave and mortal sins.

In confession, we must tell all our mortal sins, their quantity or number, the commandment or virtue sinned against, and any other circumstances that may have affected the gravity of the sin r

---

[306] NICOLAS MASCARDI, S.J. *Carta y Relación* (1670). Cited in: GUILLERMO FURLONG. *Nicolas Mascardi, S.J. y su Carta y Relación* (1670). Ed. Teoría, Buenos Aires, 1995. pp. 130-131. (Editorial translation)

changed its kind. To knowingly hold back any grave sin is to commit a horrible sacrilege. In this case, not only will none of the sins confessed be forgiven, but another one will be added: the sin of sacrilege. Consequently, during the next confession, one must accuse oneself of all previous sins: the sin not confessed and the sin committed in withholding it in the previous confession.

The mercy of God is infinite. However great our sins may be, God's mercy has no limit. If we are truly repentant of our sins, God will sincerely forgive us. "Though your sins are like scarlet, they shall be as white as snow" (*Is* 1:18). God does not want "the death of the wicked, but that the wicked turn from his way and live" (*Ezek* 33:11). This is why Jesus came: to save sinners, since "those who are well have no need of a physician, but those who are sick" (*Mt* 9:12). Thus, "there will be more joy in heaven over one sinner who repents than over ninety-nine righteous persons who need no repentance" (*Lk* 15:7). "He who doubts obtaining pardon feels that his wickedness is greater than the goodness of the Lord."[307] This is to say, he who believes that the goodness of the Lord is not able to cover his wickedness has a very small and imperfect idea of God.

This Sacrament of Reconciliation is likened to a raft which is thrown to a ship-wrecked sailor in order to save him from drowning: "It is the last raft of salvation in the middle of the tempests of this perverted world."[308] "Confession is the gate to heaven."[309]

What if someone has not committed any mortal sins, should he not go to confession? Of course he should! Even though it is not an obligation, it is very beneficial to confess venial sins and to repent once again of all our past sins. We should never forget that Penance is a sacrament that gives us the grace of God. It restores the grace lost by mortal sin and increases it as long as we

---

[307] FRIGEL GRAZIOLI. *Modelo de Confesores*. Ed. Ibérica, Madrid, 1944. p. 85. (Editorial translation)
[308] SAINT PETER JULIAN EYMARD. *Op. cit.* p. 1093. (Editorial translation)
[309] SAINT ANTHONY OF PADUA. *Sermón acerca del Alma Penitente*. II, 19. Cited in: *Los Sermones*. T.I, Ed. El Mensajero de San Antonio, Buenos Aires, 1995. p. 97. (Editorial translation)

have only committed venial sins. This is why we should confess frequently, even if we have not committed any grave sins.

"Does the one who desires to be presentable and clean in his attire only wash himself when covered with mud? As soon as a bit of dust falls upon him, he washes it off. Even though he may not be dirty, he cleans himself often for his decorum demands it."[310]

Saint John Bosco used to say that the best method to continually grow in goodness is to make good confessions and good communions. One grows in holiness by receiving these sacraments well. It was not a coincidence that Saint John Bosco was the first saint of the twentieth century who had the glory of seeing one of his disciples, the young Saint Dominic Savio, raised to the altar. Saint Dominic Savio encourages us: "resolve to make a good confession and you will see the happiness that will fill your soul."[311]

One of the last recommendations Saint Louis, King of France, made to his son Felipe was: "confess yourself frequently."[312] Confession "is the most efficacious and truly indispensable means to preserve our conscience pure and clean."[313]

In order to make a good confession, it is necessary to first make an examination of conscience[314] so as to recall the sins committed. Saint Teresa of Jesus said "in a room into which the sunlight enters strongly, not a cobweb can be hid."[315] Then, we should feel sorrow at having offended the Lord and resolve, with the help of God, to not sin again. Finally, we should tell our sins to a priest and fulfill the penance we receive.

With complete trust, we should be docile to the priest in confession. Jesus Christ said to them: "Whatever you bind on earth shall be bound in heaven, and whatever you loose on earth shall be loosed in heaven" (*Mt* 18:18). The priest is the judge. To

---

[310] FRIGEL GRAZIOLI. *Modelo de Confesores.* Ed. Ibérica, Madrid, 1944. p. 98. (Editorial translation)
[311] SAINT JOHN BOSCO. *Vida de Domingo Savio.* Ed. Ibérica, Madrid, 1944. p. 98. (Editorial translation)
[312] *Testamento espiritual a su hijo.* (Editorial translation)
[313] FRIGEL GRAZIOLI. *Modelo de Confesores.* Ed. Ibérica, Madrid, 1944. p. 96. (Editorial translation)
[314] Refer to the examination of conscience on page 321.
[315] *The Autobiography of St. Teresa of Avila.* XIX, 2.

"bind and loose," he must know the rope and the knot, that is to say, the sins, and whether there is repentance or not.

In addition to acting as a judge, the priest acts as a doctor in Reconciliation. How would he cure the souls if he did not know the sickness? He is also a teacher because he teaches, advises, and corrects. How would he be able to do this if he ignores what the penitent does not know, what he needs or his failings? Finally, the priest acts as a merciful father who seeks the spiritual welfare of his penitent children, to whom he gives the bread of the Word of God. How would he do this if he did not know what the penitent is able to assimilate?

We should tell our sins to the priest in Reconciliation with complete confidence. Not only can he never repeat them to anybody (not another priest, not the bishop, not the Pope, not even to an angel from heaven), but he also can never use, not even for the good of the Church, what he has heard from people in the Sacrament of Penance.

5. THE SACRAMENT OF THE ANOINTING OF THE SICK

Jesus also thought of the sick, who feel very alone, depressed, lack the desire to fight and suffer many temptations. For them, Jesus instituted the Sacrament of the Anointing of the Sick, which forgives their sins, increases grace, alleviates pain, provides company in solitude, strength in temptation, and health of body, provided it would help the salvation of the soul.

"Is any among you sick? Let him call for the elders of the church, and let them pray over him, anointing him with oil in the name of the Lord; and the prayer of faith will save the sick man, and the Lord will raise him up; and if he has committed sins, he will be forgiven" (*Jas* 5:14-15).

Families should not wait until the last moment to call the priest, when the sick person is already dying. For this reason, this sacrament is no longer called "extreme unction," in order that we may not think that this sacrament is reserved only for those who have no more hope of living. Rather, this sacrament is for all who suffer from a serious sickness.

The devil, who knows the immense benefits this sacrament brings to the sick, suggests false reasons that make families fail to call the priest on time.

One of these false reasons is that "the sick person will be frightened." This is a great lie, invented by the "father of lies" (*Jn* 8:44). It is exactly the opposite: the sick person finds peace and relief in the sacrament. How many people suffer atrocious agony and are only consoled when a priest arrives! This is a sign which shows that they were waiting for a priest! Even if they are frightened (something which does not happen), it is better to go to heaven, a bit frightened, than to be condemned to hell for all eternity without being frightened.

This sacrament is "a truly great mystery and one exceedingly to be sought, through which, if the faithful ask, and their sins are forgiven, it may even follow that health of body is restored..."[316]

> "Christian living is not complete without this renewed conversion, and conversion is not fully authentic without the Sacrament of Penance. Dear young people of Dublin: Christ wants to come to meet you regularly, frequently, in a personal way, in a personal encounter of loving mercy, forgiveness and healing. He wants to sustain you in your weakness and keep lifting you up, drawing you closer to his heart. As I explained in my Encyclical *Redemptor Hominis*, the encounter of this Sacrament is a right that belongs to Christ and to each of you. And so the Pope is very much in earnest when he now exhorts you: Do not deprive Christ of his right in this Sacrament, and never surrender your own."
>
> *John Paul II*
> *To the pilgrims from Dublin, Ireland*
> *August 28, 1980*

---

[316] COUNCIL OF TICINUS. *The Sacrament of Extreme Unction.* Dz. 315.

CHAPTER THREE
THE SACRAMENTS AT THE SERVICE
OF THE COMMUNITY

6. THE SACRAMENT OF HOLY ORDERS

Who are the ones who usually administer the sacraments? Who baptize, hear confessions, celebrate the Holy Mass, anoint the sick, preside over weddings, and preach the Word of God? Bishops and priests. How does Jesus give them the powers they need to act in his name and work with his authority? Through the Sacrament of the Holy Orders. In addition, this sacrament gives them the grace of their state: it equips them to carry out in holiness the difficult tasks of the priestly ministry, to conquer every danger and temptation, and to remain faithful to the promises they make to God.

The matter of this sacrament is the laying on of hands: "These [men] they set before the apostles, and they prayed and laid their hands upon them" (*Acts* 6:6). An uninterrupted chain of pastors, from the Apostles to the current bishops and priests, has made the powers of Christ extend into our present time by means of the laying on of hands. This happens in such a way that if the risen Lord Jesus Christ would appear and hear confessions alongside other priests, our sins would be just as much forgiven by these priests—who act in the person of Christ, in his name and with his power—as if they were forgiven by our Lord himself.

If Christ himself were to celebrate the Holy Mass, surrounded by all the bishops and cardinals, in a great ceremony with splendorous chant and sacred music, it would essentially be no different than a Mass celebrated by a priest who was alone, abandoned, ignored by all, without vestments and hidden from the guards in a concentration camp, with mere crumbs of bread and a little wine in a container. Essentially, both Masses are of an equal and infinite value because both are the perpetuation of the one Sacrifice of Christ. In the former, Christ would celebrate the Mass in person; and in the latter, the priest would celebrate in the person of Christ (cf. *2 Cor* 2:10), with his power and in his name because he has received the Sacrament of Holy Orders by the laying on of hands. Even if the priest were in a state of mortal sin, his powers of forgiveness and consecration remain since they are not dependent on the merit of his virtues, his intellectual capacity or his last name. The priest has these powers because he has received them from Christ. If a priest were to use his powers of forgiveness and consecration in a state of mortal sin, he would commit a horrible sacrilege, but he would still forgive and consecrate because he would do it in the person of Christ. Water flows through a silver pipe just as it does through a lead pipe. The "living water" of the grace of God flows through a holy priest just as it does through a sinful priest.

To excuse oneself from going to church and fulfilling our obligations to God because a priest is bad is stupidity. "Each of us shall give account of himself to God" (*Rom* 14:12). God will ask each of us for an account of the evil we have done and the good we have failed to do, not the evil others have done and the good they have failed to do, even if they are priests. When men present themselves before "the judgment seat of Christ, so that each one may receive good or evil" (*2 Cor* 5:10), the excuse "I didn't do good because others were doing evil" will not mean anything. For God "will render to every man according to his works" (*Rom* 2:6) and not according to the works of others.

We must always pray to God for priests, that they may be holy, and faithfully fulfill their mission. We must also pray for young men that they may not be deaf to the voice of God if he calls them to the priesthood, since "the harvest is plentiful, but the laborers are few" (*Lk* 10:2). We must not cease to pray to God for priests, "for the soul of the priest ought to be purer than the very sunbeams."[317] We must pray so that they may not forget that they are "the eyes of the Church, whose office is to weep for the evils that affect the body."[318] Finally, we must pray that they may always be sure guides who lead us on the path towards heaven, pastors who shepherd us to the good pastures of the doctrine of Christ and who are willing to give, if it were necessary, their "life

---

[317] SAINT JOHN CHRYSOSTOM. *On the Priesthood.* VI, 2.
[318] SAINT JOHN OF AVILA. *Escritos sacerdotales.* Pláticas sacerdotales (Segunda plática para clérigos), Madrid: B.A.C., 1969. p. 209. (Editorial translation)

for the sheep" (*Jn* 10:11) in order to separate them from the venomous pastures of error and heresy.

7. THE SACRAMENT OF MATRIMONY

1. MATRIMONY IN THE PLAN OF GOD

God created man, male and female, so that in living together they would have children and educate them, manifesting mutual love.

Forming a family is a very important task which involves many difficulties, such as: economic problems, differences in character and points of view, sacrifices, etc.

Our Lord Jesus Christ, "out of the great love with which he loved us" (*Eph* 2:4), instituted the sacrament of matrimony in order to not only bestow the grace of God to married couples, but to also give them a special grace which equips them to face all the difficulties of the home and triumph over them "through him who loved us" (*Rom* 8:37). Christ loved the Church as his spouse. "Husbands, love your wives, as Christ loved the church and gave himself up for her" (*Eph* 5:25). A wife must love her husband as the Church loves Christ, from the Cross until the end of time. This is why divorce is not licit.

In a Catholic marriage, a man and a woman are united forever, mutually faithful and generous in the transmission of life until separated by death.

Let us remember that Jesus performed his first miracle in Cana of Galilee, at a wedding feast. Upon the request of the Blessed Virgin Mary, Jesus turned water into wine so that the feast of the newlyweds would not be ruined. From then on, every family should always see Jesus and Mary as their best friends.

2. PREPARATION FOR MARRIAGE: THE CATHOLIC COURTSHIP

"So that the 'I do' of the spouses may be a free and responsible act and so that the marriage covenant may have solid and lasting human and Christian foundations, preparation for marriage is of prime importance. The example and teaching given by parents and families remain the special form of this preparation. The role of pastors and of the Christian community as the 'family of God' is indispensable for the transmission of the human and Christian values of marriage and family, and much more so in our era when many young people experience broken homes which no longer sufficiently assure this initiation.

'It is imperative to give suitable and timely instruction to young people, above all in the heart of their own families, about the dignity of married love, its role and its exercise, so that, having learned the value of chastity, they will be able at a suitable age to engage in honorable courtship and enter upon a marriage of their own.'"[319]

This preparation is very important because, in most cases, the failure of a marriage begins in the courtship. Young people who think they love each other and want to formalize their relationship by getting married must be aware that the entire meaning of a Catholic courtship consists in the future marriage.

CONCLUSION

Let us always draw near these rivers which descend from Calvary, bringing us the "living water" of the grace of God. Only then will our life be worth living, because each day we will grow closer to God.

---

[319] *Catechism of the Catholic Church.* 1632.

PART THREE
WHAT WE MUST DO

LIFE IN CHRIST

"What does Christ mean in your life? More than once you must have asked yourself this question and have been asked by others as well. I wish to help you with this answer which many of you may have already answered. For an idealistic young person, generous and valiant, Christ can and must be the root of your life, the central axis and point of reference of all your thoughts, decisions, and generous commitment to goodness. Search for Christ then and receive him. He is demanding; he is not satisfied with mediocrity; he does not permit indecisiveness. He is the only path towards the Father (cf. *Jn* 14:6) and he who follows him never walks in darkness (cf. *Jn* 8:12)."

John Paul II
to the youth in Caracas, Venezuela
January 28, 1985
(Editorial translation)

SECTION ONE
MAN'S VOCATION,
LIFE IN THE SPIRIT

"The Gospel is life. Your task consists in bearing witness to this life: the life of the adopted children of God. The modern man has an urgent need for this life—whether he knows it or not—just as humanity had need of the coming of Christ two-thousand years ago; people will always have this need of Jesus Christ until the end of time."

John Paul II
Vigil of prayer on the occasion of the 10th World Youth Day in Manila
January 14, 1995
(Editorial translation)

CHAPTER ONE
THE DIGNITY OF THE HUMAN PERSON

1. MAN, THE IMAGE OF GOD

"'Christ . . . makes man fully manifest to man himself and brings to light his exalted vocation' (*GS* 22 § 1).

Endowed with a spiritual soul, with intellect and with free will, the human person is from his very conception ordered to God and destined for eternal beatitude. He pursues his perfection in 'seeking and loving what is true and good' (*GS* 15 § 2).

In man, true freedom is an 'outstanding manifestation of the divine image' (*GS* 17).

Man is obliged to follow the moral law, which urges him 'to do what is good and avoid what is evil' (cf. *GS* 16). This law makes itself heard in his conscience.

Man, having been wounded in his nature by original sin, is subject to error and inclined to evil in exercising his freedom.

He who believes in Christ has new life in the Holy Spirit. The moral life, increased and brought to maturity in grace, is to reach its fulfillment in the glory of heaven."[320]

2. THE FREEDOM OF MAN

"'God willed that man should be left in the hand of his own counsel (cf. *Sir* 15:14), so that he might of his own accord seek his Creator and freely attain his full and blessed perfection by cleaving to him' (*GS* 17 § 1).

Freedom is the power to act or not to act, and so to perform deliberate acts of one's own. Freedom attains perfection in its acts when directed toward God, the sovereign Good.

---

[320] *Catechism of the Catholic Church.* 1710-1715.

Freedom characterizes properly human acts. It makes the human being responsible for acts of which he is the voluntary agent. His deliberate acts properly belong to him.

The imputability or responsibility for an action can be diminished or nullified by ignorance, duress, fear, and other psychological or social factors.

The right to the exercise of freedom, especially in religious and moral matters, is an inalienable requirement of the dignity of man. But the exercise of freedom does not entail the putative right to say or do anything.

'For freedom Christ has set us free' (*Gal* 5:1)."[321]

3. THE MORALITY OF HUMAN ACTS

"The object, the intention, and the circumstances make up the three 'sources' of the morality of human acts.

The object chosen morally specifies the act of willing accordingly as reason recognizes and judges it good or evil.

'An evil action cannot be justified by reference to a good intention' (cf. Saint Thomas Aquinas, *Dec. praec.* 6). The end does not justify the means.

A morally good act requires the goodness of its object, of its end, and of its circumstances together.

There are concrete acts that it is always wrong to choose, because their choice entails a disorder of the will, i.e., a moral evil. One may not do evil so that good may result from it."[322]

4. THE MORALITY OF THE PASSIONS

"The term 'passions' refers to the affections or the feelings. By his emotions man intuits the good and suspects evil.

---

[321] *Catechism of the Catholic Church.* 1743-1748.
[322] *Catechism of the Catholic Church.* 1757-1761.

The principal passions are love and hatred, desire and fear, joy, sadness, and anger.

In the passions, as movements of the sensitive appetite, there is neither moral good nor evil. But insofar as they engage reason and will, there is moral good or evil in them.

Emotions and feelings can be taken up in the virtues or perverted by the vices.

The perfection of the moral good consists in man's being moved to the good not only by his will but also by his 'heart.'"[323]

5. MORAL CONSCIENCE

"'Conscience is man's most secret core, and his sanctuary. There he is alone with God whose voice echoes in his depths' (GS 16).

Conscience is a judgment of reason by which the human person recognizes the moral quality of a concrete act.

For the man who has committed evil, the verdict of his conscience remains a pledge of conversion and of hope.

A well-formed conscience is upright and truthful. It formulates its judgments according to reason, in conformity with the true good willed by the wisdom of the Creator. Everyone must avail himself of the means to form his conscience.

Faced with a moral choice, conscience can make either a right judgment in accordance with reason and the divine law or, on the contrary, an erroneous judgment that departs from them.

A human being must always obey the certain judgment of his conscience.

Conscience can remain in ignorance or make erroneous judgments. Such ignorance and errors are not always free of guilt.

---

[323] *Catechism of the Catholic Church.* 1771-1775.

The Word of God is a light for our path. We must assimilate it in faith and prayer and put it into practice. This is how moral conscience is formed."[324]

"Conscience bears witness to man's own rectitude or iniquity to man himself but, together with this and indeed even beforehand, conscience is *the witness of God himself,* whose voice and judgment penetrate the depths of man's soul."[325]

---

[324] *Catechism of the Catholic Church.* 1795-1802.
[325] JOHN PAUL II. Encyclical letter *Veritatis Splendor.* 58.

CHAPTER TWO
THE HUMAN COMMUNITY

1. THE PERSON AND SOCIETY

"There is a certain resemblance between the union of the divine persons and the fraternity that men ought to establish among themselves.

The human person needs life in society in order to develop in accordance with his nature. Certain societies, such as the family and the state, correspond more directly to the nature of man.

'The human person . . . is and ought to be the principle, the subject, and the object of every social organization' (*GS* 25 § 1).

Widespread participation in voluntary associations and institutions is to be encouraged.

In accordance with the principle of subsidiarity, neither the state nor any larger society should substitute itself for the initiative and responsibility of individuals and intermediary bodies.

Society ought to promote the exercise of virtue, not obstruct it. It should be animated by a just hierarchy of values.

Where sin has perverted the social climate, it is necessary to call for the conversion of hearts and appeal to the grace of God. Charity urges just reforms. There is no solution to the social question apart from the Gospel (cf. *CA* 3, 5)."[326]

2. PARTICIPATION IN SOCIAL LIFE

"'There is no authority except from God, and those authorities that exist have been instituted by God' (*Rom* 13:1).

Every human community needs an authority in order to endure and develop.

---

[326] *Catechism of the Catholic Church.* 1890-1896.

'The political community and public authority are based on human nature and therefore...belong to an order established by God' (*GS* 75 § 3).

Authority is exercised legitimately if it is committed to the common good of society. To attain this it must employ morally acceptable means.

The diversity of political regimes is legitimate, provided they contribute to the good of the community.

Political authority must be exercised within the limits of the moral order and must guarantee the conditions for the exercise of freedom.

The common good comprises 'the sum total of social conditions which allow people, either as groups or as individuals, to reach their fulfillment more fully and more easily' (*GS* 26 § 1).

The common good consists of three essential elements: respect for and promotion of the fundamental rights of the person; prosperity, or the development of the spiritual and temporal goods of society; the peace and security of the group and of its members.

The dignity of the human person requires the pursuit of the common good. Everyone should be concerned to create and support institutions that improve the conditions of human life.

It is the role of the state to defend and promote the common good of civil society. The common good of the whole human family calls for an organization of society on the international level."[327]

3. SOCIAL JUSTICE

"Society ensures social justice by providing the conditions that allow associations and individuals to obtain their due.

---

[327] *Catechism of the Catholic Church.* 1918-1927.

Respect for the human person considers the other 'another self.' It presupposes respect for the fundamental rights that flow from the dignity intrinsic of the person.

The equality of men concerns their dignity as persons and the rights that flow from it.

The differences among persons belong to God's plan, who wills that we should need one another. These differences should encourage charity.

The equal dignity of human persons requires the effort to reduce excessive social and economic inequalities. It gives urgency to the elimination of sinful inequalities.

Solidarity is an eminently Christian virtue. It practices the sharing of spiritual goods even more than material ones."[328]

> "Marxism had promised to uproot the need for God from the human heart, but the results have shown that it is not possible to succeed in this without throwing the heart into turmoil."
>
> *John Paul II*
> *Encyclical letter Centesimus Annus, 24*

---

[328] *Catechism of the Catholic Church.* 1943-1948.

CHAPTER THREE
GOD'S SALVATION: LAW AND GRACE

1. THE NATURAL LAW

"'If you wish to enter into life, keep the commandments' (*Mt* 19:17). Only God can answer the question about the good, because he is the Good. But God has already given an answer to this question: he did so *by creating man and ordering him* with wisdom and love to his final end, through the law which is inscribed in his heart (cf. *Rom* 2:15), the 'natural law.' The latter 'is nothing other than the light of understanding infused in us by God, whereby we understand what must be done and what must be avoided. God gave this light and this law to man at creation.' He also did so *in the history of Israel,* particularly in the 'ten words,' the *commandments of Sinai,* whereby he brought into existence the people of the Covenant (cf. *Ex* 24) and called them to be his 'own possession among all peoples,' 'a holy nation' (*Ex* 19:5-6), which would radiate his holiness to all peoples (cf. *Wis* 18:4; *Ezek* 20:41). The gift of the Decalogue was a promise and sign of the *New Covenant,* in which the law would be written in a new and definitive way upon the human heart (cf. *Jer* 31:31-34), replacing the law of sin which had disfigured that heart (cf. *Jer* 17:1). In those days, 'a new heart' would be given, for in it would dwell 'a new spirit', the Spirit of God (cf. *Ezek* 36:24-28).""[329]

2. THE NEW LAW OR THE LAW OF THE GOSPEL

Since the ultimate end of man is to enjoy God—an end which exceeds man's natural capacity—it was necessary that God himself give man a law as a guide. This law exists in order to help man do what he must do and avoid what he must avoid if he wants to direct his actions in such a way that he can reach his supernatural, ultimate end—his salvation. Along with this

---

[329] JOHN PAUL II. Encyclical letter *Veritatis Splendor.* 12.

knowledge, God gives man grace to be able to fulfill his commandments.

However, since the salvation of man can only be brought about by Christ, being that "there is salvation in no one else" (*Acts* 4:12), Christ is the only one that can promulgate a law which leads absolutely everyone along the path to salvation: the new law. Our Lord is the author of this law, also called "the law of Christ" (*Gal* 6:2).

Aside from being the author of the new law, our Lord is the model for the fulfillment of this law. In Christ, we not only have a teacher to learn from, but also an example to imitate. "Christ also suffered for you, leaving you an example, that you should follow in his steps" (*1 Pet* 2:21). He himself affirmed it: "learn from me..." (*Mt* 11:29). Saint Paul wrote: "Have this mind among yourselves, which was in Christ Jesus" (*Phil* 2:5). The saints became saints precisely because they were able "to be conformed to the image of his Son" (*Rom* 8:29). This is why we should frequently ask ourselves: What would Jesus do if he were in my place? We should then act likewise.

1. THE NEW LAW IS MAINLY INFUSED AND INTERIOR

What does this new law, the law of Christ, of the Gospel, and of the New Testament, principally consist of? It consists in "faith working through love" (*Gal* 5:6). "God's love has been poured into our hearts through the Holy Spirit which has been given to us" (*Rom* 5:5). This is where all of its power resides.

"Now that which is preponderant in the law of the New Testament, and whereon all its efficacy is based, is the grace of the Holy Ghost, which is given through faith in Christ."[330] This is why it is also called the "principle of faith" (*Rom* 3:27), "the righteousness which is based on law" (*Rom* 9:31) or "the law of the Spirit of life... [which has set us] free from the law of sin and death" (*Rom* 8:2). It is the law which "set us free" (*Gal* 5:1) since "where the Spirit of the Lord is, there is freedom" (*2 Cor* 3:17). It

---

[330] SAINT THOMAS AQUINAS. *Summa Theologica.* I-II, 106, 1.

is "the perfect law, the law of liberty" (*Jas* 2:5) since it compels us interiorly and freely to do everything necessary for eternal salvation and avoid everything contrary to it.

By not placing obstacles to the action of grace, the saints were immensely free. That is why Saint Augustine said: "Love, and do what you will."[331] He who truly loves will only do what Love wants. "The gate is narrow and the way is hard, that leads to life" (*Mt* 7:14). This is the path of those who, throughout the centuries, have followed and practiced the teaching of Jesus: "If any man would come after me, let him deny himself and take up his cross and follow me" (*Mt* 16:24). Once they arrive at the summit of perfection, Saint John of the Cross says: "Here there is no longer any way because for the just man there is no law, he is a law unto himself,"[332] because "the law is not laid down for the just" (*1 Tim* 1:9). Those who act according to the Spirit of God given to us will produce fruits of "love, joy, peace, patience, kindness, goodness, faithfulness, gentleness, self-control," that is to say, they do not act against the law since "against such there is no law" (*Gal* 5:22-23). "They are a law to themselves" (*Rom* 2:14) because they always do what God wants.

In this way, the prophecies of the Old Testament are fulfilled: "I will put my law within them, and I will write it upon their hearts" (*Jer* 31:33);[333] "a new heart I will give you, and a new spirit I will put within you; and I will take out of your flesh the heart of stone and give you a heart of flesh" (*Ezek* 36:26). The law written on hearts, a new spirit and a new heart, is "the very presence of the Holy Spirit."[334]

2. THE NEW LAW IS SECONDLY WRITTEN AND EXTERIOR

Secondly, the new law consists of precepts which are exterior to man. These precepts dispose man to receive the grace of the Holy Spirit, which teaches him to receive, cultivate, and spiritually

---

[331] *Homilies on the First Epistle of John.* VII, 8.
[332] In his drawing of the Mount of Perfection found in "The Ascent of Mount Carmel." *The Collected Works of St. John of the* Cross. p. 111.
[333] Cf. *Heb* 8:8.
[334] SAINT AUGUSTINE. *On the Spirit and the Letter.* 36.

use this grace. In other words, man is disposed to practice all the virtues and gifts given to him along with grace.

For example, in the holy Gospel we are taught what we must believe in, what we must receive, what we must do and what we must pray for. The Gospel also teaches us contempt for the world. By this contempt, man is made capable of receiving the grace of the Holy Spirit. Those who love the world cannot receive "the Spirit of truth" (*Jn* 14:17). "Do you not know that friendship with the world is enmity with God?" (*Jas* 4:4).

Moreover, the new law does not only indicate what we must do; but, it also helps us to be able to do it. This new law is not only likened to a sign which indicates the way; but, it is also likened to the fuel which interiorly moves a vehicle in order to reach its destination. This assistance, this help, is the new life Christ came to bring. "I came that they may have life, and have it abundantly." (*Jn* 10:10). This new life is the grace of God, which is the life of God in us.

The new law, in reference to external things, commands us to follow what brings us to grace and to what necessarily leads to the good use of grace. Since we cannot acquire grace through our own efforts, but only through Christ, this same Lord instituted the seven sacraments by which we receive grace. This is why Christ commands us to receive the sacraments.

The good use of grace consists in doing the works of charity which are necessary to every virtue, according to the Ten Commandments. The good use of grace also prohibits us from practicing anything which entails a lack of charity, which, consequently, deprives us of grace. We will see this more fully in the section on the Ten Commandments.[335]

3. THE SERMON ON THE MOUNT

In the Sermon on the Mount,[336] our Lord Jesus Christ lays out a perfect plan of the Christian life. It is the heart of the Gospel.

---

[335] Cf. Second Section: the Ten Commandments on 221.
[336] Cf. *Mt* chapters 5, 6 and 7.

Many believe the Sermon on the Mount only consists in the eight beatitudes,[337] but these are like the doorway and prologue to the Sermon which spans three entire chapters of the Gospel of Saint Mathew.[338]

a) The Beatitudes

This prologue is known as the Beatitudes because each one of the eight phrases of Jesus begins with the word "blessed." (Beatitude, from the Latin *beatitudo*: happiness). In the Beatitudes we learn:

-the end and goal of our life: God and his Kingdom;

-the interior means to more easily reach this end; the heroic dispositions of self-denial which are most convenient in order to enter the Kingdom, already begun on earth by grace.

Our Lord only gives eight examples, being that all the heroic acts of the saints, which are acts of infused virtue perfected by the gifts of the Holy Spirit, are worthy of "beatitude." In one way or another, all of these acts can be reduced to one of the eight listed by the Lord. To be blessed means to possess the highest degree of happiness. Jesus teaches us here the way to be extremely happy because living the way he indicates is to anticipate eternal happiness. Consequently, he who lives this way has reached the highest summit of Christian perfection and holiness which can be attained in this life. "The soul is excited and encouraged to seek after and attain the evangelical beatitudes which, like the flowers that come forth in the spring time, are the signs and harbingers of eternal beatitude."[339]

1. "Blessed are the poor in spirit, for theirs is the kingdom of heaven" (*Mt* 5:3). The poor in spirit are those who have contempt for and are not attached to the riches of the world. They have contempt for all honors because they cultivate humility according to what Saint Paul wrote: "What have you that you did not receive?"(*1 Cor* 4:7).

---

[337] Cf. *Mt* 5:1-12.
[338] Cf. *Mt* chapters 5, 6 and 7.
[339] LEO XIII. Encyclical Letter *Divinum illud munus*. 9.

2. "Blessed are those who mourn, for they shall be comforted" (*Mt* 5:4). Those who weep are the ones who mortify themselves in all delectable things; those who suffer without complaint; and those who deprive themselves of worldly pleasures. The experience of this beatitude made Saint Peter of Alcántara exclaim: "O blessed penance which has merited so great a reward!"[340]

3. "Blessed are the meek, for they shall inherit the earth" (*Mt* 5:5). The meek are those who endure all difficulties with patience and do not allow themselves to be carried away by anger, fear or despair.

4. "Blessed are those who hunger and thirst for righteousness, for they shall be satisfied" (*Mt* 5:6). Those who hunger and thirst for righteousness are the ones who have a fervent desire to give their neighbor what is rightly due him and to God what is owed to him. "To hunger and thirst for righteousness is to love God," exclaimed Saint Francisco Solano.[341] The Servant of God Camila Rolón wrote: "God is with those who suffer for him; those who suffer for righteousness are called blessed."[342]

5. "Blessed are the merciful, for they shall obtain mercy" (*Mt* 5:7). The merciful are those who practice works of mercy.

6. "Blessed are the pure in heart, for they shall see God" (*Mt* 5:8). The pure in heart are those who are pure in thought, desire, word, and deed.

7. "Blessed are the peacemakers, for they shall be called sons of God" (*Mt* 5:9). The peacemakers are those who sow peace around them, which is tranquility in order, and those who receive all things, no matter how painful or unexpected they may be, as coming from the hand of God. Saint Paul declares: "God works for good with those who love him" (*Rom* 8:28).

8. "Blessed are those who are persecuted for righteousness' sake, for theirs is the kingdom of heaven" (*Mt* 5:10). Those who

---

[340] SAINT TERESA OF AVILA. *The Autobiography of St. Teresa of Avila*. XXVII, 21.
[341] Editorial translation.
[342] Letter written on October 21, 1911. (Editorial translation)

suffer persecution for justice are the ones who do not separate themselves from the goods belonging to the previous beatitudes because of some exterior attack. That is to say, they prefer to continue being poor, humble, meek, mortified, just, merciful, pure, and peaceful in spite of any persecution. In the end, as Saint Paul says, "all who desire to live a godly life in Christ Jesus will be persecuted" (*2 Tim* 3:12). Thus, Saint Peter writes, when these persecutions come "do not be surprised...as though something strange were happening to you" (*1 Pet* 4:12). Persecution is only blessed "when it is for His sake, and when the things that are said are false."[343]

Finally, the Lord exalts the dignity of the Apostles through whom the Gospel is announced.[344] By saying to them "you are the light of the world" (*Mt* 5:14), Christ teaches them how to give a good example to all. The words of Jesus were primarily directed to his disciples; but, they are also for us. Although in different degrees, Christ entrusts all of us with the vital duty of the apostolate, that is, the obligation to bring souls to God by our example, our words, our sacrifices, our prayer and our life. We must be like an overflowing chalice of our Lord Jesus Christ which pours his superabundance upon others.

"That they may see your good works and give glory to your Father who is in heaven" (*Mt* 5:16).

b) To perfectly fulfill the will of God

After this prologue, where the Lord incites us to carry out the most perfect acts of supernatural virtue and gifts of the Holy Spirit and to reconquer the world for God by our apostolate, Jesus teaches us the fundamental obligation. This obligation was essential in Christ's life and must be essential for the life of any of his disciples: the fulfillment of the will of God. "My food is to do the will of him who sent me" (*Jn* 4:34). "I have come down from heaven, not to do my own will, but the will of him who sent me"

---

[343] SAINT JOHN CHRYSOSTOM. *Homilies on the Gospel of St. Matthew.* XV, 7.
[344] Cf. *Mt* 5:13-16.

(*Jn* 6:38). Furthermore, only "he who does the will of my Father" (*Mt* 7:21) will enter the kingdom of heaven.

The will of God is expressed precisely in the Ten Commandments,[345] in the precepts of the Church,[346] and in works of mercy.[347] Jesus teaches us that we must follow all the Commandments of the Law of God by submitting our will to God's: "Think not that I have come to abolish the law...I have come not to abolish them but to fulfill them" (*Mt* 5:17). Furthermore, Christ warns us that not only are the external works of evil prohibited, but also the internal works of evil, such as sins in thought or desire. He warns us of this because external acts of sin are a consequence of internal acts of sin which come from the heart of man. An unclean interior is what "defiles a man" (*Mt* 15:18). Consequently:

-Jesus teaches that "every one who is angry with his brother shall be liable to judgment..." (*Mt* 5:22). By this, Jesus prohibits all lack of charity against our neighbors, even internal acts.

-The Lord affirms that "every one who looks at a woman lustfully has already committed adultery with her in his heart" (*Mt* 5:28). By this, Jesus condemns all sins of impurity. He who wants to be pure must have the windows of his eyes and of his mind closed to evil; otherwise, sooner or later, he will fall into grave sins, even external ones.

-Jesus teaches us the language of truth: "Let what you say be simply 'Yes' or 'No'" (*Mt* 5:37). We must "drown all manifestations of error [and of lies] in the whirlwind of truth...in order to give back to the world the joy of living"[348] (Saint Maximilian Kolbe). Likewise, we must abstain from unnecessary and vain judgments: "Do not swear at all" (*Mt* 5:34).

-"Do not resist one who is evil. But if any one strikes you on the right cheek, turn to him the other also" (*Mt* 5:39). With these words, the Lord teaches us not to act out of vengeance, but rather

---

[345] Cf. Ten Commandments are found on page 19.
[346] Cf. Precepts of the Church are found on page 20.
[347] Cf. Works of Mercy are found on page 20.
[348] Editorial translation.

to have a spirit prepared to suffer even the greatest injury or injustice, if the need should arise. "Do not return evil for evil" (*1 Pet* 3:9). "Do not be overcome by evil, but overcome evil with good" (*Rom* 12:21).

-By saying "if any one would sue you and take your coat, let him have your cloak as well" (*Mt* 5:40), Jesus teaches us not to demand our rights and our goods out of greed. If it were necessary, rather, we must be willing to give more than what we are obligated to give.

-In declaring, "love your enemies and pray for those who persecute you" (*Mt* 5:44), Jesus exhorts us to love our enemies and to be willing to do them good. "Let us hate not the person, but rather the sin" says Saint Thomas Aquinas.

In his infinite mercy, Jesus warns us about everything that leads us to sin, which is called: occasion of sin. In order to avoid internal and external sin, we must run from all grave occasions of sin, such as: immoral movies, bad friends or relatives, immoral magazines, dishonest conversations, indecent places, etc. Jesus even says: "If your right eye causes you to sin...and if your right hand causes you to sin, cut it off and throw it away" (*Mt* 5:29-30), teaching us that we must be willing to undertake great sacrifices in order to escape from occasions of sin. The occasion of sin is likened to fire: one cannot play around with it. "He who plays with fire will soon get burned." To seek after the occasion of sin is to put oneself in the near danger of sin. Furthermore, "whoever loves danger will perish by it" (*Sir* 3:26).

c) To do everything with the right intention

Jesus not only commands us to avoid evil, but also to do good. It is not enough to do good, always, everywhere and to everyone; but, we must do it with the right intention. To do something with a good intention is to do it for the love of God, "directed purely to the service and praise of His Divine Majesty."[349] If someone does something good (prayer, almsgiving, etc.) for a motive other

---

[349] LOUIS J. PUHL, S.J. *The Spiritual Exercises of St. Ignatius.* 46.

than for the love of God, such as so that others might see and think him pious or generous and speak well of him, he does not have a good intention. He does not do good for God, but for egoism. Jesus teaches that we must not practice virtues in order that men might praise us, or speak well of us, seeking merely human glory. This is completely opposed to the Gospel of Jesus. Thus, Saint Paul says: "If I were still pleasing men, I should not be a servant of Christ" (*Gal* 1:10).

The Lord points out three cases in which the glory of men is sought.

The first case is when we do good to our neighbor: "When you give alms, sound no trumpet…but when you give alms, do not let your left hand know what your right hand is doing" (*Mt* 6:2-3). Father José Gabriel Brochero, the "*Gaucho Priest*" said: "Let us consider ourselves fortunate that Jesus Christ permits us to work united with him and leave the applause to someone else."[350]

The second case is in the occasion of worshipping God: "When you pray, you must not be like the hypocrites; for they love to stand and pray in the synagogues and at the street corners, that they may be seen by men" (*Mt* 6:5). Jesus himself gave us the model for prayer when he taught us the Our Father.[351]

The third case is in relation to self-control: "When you fast, do not look dismal, like the hypocrites, for they disfigure their faces that their fasting may be seen by men" (*Mt* 6:16).

Likewise, the Lord teaches us that we must not place our ultimate end in riches: "Do not lay up for yourselves treasures on earth, where moth and rust consume and where thieves break in and steal" (*Mt* 6:19). "For what will it profit a man, if he gains the whole world and forfeits his life?" (*Mt* 16:26). When the greedy man dies, he will not be able to bring anything with him—coffins do not have pockets.

---

[350] Editorial translation.
[351] Cf. the Our Father is found on page 21.

Jesus also teaches us that we must not seek temporal things—food, drink, clothing, shelter—in such a way that we forget about God. On the contrary, we must seek him first and everything else will then be given to us: "Seek first his kingdom and his righteousness, and all these things shall be yours as well" (*Mt* 6:33). Father Francisco Castañeda interpreted with precision that the first thing we must seek after is the Kingdom of God and holiness: "above all be holy and yearn for the Kingdom of God, assured that all else will be given to you."[352] Since the just man is a holy man, he who seeks justice seeks holiness. Saint Paul teaches: "Whether you eat or drink, or whatever you do, do all to the glory of God" (*1 Cor* 10:31).

The eagerness to acquire temporal things can be disproportionate and disordered, and, therefore, sinful. This eagerness can be sinful in five ways:

1. When we make these things the goal of our life: "No one can serve two masters…you cannot serve God and mammon" (*Mt* 6:24). Or, when we serve God only in the things necessary to eat or to wear: "do not be anxious about…what you shall eat… what you shall put on" (*Mt* 6:25).

2. When we live so concerned about temporal things and seek them with such great interest that we separate ourselves from the spiritual things which we must preferentially attend to. God never forgets us: "your heavenly Father knows that you need them all" (*Mt* 6:32).

3. When we presumptuously believe that we can provide ourselves with what we need in order to live by our own efforts and without the help of God: "Which of you by being anxious can add one cubit to his span of life?" (*Mt* 6:27).

4. When we have an exaggerated fear that, even though we are doing what we should do, we will lack the necessities of life. The Lord reproves this fear based on three considerations:

---

[352] Homily in the Cathedral of Buenos Aires, 1818; cited in GUILLERMO FURLONG, S.J. *Fray Francisco de Paula Castañeda: Un testigo de la naciente Patria Argentina.* Ed. Castañeda, Buenos Aires, 1994. p. 721. (Editorial translation)

-By the great benefits God freely gives man, such as the body and the soul. "Is not life more than food, and the body more than clothing?" (*Mt* 6:25).

-By the protection God has over plants and animals without the assistance of men. "Look at the birds of the air: they neither sow nor reap nor gather into barns, and yet your heavenly Father feeds them. Are you not of more value than they?" (*Mt* 6:26). "And why are you anxious about clothing? Consider the lilies of the field, how they grow; they neither toil nor spin; yet I tell you, even Solomon in all his glory was not arrayed like one of these. But if God so clothes the grass of the field, which today is alive and tomorrow is thrown into the oven, will he not much more clothe you, O you of little faith?" (*Mt* 6:28-30). Our heroes also experience this protection in the work of independence. "We ended well because it is God who protects our cause" (Argentine hero, General Manuel Belgrano).[353]

-By Divine providence. The ignorance of this providence led the gentiles to seek temporal goods above everything "'What shall we eat?' or 'What shall we drink?' or 'What shall we wear?' For the Gentiles seek all these things" (*Mt* 6:31-32). This is of particular importance in apostolic work. Saint Marcelin Champagnat stated: "It would be a waste of time to expect success in our endeavors from our own personal efforts, talents or the help of men, because only God can bring about this success."[354]

5. When, instead of keeping *occupied*, we become inordinately *preoccupied* with the future. "Therefore do not be anxious about tomorrow...let the day's own trouble be sufficient for the day." (*Mt* 6:34). "For every matter has its time" (*Eccles* 8:6). Saint Thomas Aquinas stated: "This is why our endeavors must be directed principally to the attainment of spiritual goods, with the

---

hope that temporal goods will also be given to us, if we fulfill our duty, as long as they are in accord with our need."[355]

We must place our life in the hands of God. Saint Giuseppe Benito Cottolengo reminds us that "our duty is to accommodate ourselves to the plans of Divine Providence and fulfill the role destined for us."[356]

We cannot place our lives into better hands. Ultimately, the Lord orders internal acts with respect to our neighbor, as long as we do not judge others rashly, unjustly, or presumptuously. "Judge not, that you be not judged." (*Mt* 7:1). However, this does not mean that all judgment is prohibited. On the contrary, our Lord asks "Why do you not judge for yourselves what is right?" (*Lk* 12:57). He also states: "Do not judge by appearances, but judge with right judgment" (*Jn* 7:24). Furthermore, "the spiritual man judges all things" (*1 Cor* 2:15). "Our Lord forbids rash judgment which is about the inward intention, or other uncertain things, as Augustine states (De Serm. Dom. in Monte ii, 18). Or else He forbids judgment about Divine things, which we ought not to judge, but simply believe, since they are above us, as Hilary declares...Or again according to Chrysostom [Hom. xvii in Matt. in the Opus Imperfectum falsely ascribed to Saint John of the Cross], He forbids the judgment which proceeds not from benevolence but from bitterness of heart."[357]

However, we should never be disrespectful to God by giving our neighbor holy and divine things of which they are unworthy of: "Do not give dogs what is holy" (*Mt* 7:6).

d) How to live according to these teachings

Finally, the Lord teaches us how to carry out this sublime doctrine: "Ask, and it will be given you; seek, and you will find; knock, and it will be opened to you" (*Mt* 7:7). You must implore the help of God, frequently receive the Holy Sacraments because without grace "you can do nothing" (*Jn* 15:5).

---

[355] Editorial translation.
[356] Editorial translation.
[357] SAINT THOMAS AQUINAS. *Summa Theologica.* II-II, 60, 2, ad. I.

-"So whatever you wish that men would do to you, do so to them" (*Mt* 7:12). Charity must be practiced with everyone.

-"Enter by the narrow gate…the gate is narrow and the way is hard, that leads to life, and those who find it are few" (*Mt* 7:13-14).

-"Beware of false prophets…you will know them by their fruits" (*Mt* 7:15-16). We must be extremely careful not to be corrupted and perverted by such imposters. If Christ spoke of them it was because they exist. If Christ warned us it is because we could come across them.

-Christ reminds us, yet again, that following the Commandments is absolutely necessary in order to preserve the grace of God and enter the Kingdom of Heaven. Only "he who does the will of my Father" (*Mt* 7:21) will enter into the Kingdom of Heaven. It is not enough to have faith and manifest it by saying "Lord, Lord," nor is it enough to prophesize ("did we not prophesy in your name") nor cast out demons ("cast out demons in your name"), nor even to perform miracles ("do many mighty works in your name"). Those who do not live by the Commandments of God, even if they perform wonderful miracles, will go to hell.

Jesus Christ will say to them on the Day of Judgment: "'I never knew you; depart from me, you evildoers'" (*Mt* 7:23).

e) The Final Parable

"Every one then who hears these words of mine and does them will be like a wise man who built his house upon the rock; and the rain fell, and the floods came, and the winds blew and beat upon that house, but it did not fall, because it had been founded on the rock. And every one who hears these words of mine and does not do them will be like a foolish man who built his house upon the sand; and the rain fell, and the floods came, and the winds blew and beat against that house, and it fell; and great was the fall of it." (*Mt* 7:24-27). How admirable is this doctrine of Jesus! The Gospel itself points it out: "the crowds were astonished at his teaching" (*Mt* 7:28).

3. SIN

Our life has, in a certain way, different layers. There is vegetative life in us which we have in common with plants. This is manifested when our hair and fingernails grow, or when we nourish ourselves. We also have animal life which we have in common with animals. This is manifested in our capacity to see, hear, feel, and smell, or our ability to move, eat and sleep. In addition to these, we enjoy rational life, which we have in common with the angels. This is manifested in our capacity to know, want, or love. Finally, on a level far superior to the others, we have received Divine Life, which we have in common with God. This Divine Life is the sanctifying grace by which we participate in the Trinitarian life of God himself.

1. MORTAL SIN

When we commit a serious sin we expel God from us and we lose sanctifying grace. This is why sin is the greatest disgrace in the world. To sin gravely is the most wicked and foolish thing, terrible and criminal, absurd and abject. It is to act against the will of God. It is to make an attempt against his glory, to offend him who is infinitely good. It is to deprive oneself of the grace of God. It is to submit in slavery to the devil, to make oneself a candidate for hell.

Saint John Marie Vianney states that "if, filled with faith, we could see the depths of a soul stained by mortal sin, we would die of horror."[358] Saint Dominic Savio rightly exclaimed: "Death, but not sin;"[359] and Friar Mamerto Esquiú prayed: "May God grant me the grace to detest this evil with my whole heart and send me death before committing it."[360] José de San Martín expressed it like this: "The desire of your old friend is that God may free you from living and dying in mortal sin."[361]

---

[358] Editorial translation.
[359] Editorial translation.
[360] Editorial translation.
[361] CAYETANO BRUNO. *Historia de la Iglesia en la Argentina.* T. VIII. p. 395. (Editorial translation)

It is a mortal sin to knowingly and willingly think, desire, say, do, or omit anything against the law of God in grave matters.

Just as by grace the soul anticipates heaven, by mortal sin the soul anticipates hell. If we arrive at our death, even with only one mortal sin, we will go to hell. "What world will receive any of those who run away from Him?"[362] Whoever lives in mortal sin is condemning himself.

"Every one who commits sin is a slave to sin" (*Jn* 8:34). "Whatever overcomes a man, to that he is enslaved" (*2 Pet* 2:19). Since it is the devil who conquers man by inducing him to sin, whoever commits a mortal sin ends up subjected in servitude to the devil. "He who commits sin is of the devil" (*1 Jn* 3:8). For this reason, sinners are entangled in "the snare of the devil, after being captured by him to do his will" (*2 Tim* 2:26).

Grave sin is called mortal sin because by depriving a soul of grace, it deprives the soul of supernatural life. Mortal sin, then, becomes an anticipation of eternal death. Thus, God teaches us by saying: "The soul that sins shall die" (*Ezek* 18:20) and "sin, which leads to death" (*Rom* 6:16).

Just as we must run away from a poisonous viper since its bite will kill us, we must run away from sin: "Flee from sin as from a snake" (*Sir* 21:2).

When a Christian commits a mortal sin, he can only be forgiven if he confesses his sins before a priest. "It is true that the perfect act of contrition which justifies does exist; however, it should contain within itself the desire of confession."[363] When we confess our sins, we should say the number of times committed, what commandments they broke, and the circumstances which increase the severity of a mortal sin, to the point of changing its species. For example, the following acts are

---

[362] SAINT CLEMENT OF ROME. *Letter to the Corinthians (First Epistle).* XXVIII.
[363] SAINT PETER JULIAN EYMARD. *op. cit.* p. 1093. (Editorial translation)

mortal sins if they are committed with full consciousness and a deliberate will:[364]

-To not believe something taught by God and the Church.

-To blaspheme the Holy Name of God, the Virgin Mary or the saints.

-To not attend Mass on Sundays or on a Holy Day of obligation without a legitimate reason.

-To murder, commit suicide, or have an abortion. These are "unspeakable crimes."[365]

-To consent to evil thoughts, desires, looks, conversations, or actions against purity, fidelity, or the transmission of life.

-To steal in large sums.

-To slander or discredit a person in serious matters.

Capital sins. Some sins are called **capital sins** because they engender other sins and vices. They are pride, avarice, envy, wrath, lust, gluttony, and sloth.[366]

Sins against the Holy Spirit. "Whoever blasphemes against the Holy Spirit never has forgiveness, but is guilty of an eternal sin" (*Mk* 3:29, cf. *Mt* 12:32, *Lk* 12:10). God is always ready to forgive us; but if we do not want it, God respects our freedom and does not obligate us to accept his pardon. It is said that sins against the Holy Spirit are never forgiven because of our lack of disposition to receive forgiveness.[367] We can list six types of sins against the Holy Spirit: to despair in receiving pardon for sins, to presume we will be saved even without doing what God has commanded, to oppose the known truth, to envy the grace of another, to be obstinate in evil and reject final repentance.[368]

---

[364] Cf. FRAY LUIS DE GRANADA. *Obra Selecta. Una Suma de la vida cristiana.* II, VI; Madrid: B.A.C., 1947. p. 248-251. (Editorial translation)

[365] II VATICAN COUNCIL. *Gaudium et Spes.* 51.

[366] Cf. *Catechism of the Catholic Church.* 1866.

[367] Cf. Ibid. 1864.

[368] Cf. FRAY LUIS DE GRANADA. *op. cit.* II, VII. p. 255-257. (Editorial translation)

Sins that cry out to Heaven.[369] These include: voluntary homicide,[370] sodomy,[371] oppression of the poor,[372] mistreatment of foreigners, widows, and orphans[373] and injustice toward hired workers.[374]

2. VENIAL SIN

There is another type of sin called venial sin. This sin does not deprive the soul of the grace of God and does not condemn it to hell. Rather, it consists of a delay or deviation from the right path.

Venial sin is to think, desire, say, do or omit something that goes against the law of God in slight matters.

Venial sin is essentially different from mortal sin. The latter has a punishment of eternal hell. The former does not impede the entrance into heaven but has purgatory as a punishment, which is only for a certain period of time.

Mortal sin is only forgiven with confession (or with a perfect act of contrition which implies the intention to go to confession as soon as possible). Venial sin, on the other hand, is forgiven in many ways: through a good deed, a prayer, almsgiving, holy water, the Sign of the Cross, and also through confession (in this case it is not necessary to mention the number of venial sins committed).

Even though venial sin is not something grave, it does not mean we should stop fighting against it; but we should follow the advice of our Lord Jesus Christ: "You, therefore, must be perfect, as your heavenly Father is perfect" (*Mt* 5:48). It should not discourage us when we fall into venial sin many times, "for a righteous man falls seven times, and rises again" (*Prov* 24:16). We must fight against venial sin not only because we must always love God more, but also because venial sins can lead us to commit

---

[369] Cf. FRAY LUIS DE GRANADA. *op. cit*, II, VII. p. 257-258 (Editorial translation); Cf. *Catechism of the Catholic Church*. 1867.

[370] Cf. *Gen* 4:10.

[371] Cf. *Gen* 18:20; 19:13.

[372] Cf. *Ex* 3:7-10.

[373] Cf. *Ex* 22:20-22.

[374] Cf. *Deut* 24:14-15; *Jas* 5:4.

more serious sins: "He who despises small things will fail little by little" (*Sir* 19:1). "Dead flies make the perfumer's ointment give off an evil odor; so a little folly outweighs wisdom and honor" (*Eccles* 10:1).

Temptation, although it incites us to sin, is not sin itself. Jesus was tempted; yet "in him there is no sin" (*1 Jn* 3:5). When does a temptation become a sin? It becomes a sin when one does not reject temptation (such as a bad thought); but rather, knowing that it is bad, the temptation is entertained. Thus, one commits a mortal or venial sin according to the gravity of the matter. When a person rejects temptation, not only does he not fall into sin, but he also performs an act of virtue, since he "had the power to transgress and did not transgress, and to do evil and did not do it" (*Sir* 31:10).

3. THE CHRISTIAN BATTLE

Christian life is a battle. It is a battle against the flesh; against the world, the enemy of God; and against the devil who seeks to condemn us.

To persevere in good, we must fight against evil, working out our salvation "with fear and trembling" (*Phil* 2:12).

The Council of Trent teaches us that in order to conquer these enemies we must "fear...the combat that yet remains with the flesh, with the world, with the devil, in which [we] cannot be victors, unless with God's grace."[375]

"Has not man a hard service upon earth?" (*Job* 7:1) Did Jesus not say that he had come to bring the sword?[376] Saint Paul said of himself: "I have fought the good fight...I have kept the faith" (*2 Tim* 4:7). Furthermore, Saint Peter warns us saying: "Your adversary the devil prowls around like a roaring lion, seeking some one to devour" (*1 Pet* 5:8). "We must reach heaven exhausted. By working here exhaustively, there we will live from

---

[375] COUNCIL OF TRENT. *Decree on Justification.* Dz. 806.
[376] Cf. *Mt* 10:34.

the profits of our labor. That is why we must accumulate a solid wealth of virtues."[377]

Saint Paul says that in order to fight we must cloth ourselves with the "armor of God" (*Eph* 6:11). Let us take a closer look at this beautiful passage:

-"Stand therefore, having fastened the belt of truth around your waist" (*Eph* 6:14). The love of truth is the fundamental virtue for the Christian. "Speaking the truth in love, we are to grow up in every way into him who is the head, into Christ" (*Eph* 4:15). We must "love the truth" (*2 Thess* 2:10) and fight for it. "Strive even to death for the truth and the Lord God will fight for you" (*Sir* 4:28). In the end, this truth is Christ himself: "I am the way, and the truth, and the life" (*Jn* 14:6).

-"Put on the breastplate of righteousness" (*Eph* 6:14). Righteousness causes us to give to God and to our neighbor what is due to each respectively. This righteousness can be identified with holiness. It impels our love to be genuine, to hate what is evil, and hold fast to what is good (cf. *Rom* 12:9). Furthermore, we must not only do good, but we must also fight against evil: "The Lord loves those who hate evil" (*Ps* 97:10). Only the evil man "spurns not evil" (*Ps* 36:4); the one who does not reject evil becomes an accomplice of evil. We should "abstain from every form of evil" (*1 Thess* 5:22).

-"Shod your feet with the equipment of the gospel of peace" (*Eph* 6:15). Oftentimes, the best defense is a good offense. We must have the soul of an apostle, jealousy for the house of God, and compassion for the many souls that are in darkness.

-"Taking the shield of faith" (*Eph* 6:16). Faith "overcomes the world" (*1 Jn* 5:4). It overcomes the devil: "Resist him, firm in your faith" (*1 Pet* 5:9). Faith also overcomes the flesh: "our hearts are purified by faith."[378]

[377] BLESSED VICENTE GROSSI. (Editorial translation)
[378] SAINT AUGUSTINE. *On the Holy Spirit*. Book 1, Ch. 8, 17.

-"Take the helmet of salvation" (*Eph* 6:17). Christ is the only one who has "the words of eternal life" (*Jn* 6:68). He is the only one who saves us. This salvation comes to us by means of the holy sacraments.

-"And the sword of the Spirit" (*Eph* 6:17) which is the Word of God given by the Holy Spirit. It is a "two-edged sword" (*Heb* 4:12) which we learn from in order to be a good fencer.

"To fight belongs to men and to give glory belongs to God" (Saint Joan of Arc).[379]

---

[379] Cited in: JEAN OUSSET. *Para que Él reine*. Ed. del Cruzamante. Buenos Aires, 1980. p. 284. (Editorial translation)

SECTION TWO
THE TEN COMMANDMENTS

"Jesus tells the young man: 'If you wish to enter into life, keep the commandments' (*Mt* 19:17). In this way, a close connection is made between eternal life and obedience to God's commandments: God's commandments show man the path of life and they lead to it. From the very lips of Jesus, the new Moses, man is once again given the commandments of the Decalogue. Jesus himself definitively confirms them and proposes them to us as the way and condition of salvation."

John Paul II
Encyclical letter Veritatis Splendor, 12

INTRODUCTION

We have already mentioned that Jesus came to fulfill the commandments, not to abolish them. God does not erase with one hand what he has written with the other. It was God himself who gave the two stone tablets where the Ten Commandments were written to Moses on Mount Sinai.[380]

The first tablet contained the first three commandments, which are in reference to God. On the other, the other seven commandments were written, which are in reference to our neighbor and ourselves. Jesus will then say that any law of God can be summarized in this double commandment: "You shall love the Lord your God with all your heart, and with all your soul, and with all your mind.... [and] your neighbor as yourself. On these two commandments depend all the law and the prophets" (*Mt* 22:37,39-40). This is so, since charity is "the fulfilling of the law" (*Rom* 13:10).

Following the precepts of the Decalogue is an absolute necessity for all men in order to reach salvation. "If you would enter life, keep the commandments" (*Mt* 19:17). God, who "desires all men to be saved" (*1 Tim* 2:4), does not demand things from us that cannot be fulfilled: "His commandments are not burdensome" (*1 Jn* 5:3). "For my yoke is easy, and my burden is light" (*Mt* 11:30). "God could not possibly have enjoined impossibilities, we are admonished both what to do in easy paths and what to ask for when they are difficult," for the commandments are not grievous for the one who loves, but for the one who does not love.[381]

"Therefore do not be foolish, but understand what the will of the Lord is" (*Eph* 5:17). We will examine this by studying the commandments of the law of God one by one.

---

[380] Cf. *Ex* 20.
[381] SAINT AUGUSTINE. *On Nature and Grace.* 83.

Exodus 20:2-17	Deuteronomy 5:6-21	
I am the Lord your God, who brought you out of the land of Egypt, out of the house of bondage.	I am the Lord your God, who brought you out of the land of Egypt, out of the house of bondage	
You shall have no other gods before me. You shall not make for yourself a graven image, or any likeness of anything that is in heaven above, or that is in the earth beneath, or that is in the water under the earth; you shall not bow down to them or serve them; for I the Lord your God am a jealous God, visiting the iniquity of the fathers upon the children to the third and the fourth generation of those who hate me, but showing steadfast love to thousands of those who love me and keep my commandments.	You shall have no other gods before me…	I am the Lord your God: you shall not have strange gods before me.
You shall not take the name of the Lord your God in vain; for the Lord will not hold him guiltless who takes his name in vain.	You shall not take the name of the Lord your God in vain…	You shall not take the name of the Lord your God in vain.
Remember the Sabbath day, to keep it holy. Six days you shall labor,	Observe the Sabbath day, to keep it holy.	Remember to keep holy the Lord's Day.

and do all your work; but the seventh day is a Sabbath to the Lord your God; in it you shall not do any work, you, or your son, or your daughter, your manservant, or your maidservant, or your cattle, or the sojourner who is within your gates; for in six days the Lord made heaven and earth, the sea, and all that is in them, and rested the seventh day; therefore the Lord blessed the Sabbath day and hallowed it.		
Honor your father and your mother, that your days may be long in the land which the Lord your God gives you.	Honor your father and your mother.	Honor your father and your mother.
You shall not kill.	You shall not kill.	You shall not kill.
You shall not commit adultery.	Neither shall you commit adultery.	You shall not commit adultery.
You shall not steal.	Neither shall you steal.	You shall not steal.
You shall not bear false witness against your neighbor.	Neither shall you bear false witness against your neighbor.	You shall not bear false witness against your neighbor.

You shall not covet your neighbor's house; you shall not covet your neighbor's wife, or his manservant, or his maidservant, or his ox, or his ass, or anything that is your neighbor's.	Neither shall you covet your neighbor's wife. You shall not desire… anything that is your neighbor's.	You shall not covet your neighbor's wife. You shall not covet your neighbor's goods.

CHAPTER ONE
"YOU SHALL LOVE THE LORD YOUR GOD WITH ALL YOUR HEART, WITH ALL YOUR SOUL AND WITH ALL YOUR STRENGTH"

THE FIRST COMMANDMENT:
I AM THE LORD YOUR GOD:
YOU SHALL NOT HAVE ANY STRANGE GODS BEFORE ME

"Love the Lord your God with all your heart, and with all your soul, and with all your mind, and with all your strength" (*Mk* 12:30). "This is the great and first commandment" (*Mt* 22:38) because the end of the whole Christian life is union with God. Furthermore, that is what creates charity: "This commandment is as a sun which gives luster and dignity to all the sacred laws...All is done for this heavenly love, and all has reference to it."[382]

1. THE MEASURE OF THE LOVE FOR GOD

To love God with our whole heart means that all of our actions, not excluding even the smallest ones, must be directed to him, who is our ultimate end. "Whether you eat or drink, or whatever you do, do all to the glory of God" (*1 Cor* 10:31). It is true that our hearts will be completely transformed into God only once we have arrived in heaven; but already now it can and should be closed to anything that is contrary to the love of God.

To love God with our whole soul means that our will is totally subjected to God's will.

To love God with our whole mind means that our understanding must be completely submitted to God.

---

[382] SAINT FRANCIS DE SALES. *Treatise on the Love of God.* Trans. Dom Henry Benedict Mackey, O.S.B. Illinois: Tan Books and Publishers, Inc., 1997. X, 1.

To love God with all our strength means that we always obey him in everything we do exteriorly.

What is the measure of the love of God? "The way to love him is without measure."[383]

2. MOTIVES

And, why must we love God without measure?

-Because of his own and infinite Goodness; because of everything that he is without measure, apart from all he has done for us. Love him for who he is.

-Because of the eternal love with which God loves us. "He first loved us" (*1 Jn* 4:19). In spite of our sins, "God shows his love for us in that while we were yet sinners Christ died for us" (*Rom* 5:8). Jesus loved us "to the end" (*Jn* 13:1), to the extreme, without limits.

-Because of the natural goods God has given to us. He created us because he desired to; he holds us in being since "in him all things hold together" (*Col* 1:17); and he orders our whole life with his Providence and in carrying out his decisions.

-Because of the supernatural goods he has bestowed upon us without measure: he has called us to enjoy him in heaven; he sent his only Son to save us, to bring us sanctifying grace (along with the virtues and gifts), to found the Catholic Church so that—through her—the sacraments would distribute the divine life; and ordained our birth in a Catholic country, into a Christian home, etc.

3. WAYS TO LOVE GOD

As beautiful as it is to consider the love of God, we cannot stop at just contemplating his love for us. Love is paid with love. How should we put our love of God into practice? In two ways: loving God affectively with our will elevated by charity, and

---

[383] "On Loving God." *Bernard of Clairvaux: Selected Works*. Trans. G.R. Evans. New York: Paulist Press, 1987. I.1. p.174.

loving God effectively in the perfect fulfillment of all of the commandments. The latter will be the best test of our interior love.

1. AFFECTIVE LOVE OF GOD

The essence of the Gospel is to love God from the innermost part of our hearts. This is the end of our life. Such love is not necessarily sensible; however it can be, and many times is, sensible.

Affective love of God can be manifested in two forms. The first is pure and disinterested love. It is called a love of complacency. In this kind of love, the soul loves God not for the benefits it has received from him, but simply and only to please him, in whom the soul contemplates all imaginable perfections and excellencies. This type of love produces great joy and immense peace in the soul, "for the soul is more where it loves than where it lives."[384]

This is the love which inspired this sonnet attributed to Saint Teresa of Avila:

The promised heaven you have for me
    Does not move me, my God, to love you,
Nor does hell, so feared, move me
    To stop offending you.

> *No me mueve, mi Dios, para quererte*
> *el Cielo que me tienes prometido,*
> *ni me mueve el Infierno, tan temido*
> *para dejar por eso de ofenderte.*

You move me, Lord, it moves me to see you
    nailed to a cross and derided
It moves me to see your body so wounded
    Your insults and your death move me.

---

[384] SAINT ALBERT THE GREAT. *Cleaving to God.* 12.

Tú me mueves, Señor, muéveme el verte
clavado en una Cruz y escarnecido,
muéveme el ver tu cuerpo tan herido
muéveme tus afrentas y tu muerte.

Your love moves me in such a way that
even if there were no heaven, I would love you
And even if there were no hell, I would fear you.

Muéveme, en fin, tu amor de tal manera,
que aunque no hubiera Cielo, yo te amara
y aunque no hubiera Infierno, te temiera.

You do not have to give to me so that I love you
Because even what I hope for I wouldn't hope
Just as I do love you, I would love you.

No me tienes que dar porque te quiera,
porque aunque lo que espero no esperara,
lo mismo que te quiero, te quisiera.

The contemplative religious orders—the Trappists,
Benedictines, Poor Clares, Visitation Sisters of Saint Francis de
Sales, Carmelites, Carthusians, etc.—remind us with their silent
and eloquent testimony of the primacy and excellence of the pure
love of God. "The only favor I desire is that [my life] be broken
through love."[385] Sister Gertrudis de Nuestra Señora de Luján, the
first Argentine Benedictine, wrote to her sister: "Do you want to
know about our life? Well, to love God and give him glory at
every moment."[386] This is the same love which led Saint Francis
of Assisi to exclaim: "May I die for love of your love, since out of
love for my love you deigned to die."[387]

---

[385] SAINT THERESE OF THE CHILD JESUS. *Story of a Soul.* p. 215.
[386] Letter dated July 5th, 1927; cf. *La primera benedictina argentina.* Abadía de Santa Escolástica, 1959. p. 78. (Editorial translation)
[387] *Oracion Absorbeat*; cited in SAINT FRANCIS OF ASSISI. *Escritos y biografías, Escritos líricos.* Madrid: B.A.C., 1976. p. 61. (Editorial translation)

The other form of affective love of God leads us to praise God and to desire that all men might praise him. It is called benevolent love. Since God does not lack any good, due to the incomprehensible immensity of his abundance,[388] no one can give him any intrinsic good. However, we can give him an extrinsic good: the glory men owe him. Those who love God with a benevolent love ardently desire this. Our Lord possessed this love in a supreme degree. No one else, save Christ, could utter this passage from Scripture with so much truth: "Zeal for your house will consume me" (*Jn* 2:17).

2. EFFECTIVE LOVE OF GOD

This type of love is the great sign of the authenticity of our interior or affective love. "Love is never idle. When it exists, it always works great things; but, if it does not act, there is no such love."[389] Jesus himself taught: "If you love me, you will keep my commandments" (*Jn* 14:15). "He who has my commandments and keeps them, he it is who loves me" (*Jn* 14:21). Furthermore, Saint John said: "He who says 'I know him' [to Christ] but disobeys his commandments is a liar" (*1 Jn* 2:4). Saint Vincent de Paul would exclaim: "The good and perfect act is the true characteristic of the love of God."[390]

For the love of God, we must perfectly follow his commandments, obeying them blindly, forcing ourselves to do his will. We must avoid what they prohibit by following the spirit of the evangelical counsels, accepting with resignation everything that is desired or permitted by God. We must abandon ourselves entirely into the hands of the Lord in all that refers to what has not yet happened, in the uncertain future, short or prolonged joys and trials, the hour of our death, etc., with the certainty that "in everything God works for good with those who love him" (*Rom* 8:28).

---

[388] Cf. SAINT FRANCIS DE SALES, *Treatise on the Love of God.* V, 6.
[389] SAINT GREGORY THE GREAT. (Editorial translation)
[390] *Saint Vincent de Paul et le sacerdoce.* p. 45; cited by MAHIEU. *Probatio Charitatis.* 69. (Editorial translation)

4. RESPONSIBILITIES GIVEN IN THE FIRST COMMANDMENT

1. FAITH

Faith is the source of the whole moral life of man. "Ignorance of God is the principle and explanation of all moral deviations."[391] We must nourish and care for our faith with prudence, rejecting all that is opposed to it. There is no greater good for man than the treasure of his Christian faith. In order to preserve it, we must be ready to make any sacrifice.

2. HOPE

Hope is the surety that God will give us the strength to be able to obey his commandments and to reach heaven.

3. CHARITY

Charity aids us to love God above all things and our neighbor as ourselves.

4. DEVOTION

Devotion is the promptitude of the will to give oneself to God and to divine things. This virtue is exclusively directed to God. The devotion to the saints has its end in God, not in the saints themselves. We venerate them because of their relationship with God.

5. PRAYER

"Prayer is the elevation of the mind and heart to God in order to praise and ask him for the things necessary for our eternal salvation."[392] Saint María Josefa Rossello exclaimed that "the Christian without prayer is likened to a bird deprived of air and a

---

[391] Cf. *Rom* 1:18-32; *Catechism of the Catholic Church*. 2087.
[392] SAINT THOMAS AQUINAS, *In lib. 3 Sent.* d. 7 a. 2 q. 3. (Editorial translation)

fish outside of water."[393] Prayer is so important that we will study it on its own later.

6. ADORATION

Through adoration, we recognize the greatness of God and our littleness, submitting our will to his. Adoration must express itself externally through specific acts: sacrifice, genuflection, kneeling, the raising of our hands, etc. The worship of adoration is only offered to God and is also called *latria*. In this type of worship, we adore the Sacred Humanity of our Lord Jesus Christ since it is united to the unity of persons in God. We also adore Jesus Christ himself present in the Eucharist as true God and true man. The worship of veneration called *dulia*, is only given to the saints and the angels. We offer a special worship of *hyperdulia* to the Most Holy Virgin Mary since she surpasses the holiness and power of all the angels and saints combined.

7. THE VENERATION OF SACRED IMAGES

The divine commandment implied the prohibition of any representation of God made by human hands: "You shall not make for yourself a graven image, or any likeness of anything that is in heaven above, or that is in the earth beneath" (*Ex* 20:4).

"Nevertheless, already in the Old Testament, God ordained or permitted the making of images that pointed symbolically toward salvation by the incarnate Word: so it was with the bronze serpent, the Ark of the Covenant, and the cherubim.

The Christian veneration of images is not contrary to the first commandment which proscribes idols. Indeed, 'the honor rendered to an image passes to its prototype,' and 'whoever venerates an image venerates the person portrayed in it.' The honor paid to sacred images is a 'respectful veneration,' not the adoration due to God alone."[394]

---

[393] MONS. LUIS TRAVERSO. *Vida y Virtudes de Santa Maria Josefa Rossello, Fundadora de las Hijas de Nuestra Señora de la Misericordia en Savona.* Buenos Aires, 1959. p. 205. (Editorial translation)
[394] *Catechism of the Catholic Church.* 2130, 2132.

For this reason, sacred relics and images are given worship and veneration, since "the honor paid to the image passes on to the prototype."[395] When we venerate an image we are not worshiping the matter of the image—plaster, wood, cement, marble, cloth, paper, cardboard, etc.—but rather the one represented by the image. It is similar to a mother who kisses the picture of her son who is absent; she is not making an act of love to the paper, but rather to her son. Jews, Muslims, Protestants, those who deny the humanity of Jesus, and others, are enemies of the worship of images. The Catholic Church has always defended this practice against its adversaries because it knows that external worship is a sign of internal worship. When the former disappears, the latter is easily watered down. Furthermore, the worship of images is a fitting way for simple people to raise their minds and hearts to God. This is how it has been throughout history. Even though many people in the Middle Ages did not know how to read, when they looked upon the altar pieces and church doors, the niches and the walls of the altars which depicted scenes from sacred history, they recalled their catechism. It was like a Bible made of stone for simple people.

8. SACRIFICE

Sacrifice is the most excellent act with which we can give honor to God. The perfect sacrifice is the Sacrifice of the Cross and its renewal in the Holy Mass, by which the Sacrifice of Christ is prolonged throughout the centuries.

9. PROMISES AND VOWS

Oftentimes, a Christian must promise something to God. Baptism, Confirmation, marriage and ordination always demand these promises. Fidelity to these promises is a sign of respect and love for God. The vows to be practiced in the evangelical counsels of poverty, chastity, and obedience are greatly praised by the Church.[396]

---

[395] SAINT BASIL THE GREAT. *De Spiritu Sancto.* 45.
[396] Cf. *Catechism of the Catholic Church.* 2101-2103.

10. THE SOCIAL DUTY OF RELIGION AND THE RIGHT TO RELIGIOUS FREEDOM[397]

"On their part, all men are bound to seek the truth, especially in what concerns God and His Church, and to embrace the truth they come to know, and to hold fast to it."[398] However, "it follows that he is not to be forced to act in manner contrary to his conscience. Nor, on the other hand, is he to be restrained from acting in accordance with his conscience, especially in matters religious."[399]

5. WHAT IS PROHIBITED BY THE FIRST COMMANDMENT

-Voluntary doubt of faith.

-Incredulity: scorn for faith in revealed truth.

-Despair: when one does not hope in God's help, opposing oneself to God's goodness and mercy.

-Presumption: when someone believes he will be saved by his own strength alone, or that he will be saved without having cooperated in God's works.

-Hatred for God: this is a typically satanic sin which consists in having an aversion towards God. This sin is the origin of many of the persecutions of the Catholic Church, blasphemies, sacrileges etc. It is the greatest sin that can be committed.

-Acedia: laziness, annoyance, or tediousness in spiritual things due to the work or trouble they entail. This is numbered as one of the capital sins, which means, a sin that is the origin of numerous other sins.

-Disordered love for creatures: the inclination which causes us to prefer creatures to the Creator or to the fulfillment of God's divine will.

---

[397] Cf. *Catechism of the Catholic Church.* 2104-2109.
[398] II VATICAN COUNCIL. *Dignitatis Humanae.* 1.
[399] II VATICAN COUNCIL. *Dignitatis Humanae.* 3.

-Unlawful worship: consists in giving worship, but not in the manner prescribed by the Church.

-Idolatry: a very grave sin in which we offer a creature the adoration that exclusively belongs to God.

-Fortunetelling: the pretension of predicting future events through inappropriate means.

-Superstition: rendering inappropriate worship to God or rendering divine worship to a person or thing which is not divine. For example, black and red magic, communing with spirits, etc.

-Sacrilege: profaning something sacred. For example: consciously retaining a grave sin in confession, receiving communion in a state of mortal sin (without having confessed grave faults to a priest), etc.

-Simony: the intention of purchasing something spiritual. It is called "simony" because it is the sin committed by Simeon the Magician who wanted to give money to the Apostles so that they would give him the power to communicate the Holy Spirit to other people. Saint Peter answered him: "Your silver perish with you, because you thought you could obtain the gift of God with money!" (*Acts* 8:20).

When we give a stipend or offering for a Baptism, a marriage ceremony, a Mass, or Prayer for the Dead, we do not give it as payment for spiritual things; rather, it is given as a just cooperation to sustain the material needs of the priest who has offered a spiritual service. Jesus reminded the priests that they have "received without paying" and thus commanded them to "give without pay" (*Mt* 10:8). This is why the priest will not refuse to help someone spiritually when he or she is not able to give an offering. Nevertheless, Jesus himself authorized his ministers to receive donations "for the laborer deserves his wages" (*Lk* 10:7). Furthermore, "in the same way, the Lord commanded that those who proclaim the gospel should get their living by the gospel" (*1 Cor* 9:14).

-Atheism: rejects or denies the existence of God.

-Agnosticism: is "often equivalent to practical atheism."[400]

THE SECOND COMMANDMENT: YOU SHALL NOT TAKE THE NAME OF THE LORD YOUR GOD IN VAIN

Man must submit himself to God and render him singular reverence; not only with his heart by loving God above all things, but also with his mouth by not pronouncing God's name irreverently. On the contrary, he must proclaim the wonders of God. As Scripture says: "For out of the abundance of the heart the mouth speaks" (*Mt* 12:34).

1. WHAT IS COMMANDED

This commandment, on the positive side, prescribes:

-The praise of God: the external expression of our interior love for God. "His praise shall continually be in my mouth" (*Ps* 34:1).

-The vow is a promise made to God for a greater good. For example, fasting, praying, making a pilgrimage, almsgiving, guarding virginity, etc. If made with prudence, such vows are good and recommendable: "Make your vows to the Lord your God, and perform them" (*Ps* 76:11).

Religious make three public vows before God. By the vow of chastity, religious "have given themselves to God body and soul"[401] "for the sake of the kingdom of heaven" (*Mt* 19:12). By the vow of poverty, religious "abandon all possession of external goods, for the sake of the more excellent internal ones"[402] according to the Gospel: "If you would be perfect, go, sell what you possess and give to the poor" (*Mt* 19:21). By the vow of

400 *Catechism of the Catholic Church*. 2128.
401 SAINT CYPRIAN. (Editorial translation)
402 SAINT GREGORY THE GREAT. (Editorial translation)

obedience, religious long to imitate Jesus who "became obedient unto death" (*Phil* 2:8). Saint Roque González, S.J., a martyr from Rio de la Plata in South America, wrote to his superior from a remote place in the Paraguayan jungle: "My will is to do what your Reverence wills because in doing it I follow the will of God..., here I live dying... but I am determined to stay here, even though I may die a thousand deaths... for they will not be failures but victories."[403]

-An oath: invoking God when testifying the truth.

2. WHAT IS PROHIBITED

On the negative side, this commandment prohibits:

-Taking the name of God in vain: to pronounce the Holy Name of God, the Virgin Mary, or the saints without reason or without proper respect.

-Blasphemy: consists of insulting God, the Virgin Mary, or the saints. It is a very grave sin. While a leader of the glorious army of the Andes, General José de San Martín severely punished "anyone who blasphemed against the Holy Name of God or his Adorable Mother, or who insulted religion."[404]

-Perjury: is swearing falsely, calling upon God as a witness. This implies that either God does not know the truth or that God will testify to a lie. This is in itself a grave sin.

THE THIRD COMMANDMENT: REMEMBER TO KEEP HOLY THE LORD'S DAY

This commandment of the law of God reminds us of the serious obligation we have in rendering worship to God. To sanctify something, in the language of Scripture, means to destine it for divine worship. This commandment orders us to dedicate Sundays and Holy Days of obligation to the Lord, nourishing our

---

[403] Letter of the martyr on the mission in Paraná in the year 1614. (Editorial translation)
[404] FR. CAYETANO BRUNO. *La religiosidad de San Martín*. Ed. Don Bosco. p. 9. (Editorial translation)

spirit in prayer and strengthening it in the Holy Mass. In order to be able to better dedicate ourselves to God, he commands us to rest from physical labor.

A pastor can dispense the common law to refrain from work on these days (but not from the grave obligation to participate in the Holy Mass) if it is necessary for proper piety for God (for example, decorating the altars or preparing a procession, etc); for charity with a neighbor (alleviating the sick, distributing clothing to the poor, etc.); for personal necessity or that of others (those who work in bakeries, kitchens, transportation, in scheduled shifts, etc); or, for a great private or public benefit (legitimate and extraordinary business affairs that cannot be obtained another day, etc).

THE PRECEPTS OF THE CHURCH[405]

Since the precepts of the Church complete our obligations with God, we will study them here. There are five general precepts:

The *First Precept* ("You shall attend Mass on Sundays and on Holy Days of obligation and rest from servile labor"[406]) obliges the faithful to participate in the celebration of the Eucharist, where the Christian community is gathered together, on the day which commemorates the Resurrection of the Lord and on principle liturgical feasts which commemorate the mysteries of the Lord, the Virgin Mary and the saints.[407]

This is why the Church, since the beginning, had the custom to gather together on Sundays (in Latin the word for 'Sunday,'

---

[405] Cf. *Catechism of the Catholic Church.* 2041-2043.
[406] In the United States (Episcopal Conference of the United States, *General Decree* promulgated February 28, 2002), the Holy Days of Obligation are:
1- All Sundays of the year.
2- January 1, Solemnity of Mary, the Mother of God
3- August 15, Solemnity of the Assumption of the Blessed Virgin Mary
4- November 1, Solemnity of All Saints
5- December 8, the Immaculate Conception of Mary
6- December 25, Nativity of our Lord Jesus Christ
Also obligatory are the Ascension of our Lord and the Feast of Corpus Christi.
[407] Cf. CODE OF CANON LAW. 1246-1248.

literally means the 'day of the Lord').[408] The Church did this in order to commemorate the Paschal mystery and make Christ present always anew in the Eucharist.

The Catholic Church, under the authority granted by Christ himself, commands, under the consequence of mortal sin, that all Christians participate in the Holy Mass, and that they be physically and attentively present in the Mass. There are several reasons for this command. The Holy Mass is the principle act of Catholic worship by which we honor God. It is the Sacrifice of all sacrifices, since it has the infinite value of the Sacrifice of our Lord Jesus Christ. It is through the Mass that God bestows on us the graces necessary for salvation. The Mass is "the summit toward which the activity of the Church is directed; at the same time it is the font from which all her power flows."[409] The Mass is the best way of giving thanks to God and the irreplaceable means of achieving true union among the faithful. The Servant of God Monsieur Jose Orzali declared that "the greatest work for our sanctification is the Holy Mass."[410]

Clearly, this is not an absolute law. If there is a moderately serious situation that could cause significant discomfort or injury to our soul or the body or those of others, we are excused from the obligation to attend Mass. For example, in the case of sickness, of being a considerable distance from a church, or the obligations mothers, soldiers or police officers have to watch over those under their care.

There are people who say, "I only go to Mass when I feel like it." This statement is a sign of great foolishness and there is absolutely no excuse for it:

-Because acts of virtue are rooted in the spirit and spiritual things are not "felt."

-Because love is not, in itself, sensible. To believe that one only loves when he or she feels love is to confuse love with

---

[408] Cf. JOHN PAUL II. Apostolic letter *Dies Dominis*.

[409] II VATICAN COUNCIL. *Sacrosanctum Concilium*. 10.

[410] Ordinance dated September 14, 1914; cited by RAÚL ENTRAIGAS. *El Buen Pastor de Cuyo*. 2nd Ed., Difusión. Buenos Aires, 1963. p. 313. (Editorial translation)

passion. Even though we do not "feel" the Mass, we must still participate in Mass because it is the greatest act of love we can offer to God.

-The father of a family goes to work even when he does not "feel like it," since he must fulfill his obligations. Obligations do not depend on sensibilities, as superficial people might believe, but on the will. If we do not fulfill our obligations to God, will we fulfill our obligations to our neighbor?

-It is true that there are moments or stages in life when our sensibilities can feel a certain tediousness and dryness in religion, or even aversion to it. The saints speak of a **dark night** or of **spiritual desolation**. During these moments, there is even greater reason to persevere in the participation in the Holy Mass. These are times when the soul is purified and they generally end up becoming the threshold for a superior state in the spiritual life because during these times the soul learns to seek "God who gives consolations and not the consolations of God."[411]

The *Second Precept* ("You shall confess your sins at least once a year") assures the preparation for the Eucharist by means of the reception of the Sacrament of Reconciliation, which continues the work of conversion and forgiveness begun at Baptism.[412]

The *Third Precept* ("You shall receive the Sacrament of the Eucharist at least during the Easter season") guarantees that we receive the Body and Blood of the Lord at least once at the time of Easter,[413] the origin and center of Christian liturgy.

All Catholics who have reached the age of reason are obligated to receive communion at least once a year, preceded first by confession if in a state of mortal sin.

According to the Code of Canon Law, "this precept must be fulfilled during the Easter season,"[414] which is within the fifty days from the Sunday of the Resurrection to the Sunday of Pentecost.

---

[411] SAINT TERESA OF JESUS (Editorial translation)
[412] Cf. CODE OF CANON LAW. 989.
[413] Cf. CODE OF CANON LAW. 920.
[414] CODE OF CANON LAW. 920, 2.

This precept is also fulfilled by going to communion during the Novena of a Patronal Feast, Spiritual Exercises, Popular Missions, or any time during the year for soldiers, immigrants and pilgrims.

The *Fourth Precept* ("You shall observe the days of fasting and abstinence established by the Church") ensures the periods of asceticism and penance which prepare us for liturgical feasts. These periods also help us to acquire dominion over our instincts and acquire freedom of heart.[415]

To fast is to deprive oneself of food. We fast for three reasons:

1. To mortify the power of fleshly passions. (Saint Jerome said, "Venus shivers unless Ceres and Bacchus be with her,"[416] which, Saint Thomas Aquinas comments by saying that "lust is cooled by abstinence in meat and drink."[417])

2. So that our spirit is more easily elevated to God.

3. To make satisfaction for our sins: "Return to me with all your heart, with fasting…" (*Joel* 2:12).

"Penitential days are prescribed on which the Christian faithful devote themselves in a special way to prayer, perform works of piety and charity, and deny themselves by fulfilling their own obligations more faithfully."[418] They include:

1. Every day during Lent there is a general obligation to do some act of penance.

2. Fridays during Lent. In the United States, the tradition of abstaining from meat on these Fridays is still maintained.

---

[415] Cf. CODE OF CANON LAW. 1249-1251.
[416] SAINT JEROME. *Against Jovinianus.* II, 7.
[417] SAINT THOMAS AQUINAS. *Summa Theologica.* II-II, 147, 1.
[418] CODE OF CANON LAW. 1249.

3. All Fridays throughout the year, unless a solemnity falls on a Friday, there is the obligation to do penance. Abstaining from meat is one way to observe this obligation on these days.[419]

4. Ash Wednesday and Good Friday, when in addition to general penance and abstinence, we must also fast.[420]

The *Fifth Precept* ("You shall help to provide for the needs of the Church") obligates the Christian faithful to assist with the needs of the Church.[421]

The Catholic Church is, without a doubt, a divine reality; but it is also a human reality, like Christ who is true God and true man. As far as it is human, the Church needs material resources to fulfill its goal of extending the Kingdom of God throughout the entire world. Also, we know that "God loves a cheerful giver" (*2 Cor* 9:7) and anyone who gives "even a cup of cold water...shall not lose his reward" (*Mt* 10:42).

The state does not maintain Church buildings or care after the needs of the priests. However, the electricity, gas, utilities, etc. all need to be paid for. This is why the faithful must provide for the needs of the Church.

Often, enemies of the Church criticize the riches of the Catholic Church, especially those of the Vatican. They forget that, with almost 2,000 years of history, it is logical that the Church possesses artistic treasures of great value. Almost every great artist has wanted to bequeath something of their work to the Church. What do these enemies of the Church want to do? To demolish the dome of St Peter's—made by Michelangelo—and to remake it with sheets of fiberglass? On the contrary, beauty and riches are creations of God and as such they must be at the service of Christ the King and his Church.

---

[419] Abstinence from meat can be substituted by a work of renunciation or personal penance, or by a work of piety, mercy, charity, or Christian testimony (Episcopal Conference of the United States, *April 2001*).

[420] The law of abstinence binds those who have completed their fourteenth year [unless there is grave reason to not observe it]. The law of fasting binds those who have reached 18 years of age, until the beginning of their sixtieth year [unless there is grave reason to not observe it]. Cf. CODE OF CANON LAW. 1252.

[421] Cf. CODE OF CANON LAW. 222.

Ask a priest how much he earns each month, and then ask a doctor, a teacher, a solider, a business man, even a blue-collar worker. In this comparison, you will see how the arguments against the Church are unfounded.

CHAPTER TWO
"YOU SHALL LOVE YOUR NEIGHBOR AS YOURSELF"

The seven remaining commandments, which refer to one's neighbor, were found on the second tablet God gave to Moses.

"A new commandment I give to you, that you love one another; even as I have loved you" (*Jn* 13:34). This commandment plays a fundamental role in the Sermon on the Mount.[422] It is the most important commandment, after loving God, and it is inseparable from the first commandment. It is impossible to love God without also loving our neighbor, and vice versa: "He who loves God should love his brother also" (*1 Jn* 4:21). "If any one says, 'I love God,' and hates his brother, he is a liar; for he who does not love his brother whom he has seen, cannot love God whom he has not seen" (*1 Jn* 4:20). Furthermore, the Apostle says, "and this is love, that we follow his commandments" (*2 Jn* 6).

1. THE MEASURE OF LOVE OF NEIGHBOR

What is the measure of love of neighbor? The Lord himself taught us: "love your neighbor as yourself" (*Mt* 22:39). Moreover, Jesus commanded: "love one another; even as I have loved you" (*Jn* 13:34).

We must love our neighbor for the love of God and in this way our love will be holy. We must love our neighbor with a love that does not concede to anything evil; but must concede only to the good. In this way, our love will be just. We must love our neighbor with a love that does not seek its own benefit or pleasure; but rather, a love that effectively seeks the good of the other. In this way, our love will be a true love.

The love of charity is universal and it thus encompasses the Blessed Virgin Mary, the holy angels, the saints, the souls in

---

[422] Cf. *Mt* 5:7, 9, 21-24, 34-48; 6:14-15; 7:1-5, 12.

purgatory, and all men without exception, including sinners and even enemies. It only excludes the demons and those who are condemned to hell.

2. MOTIVES

Why must we love our neighbor? For several reasons:

-Because Christ commanded it: "Love one another; even as I have loved you" (*Jn* 13:34).

-Because our neighbor reflects the goodness of God: we must love our neighbor with the love of charity because either God is in our neighbor or for God to be in our neighbor.

-Because Christ is present in our neighbor: "That they may be one even as we are one, I in them and thou in me" (*Jn* 17:22-23). It is Jesus, then, "hidden in the depths"[423] of the soul, who should draw us to our neighbor.

-Because we are sons and daughters of the same Father. Hence, we are made brothers and sisters in Christ for the Father. This encourages us to say: "Our Father…" (*Mt* 6:9).

-Because we have the same eternal destiny: Heaven.

What characteristics should our love for our neighbors have? Saint Paul tells us: "Love is patient and kind; love is not jealous or boastful; it is not arrogant or rude. Love does not insist on its own way; it is not irritable or resentful; it does not rejoice at wrong, but rejoices in the right. Love bears all things, believes all things, hopes all things, endures all things" (*1 Cor* 13:4-7).

3. WORKS OF THE LOVE OF NEIGHBOR

What are the principle works of charity that we can do for the benefit of our neighbors? Works of mercy, of which there are many. We will outline fourteen main ones, seven of the corporal order and seven of the spiritual order.

---

[423] SAINT THERESE OF THE CHILD JESUS. *Story of a Soul.* IX.

1. Spiritual Works of Mercy

1. *Instruct the ignorant.* By teaching, we can help men come out of the darkness and into the light, from error to truth, from slavery to freedom. This does not only apply to the natural order of things; but moreover to the supernatural order, with sights set on eternal salvation, since:

The greatest science	*La ciencia más acabada*
Is for man to end in grace.	*Es que el hombre en gracia acabe.*
That at the end of the journey,	*Que al final de la jornada,*
The one who is saved, knows;	*Aquel que se salva, sabe;*
And the one who is not saved	*Y el que no,*
does not know anything.	*no sabe nada.*

Some examples of practicing this work of mercy include: being a catechist, publishing and distributing religious books, collaborating with Pontifical Mission Societies, with the Office of Missions, being an active member of Catholic Action or of another parochial group.

2. *Counsel the doubtful.* How much does good advice greatly help on the journey of life when given opportunely! We all need the advice of a person with experience, since "he who takes himself for a teacher, makes himself a disciple of the foolish."[424] This is particularly important in the spiritual life. In this way, we can see the benefit of having a good spiritual director.

3. *Admonish sinners.* "If your brother sins against you, go and tell him his fault, between you and him alone. If he listens to you, you have gained your brother. But if he does not listen, take one or two others along with you, that every word may be confirmed by the evidence of two or three witnesses. If he refuses to listen to them, tell it to the church; and if he refuses to listen even to the church, let him be to you as a Gentile and a tax collector" (*Mt* 18:15-17). "If any one among you wanders from the truth and some one brings him back, let him know that whoever brings back a sinner from the error of his way will save his soul from

---

[424] SAINT BERNARD. *Epistle* 87. 7. (Editorial translation)

death and will cover a multitude of sins" (*Jas* 5:19-20). "You become worse than the sinner if you fail to correct him."[425]

4. *Forgive offenses.* "Peter came up and said to him, 'Lord, how often shall my brother sin against me, and I forgive him? As many as seven times?' Jesus said to him, 'I do not say to you seven times, but seventy times seven'" (*Mt* 18:21-22). We must forgive for four reasons:

a) Because God commands us to;

b) To imitate Jesus who said "Father, forgive them; for they know not what they do" (*Lk* 23:34);

c) In order to follow the example of the saints;

d) For our own personal good: "if you do not forgive men their trespasses, neither will your Father forgive your trespasses" (*Mt* 6:15).

Forgiveness must be:

-prompt: "do not let the sun go down on your anger" (*Eph* 4:26);

-spontaneous: "if you are offering your gift at the altar, and there remember that your brother has something against you... go; first be reconciled to your brother" (*Mt* 5:23-24);

-without limit: "if he...turns to you seven times, and says, 'I repent,' you must forgive him" (*Lk* 17:4);

-sincere: "forgive your brother from your heart" (*Mt* 18:35);

-for the love of God.

5. *Comfort the afflicted.* This means that we must share in the sufferings of our neighbor. "Bear one another's burdens, and so fulfill the law of Christ" (*Gal* 6:2).

6. *Bear wrongs patiently.* "Forbearing one another in love" (*Eph* 4:2). "Learn to be patient in enduring the faults of others, remembering that you yourself have many that offend others. We

---

[425] SAINT THOMAS AQUINAS. *Summa Theologica.* II-II, 33, 2, Sed Contra.

wish to see perfection in others, but do not correct our own faults."[426]

7. *Pray for the living and the dead.* "Pray for one another.... The prayer of a righteous man has great power in its effects" (*Jas* 5:16).

2. Corporal Works of Mercy

1. *Feed the hungry.* "Come, O blessed of my Father...for I was hungry and you gave me food" (*Mt* 25:34-35). "How can we merit heaven if we do not give food to the hungry?" questioned Saint Martin de Porres,[427] who after performing this act of mercy, "was so overjoyed that he said that there was no greater pleasure than to give to the poor and the miserable who were deprived of this pleasure and joy."[428]

2. *Give drink to the thirsty.* "Whoever gives you a cup of water to drink because you bear the name of Christ, will by no means lose his reward" (*Mk* 9:41).

3. *Clothe the naked.* "Come, O blessed of my Father... [for] I was naked and you clothed me" (*Mt* 25:34, 36).

4. *Visit the sick.* "Come, O blessed of my Father ... [for] I was sick and you visited me" (*Mt* 25:34, 36).

5. *Shelter the homeless.* "Come, O blessed of my Father ... [for] I was a stranger and you welcomed me" (*Mt* 25:34-35). "Practice hospitality ungrudgingly to one another" (*1 Pet* 4:9). "Do not neglect to show hospitality to strangers, for thereby some have entertained angels unawares" (*Heb* 13:2). "Let all guests who arrive be received like Christ."[429]

6. *Visit the imprisoned.* "Remember those who are in prison, as though in prison with them" (*Heb* 13:3). This work of mercy encompasses everything we do to help our brothers and sisters of

---

[426] THOMAS A KEMPIS. *The Imitation of Christ.* XVI, 2.

[427] Testimony of Juan Vásquez de Parra; cited in JOSÉ ANTONIO DEL BUSTO DUTHUTBURU. *San Martín de Porres.* Pontificia Universidad Católica del Perú, 1992. p. 294. (Editorial translation)

[428] Testimony of Friar Fernando Aragonés; Ibid. p. 274. (Editorial translation)

[429] SAINT BENEDICT. *The Rule of St. Benedict,* LIII, 1.

the Silent Church, those who receive hunger as wages, those who are under the pressure of the usurers, etc.

7. *Bury the dead.* The cadaver of a Christian is something sacred, since this body was "a temple of the Holy Spirit" (*1 Cor* 6:19), and will rise gloriously.[430]

4. DISTINCTIVE MARKS OF CHRISTIAN LOVE

What are the most splendid signs of Christian charity? Love for the poor, for sinners, for our enemies, since none of these can be loved easily for exterior or selfish motives, but only for the love of God.

1. Love for the poor

"Blessed is he who considers the poor! The Lord delivers him in the day of trouble" (*Ps* 41:1).

Christ wanted to identify himself with the poor: "As you did it to one of the least of these my brethren, you did it to me" (*Mt* 25:40).

We have an obligation to generously help the poor out of love for God. This is the serious obligation of almsgiving: "But if any one has the world's goods and sees his brother in need, yet closes his heart against him, how does God's love abide in him?" (*1 Jn* 3:17). Absolute failure to obey this commandment of the Lord leads to eternal condemnation: "Depart from me, you cursed, into the eternal fire…for I was hungry and you gave me no food" (*Mt* 25:41-42). Scripture exhorts us to perform this duty actively and passively: "Do not turn your face away from any poor man, and the face of God will not be turned away from you" (*Tob* 4:7). "Water extinguishes a blazing fire: so almsgiving atones for sin" (*Sir* 3:30). "If you would be perfect, go, sell what you possess and give to the poor, and you will have treasure in heaven; and come, follow me" (*Mt* 19:21). "Sell your possessions, and give alms" (*Lk* 12:33). "When you give a feast, invite the poor, the maimed, the lame, the blind, and you will be blessed, because they cannot

---

[430] Cf. *1 Thess* 4:13-18.

repay you. You will be repaid at the resurrection of the just" (*Lk* 14:13-14). "It is the bread of the hungry that you hoard, clothing of the naked that you keep in your chest, shoes of the unshod that you leave for the moths and money of the poor that you have hidden away."[431] All the saints have greatly loved the poor and they exhort us to seek them out in order to help them. "Never forget that he who serves and assists the sick and the poor cares for and assists Christ, our Redeemer" (Saint Camillus of Lelis).[432] "To the poor, daughters, to the poor; always seek the poor!" (María Benita Arias, Argentine religious).[433]

2. Love for sinners

There are two things present in a sinner: a) his human nature, good in itself and worthy of our charitable love because he was created by God, redeemed by Christ and can be sanctified by the Holy Spirit; and b) the sin that separates him from heaven, makes him an enemy of God and should be the object of our hatred. Therefore, whoever the sinner may be, even if it is our father, mother or relative, we must hate their sin, as we read in the Gospel.[434] To hate their sin and long for their conversion is to have true charity, to truly love them.

Therefore, it is necessary to hate perversities with holy hatred in order to avoid becoming like those who fail to distinguish between the sinner and the sin and end up loving the sin itself, like the liberals do. "I hate double-minded men" (*Ps* 119:113). "I hate them with perfect hatred" (*Ps* 139:22). However, at the same time it is necessary to love sinners with holy love, seeking to do good to them, trying to show them how to love what we love and to rejoice in what we rejoice in. In this aim, we follow the example of the Lord who, because of the desire to convert sinners, ate and drank with them; and we avoid the example of the Pharisees who "were righteous and despised others" (*Lk* 18:9).

---

[431] SAINT BASIL, SAINT AMBROSE, AND SAINT THOMAS AQUINAS. (Editorial translation)

[432] Editorial translation.

[433] Cited in SANTIAGO M. USSHER. *María Benita Arias, fundadora del Instituto de las Siervas de Jesús Sacramentado, Apuntes biográficos.* El Propagador Cristiano, Buenos Aires, 1938. p.278. (Editorial translation)

[434] Cf. *Lk* 14:26.

For every Christian, every person has an almost infinite value because the only Son of God, our Lord Jesus Christ, made himself the price for man, shedding his blood for the salvation of each of them. This is why the hearts of the saints burn with the same ardent apostolic longing of Saint Paul who said, "I will most gladly spend and be spent for your souls" (*2 Cor* 12:15). "Give me souls, take all the rest,"[435] "Only one thing is necessary: to save the soul! To save the soul!"[436] Thus, the saints have done great and heroic things for the conversion of sinners.

3. Love for enemies

We are not commanded to love our enemies because they are our enemies, but in spite of the fact they are our enemies. Similarly, we are not commanded to call good what is evil, for to do so would be perverse. Furthermore, we are not required to love our enemies sensibly, but supernaturally. Those who hurt us, if converted, will be able to reach celestial glory. "But I say to you that hear, love your enemies, do good to those who hate you, bless those who curse you, pray for those who abuse you" (*Lk* 6:27-28). Hatred and all thoughts of vengeance are forbidden us because we must tolerate all who are evil and bear their injuries, so long as they are not contrary to God: "It is praiseworthy to be patient under our own wrongs, but to overlook God's wrongs is most wicked."[437]

5. SINS THAT ARE DIRECTLY OPPOSED TO THE LOVE OF NEIGHBOR

1. Hatred

"He who hates his brother is in the darkness" (*1 Jn* 2:11). "You shall not hate your brother in your heart" (*Lev* 19:17). "Anyone who hates his brother is a murderer" (*1 Jn* 3:15).

---

[435] "*Da mihi animas, coeteras tolle*" (Gen 14:21), words from the king of Sodom to Abraham which St. Francis de Sales and St. Don Bosco took as their motto for their priestly ministry.

[436] SAINT JOHN BOSCO. *El Joven cristiano*. II, article 9. (Editorial translation)

[437] SAINT THOMAS AQUINAS. *Summa Theologica*. II-II, 108, 1 ad. 2.

2. Envy

This is the sin by which we consider the good of our neighbor as an evil for ourselves, fearing being equaled or surpassed by others. The envious "shall not inherit the kingdom of God" (*Gal* 5:21).

3. Discord

Discord is the disunion of wills with God or neighbor in all that refers to what is good. God abhors whoever sows "discord among brothers" (*Prov* 6:19).

4. Contention

Contention is violent discussion with words. Do not become involved in "disputing about words, which does no good" (*2 Tim* 2:14).

5. Scandal

A scandal consists in saying or doing something that induces our neighbor to sin. "Whoever causes one…to sin, it would be better for him to have a great millstone fastened round his neck and to be drowned in the depth of the sea" (*Mt* 18:6). "The one who induces another to sin has the greater fault than the one who sins" (Origen).

Now that we have taken a look at love of neighbor in general, we will look in detail at each of the seven commandments in the Law of God which refer to this love.

THE FOURTH COMMANDMENT: HONOR YOUR FATHER AND YOUR MOTHER

"According to the fourth commandment, God has willed that, after him, we should honor our parents and those whom he has vested with authority for our good.

The conjugal community is established upon the covenant and consent of the spouses. Marriage and family are ordered to the good of the spouses, to the procreation and the education of children.

'The well-being of the individual person and of both human and Christian society is closely bound up with the healthy state of conjugal and family life' (*GS* 47 § 1)."[438]

Children must love their parents: "What can you give back to them that equal their gift to you?" (*Sir* 7:28). Children must respect their parents: "Honor your father by word and deed" (*Sir* 3:8). Furthermore, children must obey them: "Children, obey your parents in the Lord, for this is right" (*Eph* 6:1), as long as they do not command something that is a sin, in which case "we must obey God rather than men" (*Acts* 5:29). Children must also help their parents when they are in need: "Whoever forsakes his father is like a blasphemer" (*Sir* 3:16).

This commandment also obligates parents to love their children, caring for them physically and spiritually. Parents must ensure a solid future for their children and be involved in the growth of their children's interior life. In addition, parents—as spouses—must love one another, help each other and live together in peace. They must be just in the administration of goods and in all that pertains to their conjugal responsibilities and mutual fidelity. Siblings must demonstrate mutual affection, unity, edification and support for each other. Furthermore, there must be a special love due to grandparents, uncles and aunts, cousins, nieces and nephews, etc.

This commandment also obligates employers to be benevolent towards their employees: they should instruct them, correct them, and pay them a just salary. Correspondingly, this commandment obligates employees to respect, obey and be loyal to their employers.

Since the academic sphere is a prolongation of the family, the fourth commandment also obligates teachers and students to fulfill their professional duties.

Finally, this commandment requires us to have love for our country, the land of our ancestors (the word *patriotic* shares the

---

[438] *Catechism of the Catholic Church.* 2248-2251.

Latin root for *paternal*). The virtue of patriotism demands us to have a preferential love for our country, respecting and honoring its history, tradition and destiny, obeying its laws, and defending it against internal and external enemies. If a person does not love the country which he sees, how will he love the celestial homeland which he does not see? Jesus wept for his country.

"Public authority is obliged to respect the fundamental rights of the human person and the conditions for the exercise of his freedom.

It is the duty of citizens to work with civil authority for building up society in a spirit of truth, justice, solidarity, and freedom.

Citizens are obliged in conscience not to follow the directives of civil authorities when they are contrary to the demands of the moral order. 'We must obey God rather than men' (*Acts* 5:29).

Every society's judgments and conduct reflect a vision of man and his destiny. Without the light the Gospel sheds on God and man, societies easily become totalitarian."[439]

THE FIFTH COMMANDMENT: YOU SHALL NOT KILL

In a positive way, this commandment obligates us to preserve our own life. Negatively, it obligates us to avoid suicide; self-mutilation; negligence with human goods; scandals which induce others to do evil; drug abuse; the abuse of food, alcohol, tobacco or medicine; to avoid drunk driving; and to avoid speeding, etc.[440]

Likewise, it forbids us to bring death upon another person unjustly, be it by homicide, feticide (abortion), genocide, euthanasia, etc. But we also must know that "The prohibition of murder does not abrogate the right to render an unjust aggressor unable to inflict harm. Legitimate defense is a grave duty for

---

[439] *Catechism of the Catholic Church.* 2254-2257.
[440] Cf. *Catechism of the Catholic Church.* 2290.

whoever is responsible for the lives of others or the common good."[441]

Duels are also prohibited, since those who duel go intent to kill or to die, to seriously wound, or to be seriously wounded. Kidnapping and taking hostages are morally illegitimate acts. Terrorism, which is to kill without discrimination, also goes against this commandment. Torture, amputations, mutilations, or direct voluntary sterilizations (except in the case of medical or therapeutic reasons) are against the moral law.

This commandment reminds us of the obligation to work for peace and to avoid war. "The fifth commandment forbids the intentional destruction of human life. Because of the evils and injustices that accompany all war, the Church insistently urges everyone to prayer and to action so that the divine Goodness may free us from the ancient bondage of war. All citizens and all governments are obliged to work for the avoidance of war.

However, 'as long as the danger of war persists and there is no international authority with the necessary competence and power, governments cannot be denied the right of lawful self-defense, once all peace efforts have failed.'"[442]

The arms race, the accumulation of weapons (especially weapons of mass destruction, like atomic, biological or chemical weapons), the production and trading of such weapons, etc. all threaten just peace. Likewise: "Injustice, excessive economic or social inequalities, envy, distrust, and pride raging among men and nations constantly threaten peace and cause wars. Everything done to overcome these disorders contributes to building up peace and avoiding war.

'Insofar as men are sinners, the threat of war hangs over them and will so continue until Christ comes again; but insofar as they can vanquish sin by coming together in charity, violence itself will be vanquished and these words will be fulfilled: 'they shall beat their swords into plowshares, and their spears into pruning hooks;

---

[441] *Catechism of the Catholic Church.* 2321.
[442] Ibid. 2307-2308.

nation shall not lift up sword against nation, neither shall they learn war any more.'"[443]

THE SIXTH COMMANDMENT: YOU SHALL NOT COMMIT ADULTERY

By this commandment we are called to be pure in thought, word and deed. The virtue of purity, prescribed by this commandment, is one of the most beautiful and delicate. Saint Augustine gave three pieces of advice in order to practice this virtue properly: 1) pray, receive the Sacraments often—above all Penance and Communion—and have a great devotion to the Blessed Virgin Mary; 2) flee from occasions of sin against purity and reject temptations a thousand and one times; and 3) mortify the body by making it accustomed to obey the soul.

Saint Paul outlines several reasons for why we ought to preserve the purity of our body: because the body "is for the Lord...[He] will also raise us up by his power;" because our bodies are "members of Christ;" because they are "temple[s] of the Holy Spirit;" because our bodies do not belong to us, since we "were bought with a price;" and because we must "glorify God in [our bodies]" (*1 Cor* 6:12-20).

God created man and woman and gave each one of them a complementary sexuality. Furthermore, in order that they would transmit life, God made pleasure a part of the sexual union. To seek this sexual pleasure—either alone, or with another person outside of matrimony, or even by artificially impeding the transmission of life within matrimony—is a grave sin.

In this respect, one not only commits sin with bad actions, but also by consenting to bad thoughts or desires, with looks, touches, readings, obscene songs, bad conversations, pornographic movies, etc.

---

[443] *Catechism of the Catholic Church.* 2317.

We must take into consideration that "'love is the fundamental and innate vocation of every human being' (FC 11).

By creating the human being man and woman, God gives personal dignity equally to the one and the other. Each of them, man and woman, should acknowledge and accept his sexual identity.

Christ is the model of chastity. Every baptized person is called to lead a chaste life, each according to his particular state of life.

Chastity means the integration of sexuality within the person. It includes an apprenticeship in self-mastery.

Among the sins gravely contrary to chastity are masturbation, fornication, pornography, and homosexual practices.

The covenant which spouses have freely entered into entails faithful love. It imposes on them the obligation to keep their marriage indissoluble.

Fecundity is a good, a gift and an end of marriage. By giving life, spouses participate in God's fatherhood.

The regulation of births represents one of the aspects of responsible fatherhood and motherhood. Legitimate intentions on the part of the spouses do not justify recourse to morally unacceptable means (for example, direct sterilization or contraception).

Adultery, divorce, polygamy, and free union are grave offenses against the dignity of marriage."[444]

THE SEVENTH COMMANDMENT: YOU SHALL NOT STEAL

According to this commandment, we are obligated to give to each person that which, by right, belongs to them. If one commits an injustice by taking something which belongs to

---

[444] *Catechism of the Catholic Church.* 2392-2400.

another, he or she is obligated to return it. One must do this in order that his or her neighbor does not remain deprived of something which rightly belongs to him or her. Everyone has the right to use their own personal things, but without forgetting their social duties.

The following things are forbidden:

-theft or robbery, which is to take something that belongs to another;

-buying stolen things;

-fraud or deception in business, measurements, price, quality, number, size, etc;

-for workers to demand a full wage when they have not completed their work;

-for an employer to fail to pay his employees their just wages. This is a sin that cries out to heaven and reaches the ears of the Lord of hosts (cf. *Jas* 5:1-4);

-usury: for the one who commits usury commits murder;[445]

-failure to pay debts;

-hoarding: "The people curse him who holds back grain" (*Prov* 11:26).

The Catechism of the Catholic Church gives us this summary:

"'You shall not steal' (*Ex* 20:15; *Deut* 5:19). 'Neither thieves, nor the greedy…nor robbers will inherit the kingdom of God' (1 *Cor* 6:10).

The seventh commandment enjoins the practice of justice and charity in the administration of earthly goods and the fruits of men's labor.

The goods of creation are destined for the entire human race. The right to private property does not abolish the universal destination of goods.

---

[445] Cf. *Roman Catechism III*, VII listed under "Various Forms of Robbery."

The seventh commandment forbids theft. Theft is the usurpation of another's goods against the reasonable will of the owner.

Every manner of taking and using another's property unjustly is contrary to the seventh commandment. The injustice committed requires reparation. Commutative justice requires the restitution of stolen goods.

The moral law forbids acts which, for commercial or totalitarian purposes, lead to the enslavement of human beings, or to their being bought, sold or exchanged like merchandise.

The dominion granted by the Creator over the mineral, vegetable, and animal resources of the universe cannot be separated from respect for moral obligations, including those toward generations to come.

Animals are entrusted to man's stewardship; he must show them kindness. They may be used to serve the just satisfaction of man's needs.

The Church makes a judgment about economic and social matters when the fundamental rights of the person or the salvation of souls requires. She is concerned with the temporal common good of men because they are ordered to the sovereign Good, their ultimate end.

Man is himself the author, center, and goal of all economic and social life. The decisive point of the social question is that goods created by God for everyone should in fact reach everyone in accordance with justice and with the help of charity.

The primordial value of labor stems from man himself, its author and beneficiary. By means of his labor man participates in the work of creation. Work united to Christ can be redemptive.

True development concerns the whole man. It is concerned with increasing each person's ability to respond to his vocation and hence to God's call (cf. *CA* 29).

Giving alms to the poor is a witness to fraternal charity: it is also a work of justice pleasing to God.

How can we not recognize Lazarus, the hungry beggar in the parable (cf. *Lk* 17:19-31), in the multitude of human beings without bread, a roof or a place to stay? How can we fail to hear Jesus: 'As you did it not to one of the least of these, you did it not to me' (*Mt* 25:45)?"[446]

THE EIGHTH COMMANDMENT: YOU SHALL NOT BEAR FALSE WITNESS AGAINST YOUR NEIGHBOR

All Christians must live "speaking the truth in love" (*Eph* 4:15). "Therefore, putting away falsehood, let every one speak the truth with his neighbor, for we are members one of another" (*Eph* 4:25).

The following things are forbidden:

-lying: "keep far from a false charge" (*Ex* 23:7);

-simulation: a lie with the intent of causing someone to form an erroneous judgment;

-hypocrisy: the sin of the Pharisees. Between two evils, "it is less grave to sin openly than to feign holiness,"[447] because a feigned goodness is not only a lie but rather a double sin: "lack of holiness, and simulation thereof;"[448]

-defamation: to discredit a person who is absent;

-slander: to accuse someone of a wrong action they did not commit;

-rash judgment: to believe without sufficient reason that another person is in a state of sin or has bad intentions;

-gossip: to sow discord among friends;

---

[446] *Catechism of the Catholic Church.* 2450-2463.
[447] SAINT JEROME. *In Glossa Isaias.* 16, 16. (Editorial translation)
[448] SAINT THOMAS AQUINAS. *Summa Theologica.* II-II, Q 3, 4.

-false testimony: affirming something false or denying something true;

-mockery: making someone appear ridiculous in front of others;

-cursing;

-violation of a secret.

A summary of what is mandated by the eighth commandment follows:

"'You shall not bear false witness against your neighbor' (*Ex* 20:16). Christ's disciples have 'put on the new man, created after the likeness of God in true righteousness and holiness' (*Eph* 4:24).

Truth or truthfulness is the virtue which consists in showing oneself true in deeds and truthful in words, and guarding against duplicity, dissimulation, and hypocrisy.

The Christian is not to 'be ashamed of testifying to our Lord' (*2 Tim* 1:8) in deed and word. Martyrdom is the supreme witness given to the truth of the faith.

Respect for the reputation and honor of persons forbids all detraction and calumny in word or attitude.

Lying consists in saying what is false with the intention of deceiving one's neighbor.

An offense committed against the truth requires reparation.

The golden rule helps one discern, in concrete situations, whether or not it would be appropriate to reveal the truth to someone who asks for it.

'The sacramental seal is inviolable' (CIC, can. 983 § 1). Professional secrets must be kept. Confidences prejudicial to another are not to be divulged.

Society has a right to information based on truth, freedom, and justice. One should practice moderation and discipline in the use of the social communications media.

The fine arts, but above all sacred art, 'of their nature are directed toward expressing in some way the infinite beauty of

God in works made by human hands. Their dedication to the increase of God's praise and of his glory is more complete, the more exclusively they are devoted to turning men's minds devoutly toward God' (*SC* 122)."[449]

THE NINTH COMMANDMENT:
YOU SHALL NOT COVET YOUR NEIGHBOR'S WIFE

Concupiscence can be defined as any movement of the sensible appetite which goes against the work of human reason. Saint John distinguishes three types:

- concupiscence of the flesh

- concupiscence of the eyes

- the pride of life

The ninth commandment prohibits the concupiscence of the flesh and of the eyes, since "every one who looks at a woman lustfully has already committed adultery with her in his heart" (*Mt* 5:28). The concupiscence of the eyes, along with the pride of life, also applies to the tenth commandment, which is why, historically, they formed one commandment.

Since man is composed of body and spirit, there arises a struggle between the tendencies of the spirit and the tendencies of the flesh within him. However, in reality, this struggle pertains to the inheritance of sin.

Now, let us look at some means in order to combat this inordinate desire in the human being:

1. Purification of the heart:

"For out of the heart come evil thoughts, murder, adultery, fornication..." (*Mt* 15:19). The struggle against concupiscence passes through the purification of the heart. If we want to be victorious in this, we must be "clean of heart." In this way, we

---

will align our intelligence and our will to the demands of sanctity of God. Moreover, we will have the promise of seeing God face to face, as our Lord Jesus Christ clearly says in the sixth beatitude: "Blessed are the pure in heart, for they shall see God" (*Mt* 5:8).

2. The battle for purity:

-by means of the virtue and gift of chastity, which allows us to love with uprightness, gives us a great spiritual fruitfulness, and makes us totally free in order to tend to God;

-through purity of intention, which consists in seeking the will of God in everything;

-through interior and exterior purity of sight: "appearance arouses yearning in fools" (*Wis* 15:5);

-through prayer: "without the grace of God it is impossible to triumph over our concupiscence completely; and this grace of God is infallibly promised to prayer, clothed with the necessary conditions."[450]

"The Gospel of Christ constantly renews the life and culture of fallen man, it combats and removes the errors and evils resulting from the permanent allurement of sin. It never ceases to purify and elevate the morality of peoples. By riches coming from above, it makes fruitful, as it were from within, the spiritual qualities and traditions of every people and of every age. It strengthens, perfects and restores them in Christ."[451]

"The ninth commandment warns against lust or carnal concupiscence.

Purity of heart will enable us to see God: it enables us even now to see things according to God. Purification of the heart demands prayer, the practice of chastity, purity of intention and of vision. Purity of heart requires the modesty which is patience,

---

[450] ROYO MARIN, O.P. *Teología de la perfección cristiana.* Madrid: B.A.C., 1968. p. 330. (Editorial translation)
[451] II VATICAN COUNCIL. *Gaudium et spes.* 58, 4.

decency, and discretion. Modesty protects the intimate center of the person."[452]

THE TENTH COMMANDMENT: YOU SHALL NOT COVET YOUR NEIGHBOR'S GOODS

This commandment completes the ninth commandment, which deals with the concupiscence of the flesh. Together, these two commandments summarize all the precepts of the Law.

The tenth commandment prohibits coveting the belongings of others, with greater emphasis on the intentions of the heart. This coveting is born from idolatry, which is condemned in the first three precepts of the Law.

The sensible appetite compels us to desire pleasurable goods we do not possess. These goods can be good in and of themselves (for example, eating when we are hungry). However, these desires often are not in accordance with reason and they cause us to desire things that are not ours in a disordered way.

This commandment also prohibits avarice, which is an immoderate desire in the appropriation of goods.

Envy is also prohibited by the last commandment. "Through the devil's envy death entered the world" (*Wis* 2:24). For this reason, we must expel this capital sin from our hearts, which only produces "sadness at the sight of our neighbor's goods and the immoderate desire to acquire them for oneself, even unjustly."[453]

Jesus Christ exhorts his disciples to "renounce all" (*Lk* 14:33) that they have "for him and the Gospel."[454] In addition, Jesus promises the possession of the Kingdom to those who obey his exhortation. "Blessed are the poor in spirit, for theirs is the kingdom of heaven" (*Mt* 5:3). It is our duty then, to fight, with

---

[452] *Catechism of the Catholic Church.* 2529, 2531-2533.
[453] *Catechism of the Catholic Church.* 2539.
[454] Cf. *Mk* 8:35.

grace from on high in order to obtain the goods promised by God.

Therefore, if we want to possess and contemplate God, we need to mortify our concupiscences and, in this way, triumph over the seductions of pleasure, of power and of possession.

"'Where your treasure is, there will your heart be also' (*Mt* 6:21).

The baptized person combats envy through good-will, humility, and abandonment to the providence of God.

Christ's faithful 'have crucified the flesh with its passions and desires' (*Gal* 5:24); they are led by the Spirit and follow his desires.

Detachment from riches is necessary for entering the Kingdom of heaven. 'Blessed are the poor in spirit.'

'I want to see God' expresses the true desire of man. Thirst for God is quenched by the water of eternal life (cf. *Jn* 4:14)."[455]

> "*Those who love are not calculating*, they do not seek their own gain. They work quietly and without charge for their brothers and sisters, knowing that every person, whoever he or she may be, has infinite value. In Christ no one is inferior and no one is superior. All are *members of the same body*, seeking one another's happiness and wishing to build a world which embraces everyone. By gestures of concern and by our active participation in social life we bear witness before our neighbor that we want to help him to become himself and to give the best of himself, for his own personal good and for the good of the entire human community. Brotherhood rejects the desire for power, and service the temptation of power. Dear young people, you have in yourselves the extraordinary capacity of being gift, of giving love and of showing solidarity. The Lord wishes to strengthen this immense generosity which animates your hearts. I invite you to come and draw from the spring of life which is Christ, in order to discover each day ways of *serving your brothers and sisters in the midst of the society in which you must assume your responsibilities as men and women and as believers.*"
>
> *John Paul II*
> *Meeting with youth in Paris*
> *August 21, 1997*

---

[455] *Catechism of the Catholic Church.* 2551, 2554-2557.

PART FOUR
WHAT WE MUST PRAY

CHRISTIAN PRAYER

"God's help comes to you through prayer. Your union with Christ will be the secret of your effectiveness, and it is strengthened by your prayer, your conversation with God, the lifting up of your heart to him."

John Paul II
To the youth of Newfoundland (Canada)
September 12, 1984

269

SECTION ONE
PRAYER IN THE CHRISTIAN LIFE

"Through prayer you will possess Christ and be able to communicate him to others. And this is the greatest contribution you can make in your lives: *to communicate Christ to the world*...In all the circumstances of your lives, you will find that Jesus is with you— he is close to you in prayer. It is prayer that will bring joy into your lives and help you to overcome the obstacles to Christian living. Remember the words of Saint James: 'Is any one among you suffering? Let him pray.'"

John Paul II
To the youth of Wales and England
June 2, 1982

CHAPTER ONE
THE REVELATION OF PRAYER

1. WHAT IS PRAYER?

Since God is a pure and personal spirit (Father, Son and Holy Spirit) and we have a spiritual and personal soul, a flow of thoughts, affections and words can be established between God and each one of us. This is **prayer**: the elevation of the mind and the heart to God.

Saint Therese of the Child Jesus said: "For me, prayer is an aspiration of the heart, it is a simple glance directed to heaven, it is a cry of gratitude and love in the midst of trial as well as joy."[456]

Saint John Damascene taught that: "prayer is the elevation of the soul to God"[457] and also "the petition to God for necessary goods."[458]

Jesus repeatedly taught that prayer is very necessary for our spiritual life: "Watch and pray" (*Mt* 26:41); always pray and do not lose heart (cf. *Lk* 18:1); "ask, and it will be given you" (*Mt* 7:7). This is why Saint Alphonsus of Liguori taught: "Whoever prays is certainly saved. He who does not is certainly damned."[459]

1. THE REVELATION OF PRAYER IN THE OLD TESTAMENT

"God tirelessly calls each person to this mysterious encounter with Himself. Prayer unfolds throughout the whole history of salvation as a reciprocal call between God and man.

The prayer of Abraham and Jacob is presented as a battle of faith marked by trust in God's faithfulness and by certitude in the victory promised to perseverance.

---

[456] *Story of a Soul,* p. 242.
[457] *De Fide* I, 3, 24: ML 39, 1887. (Editorial translation)
[458] *De Fide* I, 3, 24: ML 39, 1887. (Editorial translation)
[459] "Importance of Prayer." *Love is Prayer. Prayer is Love.* Missouri: Liguori Publications, 1973. p. 24.

The prayer of Moses responds to the living God's initiative for the salvation of his people. It foreshadows the prayer of intercession of the unique mediator, Christ Jesus.

The prayer of the People of God flourished in the shadow of the dwelling place of God's presence on earth, the ark of the covenant and the Temple, under the guidance of their shepherds, especially King David, and of the prophets.

The prophets summoned the people to conversion of heart and, while zealously seeking the face of God, like Elijah, they interceded for the people.

The Psalms constitute the masterwork of prayer in the Old Testament. They present two inseparable qualities: the personal and the communal. They extend to all dimensions of history, recalling God's promises already fulfilled and looking for the coming of the Messiah.

Prayed and fulfilled in Christ, the Psalms are an essential and permanent element of the prayer of the Church. They are suitable for men of every condition and time."[460]

2. THE REVELATION OF PRAYER IN THE FULLNESS OF TIME

"Jesus' filial prayer is the perfect model of prayer in the New Testament. Often done in solitude and in secret, the prayer of Jesus involves a loving adherence to the will of the Father even to the Cross and an absolute confidence in being heard.

In his teaching, Jesus teaches his disciples to pray with a purified heart, with lively and persevering faith, with filial boldness. He calls them to vigilance and invites them to present their petitions to God in his name. Jesus Christ himself answers prayers addressed to him.

The prayers of the Virgin Mary, in her Fiat and Magnificat, are characterized by the generous offering of her whole being in faith."[461]

---

[460] *Catechism of the Catholic Church.* 2591-2597.
[461] *Catechism of the Catholic Church.* 2620-2622.

2. FORMS OF PRAYER

We are not only praying when we ask God for something, but we are also praying when:

-we adore God, loving him with all our heart and giving him the supreme worship due to him alone;

-we praise God, extolling and celebrating his marvels, rejoicing in them as done by Saint Francis of Assisi in his "Canticle of Creatures." Martin Fierro admired the stars and said: "and God has created them so that I can console myself in them;"[462]

-we give him thanks for all the benefits received;

-we appeal to sacred things, such as saying: "O my God, incline your ear and hear...on the ground of your great mercy" (*Dan* 9:18) or "By your coming as man, Lord save your people."[463]

Likewise, there are different ways to petition something from God:

-when the petition refers directly to something determined;

-when the petition simply presents a fact, for example "he whom you love is ill" (*Jn* 11:3);

-when the petition refers to something undetermined.

"The Holy Spirit who teaches the Church and recalls to her all that Jesus said also instructs her in the life of prayer, inspiring new expressions of the same basic forms of prayer: blessing, petition, intercession, thanksgiving, and praise.

Because God blesses the human heart, it can in return bless him who is the source of every blessing.

Forgiveness, the quest for the Kingdom, and every true need are objects of the prayer of petition.

Prayer of intercession consists in asking on behalf of another. It knows no boundaries and extends to one's enemies.

---

[462] JOSÉ HERNÁNDEZ. *Martín Fierro.* Part I, Hymn IX, 1449-1450. (Editorial translation)
[463] *Roman Missal.* Easter Vigil: Litany of the Saints.

Every joy and suffering, every event and need can become the matter for thanksgiving which, sharing in that of Christ, should fill one's whole life: 'Give thanks in all circumstances' (*1 Thess* 5:18).

Prayer of praise is entirely disinterested and rises to God, lauds him, and gives him glory for his own sake, quite beyond what he has done, but simply because HE IS."[464]

3. WHAT SHOULD WE ASK FOR?

Mainly, we must ask for the things that are necessary for our eternal salvation: to live in and persevere in grace until the end of our life, to not fall into sin or be freed from it, and to be able to receive the sacraments often.   Namely, we must pray for everything which refers to our supernatural life. Secondly, we can and must ask for temporal things, but only if they are for the greater service of God and the salvation of souls.   Often these temporal goods, such as health, money, comfort, etc., become an evil for us.   Even though God always gives us what is necessary for our eternal salvation and because he "desires all men to be saved and to come to the knowledge of the truth" (*1 Tim* 2:4), God does not always give us the temporal goods we ask for.   He does this—just as a mother would not give poison to her son even if he asked for it—because sometimes the temporal goods we ask for are harmful for us.

God is merciful when he gives us what we ask him for, and he is also just, good, and merciful when he does not give us what we ask for.   He is merciful in both cases because he is working for our good: "in everything God works for good with those who love him" (*Rom* 8:28).

4. WHOM SHOULD WE ASK FROM?

We can only make direct petitions to God, as the Psalm says: "The Lord God…bestows favor and honor" (*Ps* 84:11). Indirectly, we can and we must pray to the angels, the saints and

---

[464] *Catechism of the Catholic Church.* 2644-2649.

especially to the Blessed Virgin Mary in order that they may obtain something for us from God.

5. WHOM SHOULD WE PRAY FOR?

We must not only pray for ourselves; but, also for our neighbor. "Pray for one another, that you may be healed" (*Jas* 5:16). We must especially pray for the souls in purgatory.

We must even pray for our enemies in order that they might convert. "Love your enemies and pray for those who persecute you" (*Mt* 5:44).

6. KNOW HOW TO LISTEN

Prayer is not a monologue (where only one person speaks), but a dialogue (where two people speak). It is a dialogue between God and us, which is why we not only have to learn how to talk to God, but also how to listen to him.

Since God does not speak with sensible words, but rather with intelligible words, we should practice interior silence. We do not listen to God with the ears of our body; but rather, with the ears of the soul by means of the different movements of grace.

God, who is supremely intelligent and good, communicates himself to the soul in order to transmit what he desires. Moreover, he knows how to do it in such a way that one ends up discovering God's will or desire.

CHAPTER TWO
THE TRADITION OF PRAYER

"Prayer cannot be reduced to the spontaneous outpouring of interior impulse: in order to pray, one must have the will to pray. Nor is it enough to know what the Scriptures reveal about prayer: one must also learn how to pray. Through a living transmission (Sacred Tradition) within 'the believing and praying Church,' the Holy Spirit teaches the children of God how to pray."[465]

1. SOURCES OF PRAYER

1. THE WORD OF GOD

"The Church 'forcefully and specially exhorts all the Christian faithful... to learn 'the surpassing knowledge of Jesus Christ' (*Phil* 3:8) by frequent reading of the divine Scriptures.... Let them remember, however, that prayer should accompany the reading of Sacred Scripture, so that a dialogue takes place between God and man. For 'we speak to him when we pray; we listen to him when we read the divine oracles.'"[466]

Saint Therese of the Child Jesus, Doctor of the Church, wrote: "It is especially the *Gospels* that sustain me during my hours of prayer, for in them I find what is necessary for my poor little soul. I am constantly discovering in them new lights, hidden and mysterious meanings."[467]

2. LITURGICAL PRAYER

Liturgical prayer is the prayer of the whole Church; of the head, Christ, and of the members, ourselves.

Prayer is the work of Christ present in the Church, which gives glory to God, immolating himself especially in the Holy Sacrifice of the Mass, and sanctifing men, particularly through the

---

[465] *Catechism of the Catholic Church.* 2650.
[466] *Catechism of the Catholic Church.* 2653.
[467] *Story of a Soul.* p. 179.

sacraments. When someone baptizes, it is Christ who baptizes.[468] Christ is among us in very diverse ways, speaking to us through his Word ("Ignorance of Scripture is ignorance of Christ"[469]), and imploring and singing songs with us. "Where two or three are gathered in my name, there am I in the midst of them" (*Mt* 18:20). Thus, we can say that God is perfectly glorified and men are sanctified by the liturgy.

Liturgical prayer, since it is "an action of Christ the priest and of His Body which is the Church, is a sacred action surpassing all others; no other action of the Church can equal its efficacy."[470] Thus, we should fully, consciously and actively participate in the liturgy. We should understand the sacred rites, saturate ourselves in the spirit of the different seasons of the liturgical year, know the richness hidden in the Catholic liturgy and defend it. In one word, we should value the liturgy and make it the first priority in our life of piety.

Liturgical prayer—the Holy Mass, the Sacraments, the Divine Office, Liturgical Chant, etc—is the prayer of the whole Church who, even now from earth, takes part in the celestial liturgy: "We have such a high priest, one who is seated at the right hand of the throne of the Majesty in heaven" (*Heb* 8:1). It is through the liturgy that the Holy Spirit speaks, in some way, throughout the Church: "The Spirit helps us in our weakness; for we do not know how to pray as we ought" (*Rom* 8:26). Furthermore, Christ himself, High and Eternal priest, gives his Church the guarantee she will be heard: "If you ask anything of the Father, he will give it to you in my name" (*Jn* 16:23).

3. THE THEOLOGICAL VIRTUES

"One enters into prayer as one enters into liturgy: by the narrow gate of *faith*. Through the signs of his presence, it is the Face of the Lord that we seek and desire; it is his Word that we want to hear and keep.

---

[468] Cf. SAINT AUGUSTINE. *In Ioannis Evangelium Tractatus*. 6, 7.
[469] SAINT JEROME. Nn. 1.2: CCL 731-3. (Editorial translation)
[470] II VATICAN COUNCIL. *Sacrosanctum Concilium*. 7.

The Holy Spirit, who instructs us to celebrate the liturgy in expectation of Christ's return, teaches us to pray in *hope*... 'I waited patiently for the Lord; he inclined to me and heard my cry'...

'Hope does not disappoint us, because God's *love* has been poured into our hearts by the Holy Spirit who has been given to us.' Prayer, formed by the liturgical life, draws everything into the love by which we are loved in Christ and which enables us to respond to him by loving as he has loved us. Love is the source of prayer; whoever draws from it reaches the summit of prayer. In the words of the Curé of Ars:

'I love you, O my God, and my only desire is to love you until the last breath of my life. I love you, O my infinitely lovable God, and I would rather die loving you, than live without loving you. I love you, Lord, and the only grace I ask is to love you eternally.... My God, if my tongue cannot say in every moment that I love you, I want my heart to repeat it to you as often as I draw breath.'"[471]

2. THE WAY OF PRAYER

"Prayer is primarily addressed to the Father; it can also be directed toward Jesus, particularly by the invocation of his holy name: 'Lord Jesus Christ, Son of God, have mercy on us sinners.'

'No one can say 'Jesus is Lord,' except by the Holy Spirit' (*1 Cor* 12:3). The Church invites us to invoke the Holy Spirit as the interior Teacher of Christian prayer.

Because of Mary's singular cooperation with the action of the Holy Spirit, the Church loves to pray in communion with the Virgin Mary, to magnify with her the great things the Lord has done for her, and to entrust supplications and praises to her."[472]

---

[471] *Catechism of the Catholic Church*. 2656-2658.
[472] *Catechism of the Catholic Church*. 2680-2682.

3. TEACHERS AND PLACES OF PRAYER

"In prayer, the pilgrim Church is associated with that of the saints, whose intercession she asks.

The different schools of Christian spirituality share in the living tradition of prayer and are precious guides for the spiritual life.

The Christian family is the first place for education in prayer.

Ordained ministers, the consecrated life, catechesis, prayer groups, and 'spiritual direction' ensure assistance within the Church in the practice of prayer.

The most appropriate places for prayer are personal or family oratories, monasteries, places of pilgrimage, and above all the church, which is the proper place for liturgical prayer for the parish community and the privileged place for Eucharistic adoration."[473]

> "The true centers of the world and of the history of salvation are not the active capitals of politics and economics, of money and worldly power. The authentic centers of history are the silent places of prayer, where men gather to pray. In these places, the encounter of this world with the celestial world, of the pilgrim Church on earth with the eternal and triumphant Church in heaven, are carried out in a particularly intensive way. In these places of prayer, something greater and more decisive takes place for the life and death of the great capitals, places believed to be the heartbeat of time and the center where the history of the world revolves around."
>
> *John Paul II*
> *Act of Entrustment of Germany to the Virgin of Kevelaer*
> *May 2, 1987*
> *(Editorial translation)*

---

[473] *Catechism of the Catholic Church.* 2692-2696.

CHAPTER THREE
THE LIFE OF PRAYER

1. EXPRESSIONS OF PRAYER

In order to help us understand the necessity of a life of prayer for a Christian, Saint Gregory the Nazianzen declared that "we ought to think of God even more often than we draw our breath."[474]

"The Church invites the faithful to regular prayer: daily prayers, the Liturgy of the Hours, Sunday Eucharist, the feasts of the liturgical year.

The Christian tradition comprises three major expressions of the life of prayer: vocal prayer, meditation, and contemplative prayer. They have in common the recollection of the heart."[475]

2. LEVELS OF PRAYER

Progress in prayer coincides with the advancement of the soul along the path of holiness. Holiness consists in the union of the soul with God by love. Prayer is the fruit which springs from the love of God. The more you love, the more you pray.

The Christian life, like all life, tends to its development. The seed of eternal life deposited in our souls at Baptism—grace, virtues, and gifts—carries in itself a power for growth which only ceases when it blooms in the fullness of glory, in heaven. Therefore, grace is the prelude to eternal life; it is eternal life already begun. The life of holiness, which is born at Baptism and culminates in heaven, has different levels according to the level of intensity of the love for God manifested in that life. Since this intensity of love is manifested principally in prayer—the one who loves wants to be in communication with the beloved—we can know the level of virtue of a person based on the level of prayer in their life.

---

[474] SAINT GREGORY THE NAZIANZEN, *Orations* 27, 5.
[475] *Catechism of the Catholic Church.* 2720-2721.

Christian life is essentially one—because one is the grace, which is the essence of Christian life. However, Christian life has two fundamental stages. In the first stage, man's reason illumined by faith plays the dominant role. This stage is called **ascetic** because in it, man makes an active effort to reach perfection and the exercise of the supernatural virtues (although the gifts of the Holy Spirit are also active in this stage). In the second stage, called **mystical**, the Holy Spirit plays the primary role by means of his seven gifts. In this stage, man has a more passive role. In other words, man allows God to work in his soul. In both stages, man—with the help of grace—performs acts that are truly supernatural. In the first stage, these acts are human, containing imperfections. On the other hand, in the second stage, these acts are divine: perfect. Let us take a look at an example in order to clarify what we have mentioned. Imagine our souls as harps containing many strings which represent supernatural virtues. When we pluck the strings ourselves, we are in the predominantly ascetic stage. When the strings are plucked by the Holy Spirit, we are in the predominately mystical stage.

Let us analyze these stages in greater detail by taking into account how they are expressed in the different levels of prayer.

1. THE PREDOMINANTLY ASCETIC STAGE

Level One: Vocal Prayer

Vocal prayer is prayer expressed with words pronounced with attention and piety. "If a person does not think Whom he is addressing, and what he is asking for, and who it is that is asking and of Whom he is asking it, I do not consider that he is praying at all even though he be constantly moving his lips."[476] In a certain way, everything done in the grace of God is prayer, as Saint Paul said: "So, whether you eat or drink, or whatever you do, do all to the glory of God" (*1 Cor* 10:31). In this way, prayer should be continuous, unceasing, uninterrupted: "Pray constantly"

---

[476] SAINT TERESA OF AVILA. *Interior Castle*. Trans. and Ed. E. Allison Peers. New York: Doubleday, 1961. First Mansion, Ch. I, p. 32.

(*1 Thess* 5:17). "They ought always to pray" (*Lk* 18:1) and "in every place" (*1 Tim* 2:8).

However, the ordering of all our activities to the glory of God is only prayer in a general sense. God also asks us to pray in a more strict sense. This prayer cannot be unceasing because other obligations call for our attention. However, it should last for as long as it is appropriate and useful for rousing up our internal fervor and not any longer. When Jesus tells us we should go into our room and "shut the door and pray...in secret" (*Mt* 6:6), he is not prohibiting us from praying publicly. What Jesus does not want is that we pray in order that men might praise us instead of praying for the glory of God. Likewise, when Jesus teaches: "In praying do not heap up empty phrases as the Gentiles do; for they think that they will be heard for their many words" (*Mt* 6:7), he is not prohibiting us from praying a lot, but from babbling. The Lord himself gave us an example of prolonged prayer when he spent entire nights in prayer.[477] "For in most cases prayer consists more in groaning than in speaking, in tears rather than in words."[478] It is not necessary to use already constructed formulas in order to speak with God; rather, it is fitting to speak to God in a simple manner, just as how a small child speaks with his father.

a) As far as the formulas for vocal prayer go, the best ones are the ones used by the Church: the Our Father,[479] the Hail Mary,[480] the Glory Be, the prayers of the Mass, and the Sign of the Cross,[481] etc.

b) Other prayers we should pray often are:[482]

---

[477] Cf. *Lk* 6:12.
[478] SAINT AUGUSTINE. *Letter 130.* X, 20.
[479] Cf. the Our Father is found on page 21.
[480] Cf. the Hail Mary is found on page 21.
[481] Cf. the Glory Be is found on page 286.
[482] Prayers taken from the *Compendium of the Catechism of the Catholic Church.*

1. The Hail Holy Queen

Hail Holy Queen, Mother of Mercy, our life, our sweetness and our hope. To thee do we cry poor banished children of Eve. To thee do we send up our sighs, mourning and weeping in this valley of tears. Turn then, most gracious advocate, thine eyes of mercy toward us and after this our exile, show unto us the blessed fruit of thy womb, Jesus. O clement, O loving, O sweet Virgin Mary. Pray for us O Holy Mother of God, that we may be made worthy of the promises of Christ. Amen.

2. The Glory Be

Glory be to the Father, and to the Son and to the Holy Spirit as it was in the beginning, is now and ever shall be world without end. Amen.

3. The Invocation to the Holy Spirit

Come, Holy Spirit, fill the hearts of Thy faithful and enkindle in them the fire of Thy love. Send forth Thy Spirit and they shall be created. And Thou shall renew the face of the earth.

Let us pray: O God, Who by the light of the Holy Spirit, did instruct the hearts of Thy faithful, grant that by that same Holy Spirit, we may be truly wise and ever rejoice in His consolation, through Christ our Lord. Amen.

4. The Act of Faith

O my God, I firmly believe that Thou art one God in three divine Persons, Father, Son, and Holy Spirit; I believe that Thy divine Son became man and died for our sins, and that He shall come to judge the living and the dead. I believe these and all the truths that the holy Catholic Church teaches, because Thou hast revealed them, Who canst neither deceive nor be deceived. Amen.

5. The Act of Hope

O my God, relying on Thy almighty power and infinite mercy and promises, I hope to obtain pardon of my sins, the help of Thy grace, and life everlasting, through the merits of Jesus Christ, my Lord and Redeemer. Amen.

6. The Act of Love

O my God, I love Thee above all things, with my whole heart and soul, because Thou art all-good and worthy of all love. I love my neighbor as myself for the love of Thee. I forgive all who have injured me, and ask pardon of all whom I have injured. Amen.

7. The Acts of Contrition[483]

O my God, I am heartily sorry for having offended Thee, and I detest all my sins, because of Thy just punishments, but most of all because they offend Thee, my God, Who are all-good and deserving of all my love. I firmly resolve, with the help of Thy grace, to sin no more and to avoid the near occasions of sin.

My God, I am sorry for my sins with all my heart. In choosing to do wrong and failing to do good, I have sinned against Thee whom I should love above all things. I firmly intend, with Thy help, to do penance, to sin no more, and to avoid whatever leads me to sin. Our Savior Jesus Christ suffered and died for us. In His name, my God, have mercy.

O my God, I am heartily sorry for having offended Thee, and I detest all my sins, because I dread the loss of Heaven and the pains of Hell, but most of all because they offend Thee, my God, Who art all good and deserving of all my love. I firmly resolve, with the help of Thy grace to confess my sins, to do penance and to amend my life. Amen.

Level Two: Meditation

Meditation consists in reflecting on a certain truth of our faith, penetrating it, loving it, and trying to practice it. The vast majority of sinners live in sin because of a lack of reflection: "The whole land is made desolate, but no man lays it to heart" (*Jer* 12:11).

Meditation is conducive for salvation and absolutely essential for the soul that desires holiness.

The methods of meditation are very useful. Just as the lines in a notebook help us to write neatly, these different methods help us to learn how to meditate in an appropriate and orderly way.

We can think of meditation as a conversation: 1) we make the introductions; 2) we talk about the main topic of conversation;

---

[483] Listed are three versions of the Act of Contrition.

and 3) we allow our hearts to speak, making acts of thanksgiving, etc.

1. Preparation:

-We must adore God who is present.

-We must tell him that everything we do during this time of prayer will be for his glory and not our own.

-Imagine something in reference to what we will meditate.

-Ask the Lord for the grace proper to the meditation we are going to do.

2. The body of the meditation:

-We must bring to mind the object or topic we have chosen to meditate on, along with all its circumstances.

-We must then use our intellect to consider and reflect on each one of the aspects of the truth being meditated upon, remaining on each point until the soul is satisfied. We must be like a bee on a flower, extracting all the supernatural nectar from the truths we mediate; not like a butterfly, who passes over these truths superficially.

-Finally, we must employ the will to consent to the truths meditated upon and to the proposal of practical goals. We must allow our heart, which has been filled with God, to expand in affection.

3. Conclusion:

-This is perhaps the most important part of the meditation: the colloquy or conversation. Sometimes, we can begin directly with the conversation, without going through the "body" of the meditation. The colloquy can be done with God the Father, with Jesus Christ, with the Most Holy Virgin, with a particular saint, with all of them, etc. "The colloquy is made by speaking exactly as one friend speaks to another, or as a servant speaks to a master, now asking him for a favor, now blaming himself for some misdeed, now making known his affairs to him, and seeking advice in them."[484] Saint Teresa would say: "the important thing is not to think much, but to love much."[485]

Level Three: Affective Prayer

In affective prayer, more importance is given to the affections of the will than the reflection of the intellect. It is a simplified meditation and directed to the heart.

Advice for practicing this prayer:

-Do not stop reflection except when it produces affection;

-Do not force affections. If they disappear, go back to reflection;

-Do not hurry from one affection to another;

-Try to simplify your affections so that they gain intensity;

-Remember that affections reside principally in the will and not in sensibility.

Level Four: Prayer of Simplicity

This kind of prayer is a simple look, attention or loving gaze toward God or the things of God. One day, the Curé d'Ars, upon seeing a parishioner who spent many hours before the Tabernacle, asked him what he did during all that time. The parishioner answered him saying: "I look at him and he looks at me."[486]

This level of prayer can be summed up in looking and loving.

Practical advice:

-Do not go ahead of yourself, attempting to arrive at this type of prayer ahead of time;

-Do not remain in meditative prayer if you feel drawn to the loving gaze of God;

[484] LOUIS J. PUHL, S.J. *The Spiritual Exercises of St. Ignatius.* 54.
[485] SAINT TERESA OF AVILA. *Interior Castle.* Fourth Mansion, Ch. I, p. 76.
[486] *Catechism of the Catholic Church.* 2715.

-Attain this attention to God without violence and with gentleness; but by fighting against distractions and stupefactions;

-Do not be frightened by dryness and aridity.

We will have proof that the prayer we are doing is pleasing God if we notice a progress in all virtues, especially in love of the cross.

2. THE PREDOMINANTLY MYSTICAL STAGE

All baptized peoples are called, remotely and sufficiently, to mystical prayer. All Christians are called to such a state because "the Holy Spirit…has been given to us" (*Rom* 5:5), along with his seven gifts.

Just as Jesus calls us to a high level of holiness, "be perfect, as your heavenly Father is perfect" (*Mt* 5:48), he also calls us to a high level of prayer.

Mystical prayer is absolutely normal in the Christian life.

It is not an extraordinary charism, like the performance of miracles or prophesying; nor is it something reserved only for religious in the contemplative life. Rather, it is the normal development of the life of grace we all can and should try to attain. It is a superior stage to the same and unique supernatural life we were given at Baptism. At this stage, prayer is known as infused contemplation. The Holy Spirit grants the grace of infused prayer when and how he desires to: "It depends not upon man's will or exertion, but upon God's mercy" (*Rom* 9:16). However, it is up to us to have a disposition which allows the Holy Spirit to act: with a growing purity of intention, simplicity of spirit, humility of heart, deep recollection, practice of the virtues, perseverance in prayer, filial devotion to the Virgin and great love for the cross. Saint Paul of the Cross said: "How does a soul prepare itself for infused prayer? Being a gratuitous gift of God, one cannot pretend to lead the soul to it by force. All the care of the teacher consists in elevating it to infused prayer through a great habit of virtue and true humility of heart, of knowledge of its own nothingness, of despising itself, of true blind obedience— helping it conceive the great love for this virtue at all cost—of true and perfect abnegation of its own will in everything, and of personal mortification in its own inclinations, sympathies and antipathies. These are the fundamental virtues for the spiritual edifice and for obtaining the gift of holy prayer and union with God: otherwise, one builds on sand."[487]

CONTEMPLATION: The next levels of prayer

What does contemplation consist of? Let us leave the answer to the saints who experienced it:

-"it is a delicious admiration of the resplendent truth;"[488]

-"it is a holy intoxication that separates the soul from the caducity of temporal things;"[489] "it is an anticipation of the sweet eternal joys;"[490]

-it "regards the simple act of gazing on the truth" which "terminates in the affections;"[491]

-it is "a science of love, which...is an infused loving knowledge that both illumines and enamors the soul, elevating it step by step to God, its Creator;"[492]

-"contemplation is no other thing than a loving, simple and permanent attention of the spirit to divine things;"[493] "a perception of God...proceeding from love, and tending to love."[494]

In contemplative prayer different levels also exist, which are:

Level Five: Infused Recollection

It is "a certain interior recollection of which the soul is sensible;...thus the soul, withdrawing into itself, seeks to go away from the tumult of its outward senses, and accordingly it drags them away with itself; for it closes the eyes on purpose that it may

---

[487] Letter dated October 24, 1764. (Editorial translation)

[488] Cf. RIBET. *La mystique divine.* t. I, p. I, c. I. (Editorial translation)

[489] Author of *De Spiritu Santo et Anima* (c. 32), attributed to SAINT AUGUSTINE. (Editorial translation)

[490] Author of *Scala Claustralium* (c. I), attributed to SAINT BERNARD. (Editorial translation)

[491] Cf. SAINT THOMAS AQUINAS. *Summa Theologica.* II-II, 180, 3, ad. 1 and ad. 3.

[492] "Dark Night of the Soul." *The Collected Works of St. John of the Cross.* II, XVIII, 5.

[493] SAINT FRANCIS DE SALES. *Treatise on the Love of God.* VI, 3.

[494] FATHER LUIS LALLEMANT. *La doctrine spirituelle Princ.* 7 c. 4 a. 5. (Editorial translation)

neither see, nor hear, nor understand anything but that whereon the soul is then intent, which is to be able to converse with God alone."[495]

Level Six: Prayer of Quiet

This prayer is an interior experience of the presence of God which captivates the intellect and the will, and, at the same time, fills the soul and the body with a truly ineffable sweetness and delight.

Level Seven: Simple Union

This level of prayer is practiced when all of the interior potencies are captivated and occupied in God. It is not only the intellect and the will; but also the memory and the imagination.

Level Eight: Ecstatic Union or Spiritual Betrothal

One arrives at this sublime level when not only are the potencies of the soul and the interior senses suspended in God, but when the exterior physical senses are intimately united with God.

Level Nine: Transforming Union or Spiritual Marriage

"For it is a total transformation in the Beloved; in which each surrenders the entire possession of self to the other with a certain consummation of the union of love. The soul thereby becomes divine, God through participation, insofar as is possible in this life."[496]

We believe that it is very important that you know all of the marvelous unfolding of the divine life, from Baptism to spiritual marriage, in order that your flight be that of an eagle and not of a chicken. Christ did not come to earth to bring us a rickety, narrow and sterile life; but rather Christ came in order that we might "have life, and have it abundantly" (*Jn* 10:10). Be eagles and not chickens!

---

[495] *The Autobiography of St. Teresa of Avila*. Relation VIII, 3.
[496] "The Spiritual Canticle." *The Collected Works of St. John of the Cross*. XXII, 3.

3. THE BATTLE OF PRAYER: DIFFICULTIES

There are two principle difficulties often met in prayer: distractions and dryness or aridity.

a) **Distractions** are images or thoughts foreign to prayer which impede us from giving it the required attention.

These distractions can be voluntary or involuntary. We commit a fault only if they are voluntary. If they are involuntary, it is enough to, once noticed, peacefully return to rectify our intention ("Lord, I only want to adore you") and patiently persevere in prayer. Even if one is involuntarily distracted many times, if he remains firm in prayer, always returning to the intention to pray, his prayer is worth much because, in addition to being a prayer, it is a true penance offered to God.

b) **Dryness or aridity** is a certain discouragement in prayer; a type of sensation which the soul experiences as if it were talking to a wall, along with the impression that it will obtain as much fruit as it would from watering a rock. It is as if God made himself deaf, or as if, still worse, he refused to help us. Saint María Josefa Rosello characterized this state very well by saying it was "like chewing tow."[497] If this dryness is prolonged for a long time and it cannot be attributed to natural causes (such as physical fatigue, a lack of formation, or lukewarmness in the service of God), then it is a test from God who takes away consolations and sensible devotion in order that we might not attach ourselves to them, but to him. Our disposition should be that of Saint Therese of the Child Jesus: "God will tire of testing me before I stop placing my confidence in Him."[498]

Instead of shortening prayer, we must lengthen it, making even greater sacrifices.

The state of aridity often coincides with diverse and bothersome temptations of all kinds. For example, the inclination to blaspheme, to commit a sacrilege or impurity, etc.

---

[497] MONS. LUIS TRAVERSO. *Vida y virtudes de la Santa María Josefa Rosello*. Buenos Aires, 1959. p. 205. (Editorial translation); *tow* is the coarsest part of hemp and flax.

[498] Letter 1. (Editorial translation)

Consequently, it deals with a coinciding temptation from the devil who tries to attack us and stop us from reaching a state of greater perfection to which, without a doubt, God desires to take us by means of the cross. If we, with the help of the grace of God, resist these temptations without looking for human consolations, divine consolations will abundantly rain down upon us, since "the calm comes after the storm." The just one lives by faith, not by what the body feels. We must persist in prayer even if it be "against the flesh."[499]

> "Truly, by means of prayer and the intercession of Mary, Mother of Jesus, the grace of Jesus Christ inundates your heart and gives you strength to stand firm in your Christian vocation, which consists in following Christ, accepting his path, living by his word and applying the Gospel to all the real circumstances of daily life."
>
> *John Paul II*
> *To youth in Wales and England*
> *September 4, 1983*
> *(Editorial translation)*

---

[499] Cf. LOUIS J. PUHL, S.J. *The Spiritual Exercises of St. Ignatius.* 313-336.

SECTION TWO
THE PRAYER OF THE LORD:
THE "OUR FATHER"

"I want you to realize the great opposition which exists...in order that you may confront, with realism and confidence, the challenge presented to you by being Christian young people in the world of today. Being that there is 'great opposition,' you must use the necessary means in order to remain firm and persevere. You must pray. You must pray daily. You must pray alone with God and also with each other. You must pray in union with our Lord Jesus Christ especially on Sundays, each Sunday, by taking part in the Eucharistic offering of Jesus to his Father. You must invoke the power of his death and resurrection, a power he is capable of manifesting when you ask him using these simple words: 'Give us this day our daily bread...deliver us from evil.'"

John Paul II
To youth in Wales and England
September 4, 1983
(Editorial translation)

THE "OUR FATHER"

The Our Father is the most perfect prayer, composed by Jesus himself.[500] It contains all we must ask for and the order we must ask for it. Its introduction, "Our Father, who art in heaven," becomes a background accompanying the entire prayer.

"Father:" to rouse our confidence in him, remembering his love, his gentleness, and his care for us, his children.

"Father:" not a cruel person who takes joy in punishing us; not a tyrant who enslaves us; not a jailer who tortures us; not a usurer who takes without giving; not a merchant who calculates...but a "Father," with a capital F.

"Our Father...:" not only my father since we are all brothers and sisters and we must love each other with charitable love.

"Who art in heaven...:" we express God's transcendence, majesty and the power he has to do good for us and to give us what we ask of him.

After this introduction, the petitions begin. There are seven:

1) "Hallowed be thy name." We ask for the glorification of God, who is our ultimate end, loving God as he is in himself. We ask that his name be sanctified by all peoples, which is to say, that all men may glorify God, acknowledge his holiness, and propagate his glory to all of humanity.

This is what Saint Ignatius of Loyola desired: to do everything "for the greater glory of God."[501] It is the summit of Christian perfection: "only the honor and glory of God dwells on this mount."[502]

2) "Thy kingdom come." We ask that we might reach the glory of God's Kingdom, which is the end of our Christian life. We ask

---

[500] Cf. *Mt* 6:9.

[501] The motto of the shield of the Society of Jesus: *Ad Maiorem Dei Gloriam.*

[502] Phrase St. John of the Cross placed at the top of his drawing of Mount Carmel, the summit of the mount of holiness. Taken from SAINT JOHN OF THE CROSS. "The Ascent to Mount Carmel." *The Collected Works of St. John of the Cross.* p. 111.

that we might enjoy the glory of God, loving one another in him, rousing up in us the desire for the Kingdom. We ask for the grace of God, which is the next greatest thing we could ask for after the glory of God. We also ask that he would come to reign in fullness by his Second Coming.

After teaching us to desire and ask for the supernatural ultimate end, the primary end (the glory of God) as well as the secondary end (our own sanctification), Jesus teaches us to desire and ask for the means which directly enable us to reach this end.

3) "Thy will be done, on earth as it is in heaven." This is the direct and primordial mean for reaching the end: fulfilling the commandments of the law of God, which is to obey God, submitting ourselves to his will. Furthermore, our obedience must be as perfect as that of the angels in heaven. On earth, men's obedience to God must be like a reflection of the obedience of the angels and the saints in heaven.

4) "Give us this day our daily bread." This is a direct, although secondary, means for reaching our end. It refers to everything that can help us to merit eternal life.

We can understand "bread" as the Eucharist (and with it the rest of the sacraments) and also as "material bread" (and with it everything necessary for life). We ask for the direct, although secondary, means to reach the end.

Next, the Lord teaches us to ask for the indirect means to get to heaven, which implies the removal of obstacles which could impede us from reaching heaven. There are three obstacles:

5) "Forgive us our trespasses, as we forgive those who trespass against us." The first and the principal obstacle which directly excludes us from the Kingdom of Heaven is sin. In order for God to forgive us, we must wholeheartedly forgive those who have offended us.

6) "Do not let us fall into temptation." The second obstacle is temptation, which is like the antechamber of sin and it can keep us from fulfilling the will of God. We do not ask to be free from temptations, but to not be conquered by them.

7) "But deliver us from evil." The last obstacle is made up by the rest of the calamities and sufferings of life which can disturb our soul. We especially ask to be free from "the evil one," Satan, who tirelessly seeks to separate us from God.

Let us always pray the prayer Jesus taught us. In its few words "are enshrined all contemplation and perfection."[503]

> "But in order to do this [to build a civilization based on love] you need God's help. And God's help comes to you through prayer. Your union with Christ will be the secret of your effectiveness, and it is strengthened by your prayer, your conversation with God, the lifting up of your heart to him. But Jesus has also provided for your needs through the Sacraments of the Church, particularly the Eucharist and the Sacrament of Penance. The conversion of your hearts is brought about by Christ's action and Christ reaches out to you in his Sacraments, which will always be for you an expression and celebration of your faith and your life in Christ."
>
> *John Paul II*
> *To the youth of Newfoundland (Canada)*
> *September 12, 1984*

---

[503] SAINT TERESA OF AVILA. *The Way of Perfection.* Trans. and Ed. E. Allison Peers. New York: Doubleday, 1964. XXXVII, I; cf. 42, 5.

EPILOGUE

Dearest youth:

Here we must say goodbye. I pray to God and to his Holy Mother that you have listened carefully to the call of God, who has called us through his grace (cf. *Gal* 1:15), "to be saints" (*1 Cor* 1:2; cf. *Rom* 1:7). This is why "he chose us in him before the foundation of the world, that we should be holy and blameless before him" (*Eph* 1:4).

God wants all of us to become saints, without exceptions: priests and laity, men and women, the ignorant and the wise, the rich and the poor, the youth and the adults, the weak and the powerful...everyone. "For this is the will of God, your sanctification" (*1 Thess* 4:3). "Be holy, for I am holy" (*Lev* 11:44), since "God has not called us for uncleanness, but in holiness" (*1 Thess* 4:7).

God does not call us to just any "holiness," for example the holiness of the hypocrites; but to a Christian holiness. God calls us to a holiness that consists in the participation in the life of Jesus Christ; a holiness he reveals to us by his examples and teaches us by his Words. We have been "called to belong to Jesus Christ" (*Rom* 1:6), "in the grace of Christ" (*Gal* 1:6). In other words, holiness consists in fully imitating Jesus Christ, in perfectly carrying out the Will of God, and in uniting oneself to God by love—all which are ways of saying the same thing.

God calls us to supernatural holiness, a holiness superior to the strength of our nature. This is why Jesus tells us: "Apart from me you can do nothing" (*Jn* 15:5). Note that Jesus does not say that we can do little, or a lot, but nothing. We cannot do anything in the supernatural order without the grace of Christ. Our holiness is not like God's holiness which flows from his own nature. Rather, our holiness is a participation in God's holiness and it infinitely exceeds all of our appetites and desires. This holiness is gratuitous; God gives it to us because he desires to:

"Not that we are sufficient of ourselves to claim anything as coming from us; our sufficiency is from God" (*2 Cor* 3:5).

God calls us to a holiness of expiation, proper to our state as creatures who have fallen into sin. It is not like the holiness God required of our first parents, who were "created in justice and holiness." We are born in sin and, even after Baptism, we are more inclined to evil than to good. Our holiness is a holiness of redeemed sinners. We must fight against disordered passions; we must go by way of the cross; we must mortify ourselves, loving poverty, humiliation and pain. Nor is this the holiness of heaven; there the blessed cannot sin. Here, we still have to fight against the devil, "against the spiritual hosts of wickedness" (*Eph* 6:12), and against the evil world, "if they persecuted me, they will persecute you" (*Jn* 15:20). This is why we must work out our salvation "with fear and trembling" (*Phil* 2:12). Saint Paul said: "I pommel my body and subdue it, lest after preaching to others I myself should be disqualified" (*1 Cor* 9:27). Moreover, Jesus himself taught that "unless you repent you will all likewise perish" (*Lk* 13:3). Ours is a holiness of expiation. "The sinners must work as saints."[504]

God calls us to a great holiness: "Be perfect, as your heavenly Father is perfect" (*Mt* 5:48). The reason few reach great holiness is "not that God wishes only a few of these spirits to be so elevated; he would rather want all to be perfect, but he finds few vessels that will endure so lofty and sublime a work."[505] "Remember, the Lord invites us all; and, since He is Truth Itself, we cannot doubt Him."[506] We must not be content with the flight of a chicken, but we must long to fly like eagles. We must not let ourselves be overwhelmed by difficulties, since "God is faithful, and he will not let you be tempted beyond your strength, but with the temptation will also provide the way of escape, that you may be able to endure it" (*1 Cor* 10:13). Our spirit must not fall due to the harshness of the fight which "in your struggle

---

[504] G. K. CHESTERTON, *La hostería volante*. VI. (Editorial translation)
[505] SAINT JOHN OF THE CROSS. "The Living Flame of Love." *The Collected Works of St. John of the Cross*. Stanza 2, 27.
[506] SAINT TERESA OF AVILA. *The Way of Perfection*. XIX, p. 145.

against sin you have not yet resisted to the point of shedding your blood" (*Heb* 12:4). "The kingdom of heaven has suffered violence, and men of violence take it by force" (*Mt* 11:12). "We are small, but we can transform ourselves into great souls. The saints always elevated themselves to supreme heights."[507]

God calls you and me, in particular, by first and last name: "I live by faith in the Son of God, who loved me and gave himself for me" (*Gal* 2:20); and he calls us now, in the present moment: "Now is the acceptable time; behold, now is the day of salvation" (*2 Cor* 6:2), "the appointed time has grown very short" (*1 Cor* 7:29). He calls you, now, even if you were the only person in the world trying to perfect yourself. Since it is God who calls and since God calls who he wants, you must answer him: "Lord, what do you want me to do?" (cf. *Acts* 9:10). "Here I am...Speak, Lord, for your servant hears" (*1 Sam* 3:5). Do not leave for tomorrow what you can do today.

The plan God has in mind from all of eternity and which is unwaveringly fulfilled in time is that everything, absolutely everything, is ordered for the good of the chosen ones, which concurs with the profit of the saints. "In everything God works for good with those who love him, who are called according to his purpose" (*Rom* 8:28). God, who governs all things, arranges all things toward his saints. Saint Paul has a very beautiful text which can serve as a golden clasp for our Catechism. Addressing the faithful in Corinth and exhorting them to holiness, he says: "For all things are yours, whether Paul or Apollos or Cephas or the world or life or death or the present or the future, all are yours; and you are Christ's; and Christ is God's" (*1 Cor* 3:21-23).

"For all things are yours, whether Paul or Apollos or Cephas," which is to say, the members of Christ, including the Roman Pontiff; since, the faithful are not for the Apostles, but the Apostles for the faithful. The world, life, death, the present, the future are all directed by God and ordered for his saints: "the world," which serves to satisfy the needs of the faithful and helps

---

507 CARDINAL JOSEPH MINDSZENTY. *Memoirs*. (Editorial translation)

them to know God; "life or death," which is to say, all the good and evil of this world; "the present," which we can use to gain merit; "the future," which is reserved for us as a reward; everything, absolutely everything, even that which seems most non-transcendent. Since everything the saints do, they do for Christ "and you are Christ's," and Christ, as man, orders all things to God, all things are yours. You are Christ's and Christ is God's.

O Mary, Mother and Queen of all the Saints, help us! Reproduce in us the image of your Son.

May we not be deaf to Christ's call, because the only sadness is to not become saints. May his will be done.

Onward! Always onward! Hail Mary and onward!

APPENDICES

APENDIX A:
TO BE MEMORIZED

PART ONE:
WHAT WE MUST BELIEVE

1) *What prayer summarizes what we must believe and say?*

What we must believe is summarized in the Creed and it says: see page 16.

2) *What is God?*

God is the being infinite in all perfection, creator of heaven and earth, who rewards those who are good and punishes those who are evil.

3) *What does infinite in all perfection mean?*

It means that he is the most excellent and admirable being that we could describe or think of, who contains all perfections: goodness, wisdom, power, justice, and love without measure.

4) *Who is God?*

God is Father, he is Son and he is Holy Spirit; three distinct persons in one true God.

5) *Are the persons of the Most Holy Trinity the same?*

No. We confess the uniqueness of the persons: The Father is the Father, he is neither the Son nor the Holy Spirit; the Son is the Son, he is neither the Father nor the Holy Spirit; the Holy Spirit is the Holy Spirit, he is neither the Father nor the Son.

6) *Is there a lack of union in the essence of the Most Holy Trinity?*

No. We confess unity in the essence: the Father is God, the Son is God, and the Holy Spirit is God. They are not three Gods, but only one God.

7) *Is there inequality of majesty in the Most Holy Trinity?*

No. We confess the equality in majesty. The Father is just as much God as the Son is and the Holy Spirit is; the Son is just as much God as the Father is and the Holy Spirit is; the Holy Spirit is just as much God as the Father is and the Son is.

8) *Where is the Most Holy Trinity?*

The Most Holy Trinity is in heaven, on earth, and everywhere.

9) *Do the Father, the Son and the Holy Spirit see everything?*

The Father, the Son and the Holy Spirit do see everything, even our thoughts.

10) *Why is God Creator?*

God is Creator because he has made everything out of nothing, including the angels and men.

11) *What are angels?*

Angels are purely spiritual beings, gifted with intelligence and will.

12) *Why did God create men?*

God created men in order that they might know him, love him, and serve him in this life so as to enjoy God in heaven.

13) *What did our first parents do?*

Our first parents sinned by disobeying God. When they sinned, our first parents and their descendants were deprived of sanctifying grace.

14) *Is it possible to pull ourselves out of sin by our own strength?*

No. It is impossible to pull ourselves out of sin. We need God to give us his grace in order to be freed from sin.

15) *Who is the Savior who saves us from our sins?*

The Savior who saves us from our sins is our Lord Jesus Christ.

16) *Who is our Lord Jesus Christ?*

Our Lord Jesus Christ is the Second Person of the Most Holy Trinity who became man.

17) *How many natures and persons are there in Jesus Christ?*

In Jesus there are two natures: the divine and the human. Only one person, the divine person, unites both natures.

18) *Who are the Father and Mother of Jesus Christ?*

The Father of Jesus Christ is the Eternal Father, the First Person of the Most Holy Trinity. The Mother of Jesus Christ is the Blessed Virgin Mary.

19) *Why did Jesus Christ die on the cross?*

Jesus Christ died on the cross in order to save us from sin and its consequences, and to give back the sanctifying grace we had lost.

20) *What did Jesus Christ do in order for salvation to reach us?*

In order that salvation would reach us, Jesus Christ founded the one true Roman Catholic Apostolic Church, granting her the sacraments through which he communicates sanctifying grace to us.

21) *What is the holy Catholic Church?*

The holy Catholic Church is the Mystical Body of Christ, formed by the Pope, the bishops, priests, and faithful, who have the mission of continuing the work of Christ, glorifying God and saving man.

22) *Who is the head of the Church founded by Jesus Christ?*

The Church founded by Jesus Christ has Christ himself as its invisible head. The visible head is the Pope, the successor of Saint Peter.

23) *What are the four marks of the Church founded by Jesus Christ?*

The Church founded by Jesus Christ is One, Holy, Catholic and Apostolic.

24) *What gives life to the Catholic Church?*

The life that vivifies the Catholic Church is the sanctifying grace that comes from the sacraments worthily received.

25) *Are all Catholics saints?*

All Catholics should be saints. However, by sinning, by our own account, we are separated from the life of the Church. God permits the evil of men in the Church in order that we might unite ourselves to him, that we might win more merit for eternal life and because he respects the freedom of man.

26) *What is sanctifying grace?*

Sanctifying grace is a gift from God that allows us to participate in his divine nature, becoming children of God and, therefore heirs of heaven.

27) *Along with sanctifying grace, what else is given to us?*

Along with sanctifying grace, the theological virtues, the infused moral virtues and the seven gifts of the Holy Spirit are given to us.

PART TWO:
WHAT WE MUST RECEIVE

28) *What things must we receive?*

We must receive sanctifying grace which comes to us by means of the sacraments.

29) *How many sacraments does the Church have and what are they?*

There are seven sacraments of the Church: Baptism, Confirmation, Eucharist, Penance or Confession, Extreme Unction or the Anointing of the Sick, Holy Orders, and Matrimony.

30) *Which is the first and most necessary sacrament?*

The first and most necessary sacrament is holy Baptism, which gives us the grace and the indelible mark of Christians; it makes us become children of God and heirs of heaven.

31) *Why is Baptism so important?*

Baptism is so important because someone who is not baptized cannot receive any other sacrament. Consequently, in a case of necessity, anyone can and must baptize.

32) *In case of necessity, how must one baptize?*

In case of necessity, in order to baptize, you pour water over the head of the person being baptized while saying, with the intention of baptizing: "(Name), I baptize you in the name of the Father, the Son and the Holy Spirit."

33) *What is the Eucharist?*

The Eucharist is the sacrament that really, truly and substantially contains the Body, Blood, Soul and Divinity of our Lord Jesus Christ, under the appearance of bread and wine.

34) *Where does this sacrament take place?*

This sacrament takes place in the Holy Mass. The Holy Mass consists of two parts: 1.) The Liturgy of the Word and 2.) The Liturgy of the Sacrifice. The Liturgy of the Sacrifice is then divided into three main parts: the presentation of the gifts, (the Offertory), the consecration and communion.

35) *What is the host before the consecration?*

Before the consecration, the host is bread.

36) *What is the Host after the consecration?*

After the consecration, the Host is the Body of Jesus Christ, along with his Blood, Soul, and Divinity.

37) *What is there in the chalice before the consecration?*

Before the consecration, there is a bit of wine with some drops of water in the chalice.

38) *What is there in the chalice after the consecration?*

After the consecration, the Blood of Christ, along with his Body, Soul and Divinity, is in the chalice.

39) *After the consecration is there bread in the Host or wine in the chalice?*

No. After the consecration, the substance of the bread and the wine no longer remain, but only their accidents, that is the appearances of bread and wine, such as taste, scent, color, weight, size, and shape.

40) *When does the bread and wine become the Body and Blood of our Lord Jesus Christ?*

The bread and wine become the Body and Blood of our Lord Jesus Christ during the Holy Mass at the moment of the consecration.

41) *What is this conversion of the substance of bread and wine into the Body and Blood of Jesus Christ called?*

This conversion of the substance of bread and wine into the Body and Blood of Jesus Christ is called **transubstantiation**.

42) *In addition to the transubstantiation of the bread and wine, what else happens in the Holy Mass?*

In addition to the transubstantiation of the bread and wine, the Sacrifice of Christ on the cross is perpetuated in the Holy Mass.

43) *Is the Sacrifice of the Mass the same Sacrifice of the Cross?*

Yes, the Sacrifice of the Mass is the same and identical Sacrifice of the Cross because in the Mass, Jesus Christ himself is offered and sacrificed in an unbloody manner, under the species of bread and wine.

44) *What is necessary to make a good communion?*

Three things are necessary to make a good communion:

1- To be in the state of grace of God, which is to be without mortal sin.

2- To fast one hour before receiving communion.

3- To know who we are going to receive and approach communion with devotion.

45) *What is Penance, Confession or Reconciliation?*

Penance, Confession or Reconciliation is the sacrament by which the sins committed after Baptism are forgiven.

46) *What is necessary to make a good confession?*

Five things are necessary to make a good confession:

1- An examination of conscience.

2- Contrition for our sins.

3- Purpose of amendment.

4- To confess all our sins to a priest.

5- To do the penance given by the confessor.

PART THREE:
WHAT WE MUST DO

47) *What must we do?*

We must do everything prescribed for us in the Commandments of the law of God, the precepts of the Church and in the works of mercy.

48) *What are the Commandments, the precepts and the works of mercy, and how many are there?*

The Commandments are 10:

See page 19

The precepts are 5:

See page 20

The works of mercy are 14:

7 Spiritual See page 20

7 Corporal See page 20

49) *What is mortal sin?*

Mortal sin is to think, desire, say, do or knowingly omit something which goes against the law of God in a grave matter. This sin deprives us of sanctifying grace.

50) *What is the punishment deserved for mortal sin?*

The punishment deserved for mortal sin is eternal hell.

51) *How is mortal sin forgiven?*

Mortal sin is forgiven by the Sacrament of Penance. If there is not a priest close by, mortal sin is forgiven by a perfect act of contrition together with the intention of going to confession as soon as possible.

52) *What is venial sin?*

Venial sin is to think, desire, say, do or omit something against the law of God in slight matters.

53) *What is original sin?*

Original sin is the sin that Adam and Eve committed in the beginning of humanity, and which all of their descendants are born with. It is only forgiven by Baptism.

PART FOUR:
WHAT WE MUST PRAY

54) *What is the sign of a Catholic?*

The sign of a Catholic is the Sign of the Cross:

Before beginning prayer, it is suitable to make the Sign of the Cross. It is made upon oneself by bringing the fingers of your right hand toward your forehead, saying "In the name of the Father;" next bring them toward your chest, saying "and the Son" (which traces the vertical beam of the cross); next bring the same hand toward your left and then right shoulder, saying, "and the Holy Spirit" (which traces the horizontal beam of the cross); and, at the end, you say "Amen," which means: "So be it." To make the Sign of the Cross upon yourself is called *blessing oneself.*

55) *What prayer did our Lord Jesus Christ teach us?*

Our Lord Jesus Christ taught us the Our Father: See page 21.

56) *What is the most beautiful praise we can give to the Blessed Virgin Mary?*

The most beautiful praise we can give to the Blessed Virgin Mary is the Hail Mary: See page 21

This is the most beautiful praise because it reminds her of the moment when the Angel Gabriel announced that she was to become the Mother of our Lord Jesus Christ.

APENDIX B:
TO USE THE SACRED SCRIPTURE

CONCRETE MIRACLES OF JESUS

1. COSMIC MIRACLES (9)

	Matthew	Mark	Luke	John
1. Changing water into wine				2:1
2. First miraculous catch of fish			5:1	
3. Calming of a storm	8:23	4:35	8:22	
4. First multiplication of bread	14:13	6:30	9:10	6:1
5. Walking on water	14:22	6:45		6:16
6. Second multiplication of bread	15:32	8:1		
7. Coin found in a fish	17:24			
8. Withering of the cursed fig tree	21:18	11:12		
9. Second miraculous catch of fish				21:1

2. RESURRECTIONS (3)

	Matthew	Mark	Luke	John
10. The son of the widow of Nain			7:11	
11. Jairo's daughter	9:18	5:21	8:40	
12. Lazarus				11:1

3. MIRACULOUS HEALINGS (16)

	Matthew	Mark	Luke	John
13. The son of the courtesan				4:46
14. Peter's mother-in-law	8:14	1:29	4:38	
15. A leper	8:1	1:40	5:12	
16. The paralytic by the pool of Bethsaida.				5:1
17. A paralytic in Capernaum	9:1	2:1	5:17	
18. The man with the withered hand	12:9	3:1	6:6	
19. The paralytic servant of the centurion	8:5		7:1	
20. The crippled woman			13:10	
21. The hemorrhaging woman	9:20	5:25	8:43	
22. Two blind men	9:27			
23. A deaf-mute		7:31		
24. The blind man of Bethsaida		8:22		
25. Ten lepers			17:11	
26. The man blind from birth				9:1
27. Two blind men from Jericho	20:29	10:46	18:35	
28. Malcus' ear			22:50	

4. EXPULSIONS OF DEMONS (7)

	Matthew	Mark	Luke	John
29. A possessed man from Capernaum		1:21	4:31	
30. A blind and mute man with a demon	12:22			
31. The possessed man from Gadarenes	8:28	5:1	8:26	
32. The possessed mute	9:32		11:14	
33. The man with dropsy			14:1	
34. The daughter of the Canaanite woman	15:21	7:24		
35. The possessed lunatic	17:14	9:14	9:37	

5. MIRACLES OF MAJESTY (4)

	Matthew	Mark	Luke	John
36. Expulsion of the merchants from the Temple	21:12	11:15	19:45	2:13
37. Liberation from the hands of the Nazarenes			4:28	
38. Transfiguration	17:1	9:2	9:28	
39. Fall of the enemies in Gethsemane				18:4

PROPHECIES OF JESUS:

1. HE KNOWS HIDDEN THOUGHTS

1. Intimate knowledge of the past life of Nathaniel	*Jn 1:43-50*
2. The present and past sins of the Samaritan woman	*Jn 4:17-25*
3. The whisperings of the scribes when he healed the paralytic	*Lk 5:22*
4. The judgments of the Pharisee on the sinful woman who anointed him	*Lk 7:36-50*
5. The ambitious discussion of the Apostles at the table	*Lk 9:46-48*
6. The censures of the scribes for breaking the Sabbath	*Lk 6:6-11*
7. The blasphemies of the Pharisees on dealings with demons	*Mt 12:25*
8. The betrayal of Judas	*Jn 13:27*
9.The incomprehension of the disciples about the leaven of the Pharisees	*Mt 16:8*
10. Saint John says that Jesus needed no one to bear witness of man because he knew what was in man	*Jn 2:25*
11. The disciples tell him: "now we know that you know all things, and need none to question you; by this we believe that you came from God."	*Jn 16:30*

2. HE KNOWS WHAT HAPPENS AT A DISTANCE

1. He sees the coin hidden in the mouth of the fish	*Mt 17:27*
2. He sees the donkey with a colt that the disciples would find	*Mt 21:2*
3. He sees Lazarus dead from a far away region	*Jn 11:11-15*

3. HE KNOWS WHAT WILL HAPPEN IN THE FUTURE

a) With respect to his own person

1. He would suffer and die in Jerusalem	*Lk 13:33*
2. He knows when… at the feast of Passover	*Mt 20:17-18*
3. Brought before the priests, the scribes, etc.	*Lk 22:66-71 & parallels*
4. Punished with death	*Mt 20:18*
5. Turned over to the gentiles	*Mt 20:19*
6. Spat upon, flogged and crucified	*Mt 20:19, 32*
7. Condemned to death on a cross	*Mt 20:19*
8. He would rise	*Mt 20:19 & parallels*

b) With respect to his disciples

1. The flight of the disciples	*Mt 26:31 & parallels*
2. The triple denial of Peter	*Mt 26:34 & parallels*
3. The betrayal of Judas	*Mt 26:21-25 & parallels*
4. The memory of Mary wherever the Gospel is preached	*Mt 26:6-13 & parallels*
5. Crucifixion and death of Saint Peter	*Jn 21:18-19*

c) About the Church

1. The coming of the Holy Spirit	*Jn 14:13ff, Lk 24:49, Acts 1:8*
2. The calling of the gentile nations	*Mt 8:10-12; 12:18; Lk 2:32*
3. The propagation of the Gospel	*Mk 13:10 & parallels*
4. The disciples will work miracles	*Lk 10:19, Mk 16:17*
5. Heresies, internal divisions (as we see in the parable of the weeds) will spring up in the Church due to false prophets.	*Mt 7:15-22; 13:36; 13:17-49; 16:18; 24:4*
6. The perpetual nature of the Church, due to the solid foundation and special help	*Mt 28:20*

d) With respect to the Jewish people

1. The fall of Jerusalem	*Lk 21:20-24 & parallels*
2. One generation will not pass	*Mt 24:34*
3. It would be besieged	*Lk 19:43; 21:20 & parallels*
4. The tribulations and pain that the Jewish people would suffer	*Mt 24:19-21*

5. With respect to the citizens: that they would be brought captive to other nations.	*Lk 21:24 & parallels*
6. With respect to the Temple: that it would be destroyed. All of this happened on a large scale in the year 70 AD. It is recorded by historians Tacitus, Suetonius and the Jewish historian Flavius Josephus. Still today the victory over the Jews can still be seen today in relief on the Arch of Triumph in Rome and on a Vespacian coin with the inscription: "Judea capta!" (Judea Conquered).	*Mt 24:2*
7. With respect to the city: your house will be left deserted.	*Lk 13:35*
8. Jerusalem trampled underfoot by the gentiles until the times of the gentiles are fulfilled.	*Lk 21:24*

THE PARABLES OF JESUS

	Matthew	Mark	Luke	John
1. Wind and Spirit		.		*3:8*
2. The serpent in the wilderness				*3:14*
3. The light of the world				*3:19*
4. The Friend and the Bridegroom				*3:29*
5. The flowing water				*7:38*
6. Doctor, heal yourself			*4:23*	
7. The wedding			*5:34*	
8. Doctor and sick person	*9:12*	*2:17*	*5:31*	
9. Unshrunk cloth on an old garment	*9:16*			
10. Old and new wineskins	*9:17*			
11. Old and new wine			*5:39*	
12. The sheep in the pit	*12:11*			
13 The beatitudes	*5:1*			
14. The salt of the earth	*5:13*	*9:50*	*14:34*	
15. The light and the world	*5:14*			
16. A city on a hill	*5:14*			
17. The lamp and the basket	*5:15*		*11:33*	
18. Delayed sacrifice	*5:23*			
19. The eye and the body	*6:22*			
20. The two masters	*6:24*			
21. Birds and Ravens	*6:26*		*12:24*	
22. Lilies of the field	*6:28*		*12:27*	
23. Solomon and the lilies	*6:29*		*12:27*	
24. The speck and the log	*7:3*		*6:41*	
25. Pearls and swine	*7:6*			
26. The son who asks	*7:9*			
27. The gate and the way	*7:13*		*13:24*	
28. Ravenous wolves	*7:15*			

29. Trees and fruit	*7:17*		
30. The wise builder	*7:24*		
31. The reed swayed by the wind	*11:7*		
32. Dancing and weeping	*11:16*		*7:32*
33. The two debtors			*7:41*
34. The sower	*13:1*	*4:1*	*8:4*
35. Salt and Light	*5:15*		
36. The seed			*8:11*
37. The weeds and the wheat	*13:24*		
38. The mustard seed	*13:31*	*4:31*	*13:18*
39. The leaven	*13:33*		
40. The pearl and the treasure	*13:44*		
41. The fishing net	*13:47*		
42. The trained scribe	*13:52*		
43. Sheep without a shepherd	*9:36*	*6:34*	
44. The harvest and the laborers	*9:37*		*10:2*
45. Sheep and wolves	*10:16*		
46. Serpents and doves	*10:16*		
47. Imperishable food			*6:27*
48. Impurity from within	*15:11*	*7:15*	
49. Blind leading the blind	*15:14*		*6:39*
50. Things that defile	*15:19*	*7:21*	
51. Children and dogs	*15:26*	*7:27*	
52. Signs	*16:2*	*8:12*	
53. The keys to the kingdom	*16:19*		
54. Faith, a small seed	*17:20*		
55. Jesus and the temple tax	*17:25*		
56. The lost sheep	*18:10*		
57. The debtor forgiven	*18:23*		
58. Where to lay the head	*8:20*		*9:58*
59. The hand to the plow			*9:62*
60. Lambs among wolves			*10:3*
61. The good Samaritan			*10:30*
62. The light of life			*8:12*
63. The slave and the son			*8:35*
64. The good shepherd			*10:1*
65. The insistent friend			*11:5*
66. The sieve of Satan			*22:31*
67. Disunion in kingdoms	*12:25*	*3:23*	*11:17*
68. Disunion in the house		*3:25*	
69. The strong man bound	*12:29*	*3:27*	*11:21*
70. Unmarked graves			*11:44*
71. The master is great	*10:24*		*6:40*
72. Not a hair will fall	*10:30*		*12:7*
73. The rich young man	*19:16*		*10:25*
74. Little flock			*12:32*
75. Master and thief	*24:43*		*12:39*
76. Master and servant	*24:45*		*12:37*
77. The barren fig tree			*13:6*

78. A great tree			*13:18*	
79. Leaven measured			*13:20*	
80. The closed door			*13:25*	
81. Hen and Chicks	*25:37*		*13:34*	
82. The first place			*14:7*	
83. True friendship				*15:14*
84. The great banquet			*14:15*	
85. The royal feast	*22:2*			
86. The king in war			*14:31*	
87. The man who builds a tower			*14:28*	
88. The lost sheep			*15:3*	
89. The lost coin			*15:8*	
90. The prodigal son			*15:11*	
91. The shrewd manager			*16:1*	
92. The rich man and Lazarus			*16:19*	
93. The mulberry tree in the sea			*17:6*	
94. The good and faithful servant			*17:7*	
95. Corpse and vultures	*24:28*		*17:37*	
96. The persistent widow			*18:1*	
97. The Pharisee and the publican				
98. Let the little children	*19:13*	*10:13*	*18:15*	
99. The camel and the needle	*19:24*	*10:25*	*18:25*	
100. Laborers in the vineyard	*20:1*			
101. Death and sleep				*11:11*
102. The chalice of suffering	*20:22*	*10:38*		*18:11*
103. The ten pounds			*19:11*	
104. The mountain in the sea	*21:21*	*11:23*		
105. The different sons	*21:28*			
106. The tenants in the vineyard	*21:33*	*12:1*		
107. The gnat and the camel	*23:24*			
108. Whitewashed tombs	*23:27*			
109. If the grain does not die				*12:24*
110. Lightning	*24:27*			
111. The lesson from the fig tree	*24:32*	*13:28*	*21:29*	
112. Like the great flood	*24:37*			
113. The foolish virgins	*25:1*			
114. The talents	*25:14*			
115. The sheep and goats	*25:32*			
116. The powerful			*22:26*	
117. In the form of a slave				*13:16*
118. The stricken shepherd	*26:31*	*14:27*		
119. The vine and the branches				*15:1*
120. Master and servant				*15:20*
121. A woman giving birth				*16:21*

APENDIX C:
PRACTICAL INSTRUCTIONS
FOR CONFESSION

1. BEFORE CONFESSION

Jesus, my Savior, give me the grace to make a good confession in order to gain forgiveness for my sins and to save my soul.

Most Holy Virgin, Mother of Jesus and my Mother, obtain for me from your Son Jesus the grace to know all my sins and to sincerely confess them.

Examination of Conscience

Ask yourself: How long has it been since the last time I went to confession? Did I do it well? Did I forget to mention any grave sins? Did I knowingly keep something back? Did I do the penance the confessor gave me?

Then try to remember all of the sins you have committed since your last good confession. If you have committed any grave sins, think of how many times you committed them. If you do not know their exact number, give at least an approximate number. If the previous time you did not make a good confession and you held back a serious sin because of embarrassment, this time tell the confessor that last time you confessed badly and then tell him the sin that you held back.

FIRST COMMANDMENT: Have I prayed my prayers in the morning and at night? Have I studied the catechism well? Have I been in anti-religious company?

SECOND COMMANDMENT: Have I sworn something false in the name of God? How many times? Have I said anything irreverent about God, the Virgin or the Saints? How many times?

THIRD COMMANDMENT: Have I missed Mass on a Sunday or a Holy Day of obligation, or have I arrived so late that I did not fulfill the precept? Have I worked on Sunday when it was not necessary?

FOURTH COMMANDMENT: Have I disobeyed my parents? Have I talked back? Have I made them angry? Have I lacked respect for a teacher, priest, or elder? Do I love my country and do I sacrifice myself for her?

FIFTH COMMANDMENT: Have I fought with my siblings or peers? Have I harbored hate or resentment for them? Have I been proud... envious?

SIXTH AND NINTH COMMANDMENTS: Have I consented to having bad thoughts or desires? How many times? Have I conversed about impure things? How many times? Have I looked at indecent things? How many times? Have I done bad things? How many times? Alone or with others?

SEVENTH AND TENTH COMMANDMENTS: Have I stolen anything? Have I accepted stolen things? Have I stolen money from my parents?

EIGHTH COMMANDMENT: Have I seriously gossiped? How many times? Have I lied? Have I seriously slandered anyone? How many times? Have I made rash judgments? How many times?

PRECEPTS OF THE CHURCH: Have I confessed and received communion at least once a year, in the season of Easter? Have I failed to fast, or have I eaten meat on a day of abstinence?

After the examination of conscience pray the Act of Contrition with your head bowed.

2. DURING CONFESSION

Begin your confession kneeling in the confessional and there the following will happen:

1. The receiving of the penitent. The priest will receive you with love and kindness. Then you will make the Sign of the Holy Cross, saying: "In the name of the Father, the Son and the Holy Spirit, Amen."

2. The invitation into confidence. The priest will do this and then you will say "Amen."

3. Reading of the Word of God.

4. Confession of your sins. Beginning by saying how long it has been since your last confession, you will then say all the sins that you remember and the priest will help you, if he deems it to be necessary, to make an integral confession. Then he will give you some advice.

5. Acceptance of the penance. The priest will give you penance and you will accept it saying "thank you Father" or something similar.

6. Prayer of the penitent. You will show your contrition by praying the Act of Contrition.

7. Formula of Absolution. In the name and with the power of Christ, the priest will give you absolution, which forgives your sins.

8. Thanksgiving. The priest will say: "Your sins are forgiven, you may go in peace," and you will answer: "Thanks be to God."

9. Dismissal of the penitent. The priest will say "The Lord has forgiven your sins. Go in peace."

(It is not necessary to remember all of this to go to confession. Go with confidence that the priest will help you to make a very good confession.)

3. AFTER THE CONFESSION

After the confession, before all else, give thanks to the Lord for the inestimable benefit of his pardon. Then you will immediately do the penance that the confessor assigned you, and you will renew your intention to flee from sin and from occasions of sin.

APENDIX D:
HOW TO PRAY THE ROSARY[508]

Pray five mysteries of the Rosary every day. Also carry a rosary with you.

How to pray the Rosary:

1) Make the Sign of the Cross.

"In the Name of the Father, and of the Son, and of the Holy Spirit. Amen.'

2) Pray the Apostle's Creed: "I believe in God, the Father the almighty…"

3) Pray 1 Our Father, 3 Hail Marys and 1 Glory Be, as shown in the diagram.

4) In the first mystery we remember… (Name the first mystery of the day.)

5) Pray 1 Our Father, 10 Hail Marys, and 1 Glory Be.

At the end of every mystery pray:

"Oh my Jesus, forgive us our sins. Save us from the fires of hell. Lead all souls to heaven, especially those most in need of Your Mercy" (as Our Lady asked at Fatima).

6) Continue praying in the same way for the 2nd, 3rd, 4th and 5th mysteries.

7) Then we consecrate ourselves to the Blessed Virgin by praying a Hail Holy Queen. (page 286)

---

[508] Cf. *Compendium of the Catechism of the Catholic Church.*

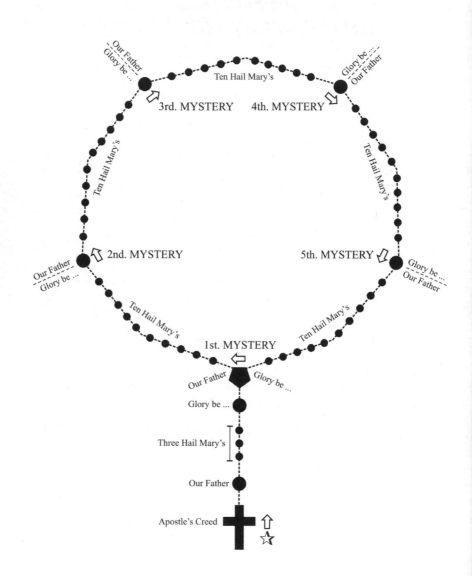

The Five Joyful Mysteries (Monday and Saturday)
1. The Annunciation
2. The Visitation
3. The Birth of our Lord
4. The Presentation of our Lord in the Temple
5. The Finding of the Child Jesus in the Temple

The Five Luminous Mysteries (Thursday)
1. The Baptism in the Jordan
2. The Wedding at Cana
3. The Proclamation of the Kingdom of God
4. The Transfiguration
5. The Institution of the Eucharist

The Five Sorrowful Mysteries (Tuesday and Friday)
1. The Agony in the Garden
2. The Scourging at the Pillar
3. The Crowning with Thorns
4. The Carrying of the Cross
5. The Crucifixion

The Five Glorious Mysteries (Wednesday and Sunday)
1. The Resurrection
2. The Ascension of our Lord
3. The Descent of the Holy Spirit
4. The Assumption of our Lady into heaven
5. The Coronation of the Blessed Virgin Mary

After the Rosary, you can pray the Litany of the Blessed Virgin:

Lord, have mercy,	*Lord, have mercy*
Christ have mercy,	*Christ, have mercy*
Lord have mercy,	*Lord, have mercy*
Christ hear us,	*Christ, hear us*
Christ graciously hear us,	*Christ graciously hear us*
God the Father of heaven,	*Have mercy on us.*
God the Son, Redeemer of the world,	*Have mercy on us.*

God the Holy Spirit,	*Have mercy on us.*
Holy Trinity, one God,	*Have mercy on us.*
Holy Mary,	*Pray for us.*
Holy Mother of God,	*Pray for us.*
Holy Virgin of virgins,	*Pray for us.*
Mother of Christ,	*Pray for us.*
Mother of divine grace,	*Pray for us.*
Mother most pure,	*Pray for us.*
Mother most chaste,	*Pray for us.*
Mother inviolate,	*Pray for us.*
Mother undefiled,	*Pray for us.*
Mother most amiable,	*Pray for us.*
Mother most admirable,	*Pray for us.*
Mother of good counsel,	*Pray for us.*
Mother of our Creator,	*Pray for us.*
Mother of our Savior,	*Pray for us.*
Virgin most prudent,	*Pray for us.*
Virgin most venerable,	*Pray for us.*
Virgin most renowned,	*Pray for us.*
Virgin most powerful,	*Pray for us.*
Virgin most merciful,	*Pray for us.*
Virgin most faithful,	*Pray for us.*
Mirror of justice,	*Pray for us.*
Seat of wisdom,	*Pray for us.*
Cause of our joy,	*Pray for us.*
Spiritual vessel,	*Pray for us.*
Vessel of honor,	*Pray for us.*
Singular vessel of devotion,	*Pray for us.*
Mystical rose,	*Pray for us.*
Tower of David,	*Pray for us.*
Tower of ivory,	*Pray for us.*
House of gold,	*Pray for us.*
Ark of the Covenant,	*Pray for us.*
Gate of heaven,	*Pray for us.*
Morning star,	*Pray for us.*
Health of the sick,	*Pray for us.*
Refuge of sinners,	*Pray for us.*
Comforter of the afflicted,	*Pray for us.*
Help of Christians,	*Pray for us.*

Queen of Angels,	*Pray for us.*
Queen of Patriarchs,	*Pray for us.*
Queen of Prophets,	*Pray for us.*
Queen of Apostles,	*Pray for us.*
Queen of Martyrs,	*Pray for us.*
Queen of Confessors,	*Pray for us.*
Queen of Virgins,	*Pray for us.*
Queen of all Saints,	*Pray for us.*
Queen conceived without original sin,	*Pray for us.*
Queen assumed into heaven,	*Pray for us.*
Queen of the most holy Rosary,	*Pray for us.*
Queen of peace,	*Pray for us.*

Lamb of God, Who takes away the sins
of the world: *Spare us, O Lord.*
Lamb of God, Who takes away the sins
of the world: *Graciously hear us, O Lord.*
Lamb of God, Who takes away the sins
of the world: *Have mercy on us.*

Pray for us, O Holy Mother of God:
That we may be made worthy of the promises of Christ.

Prayer

Grant, we beseech Thee, O Lord God, that we thy servants may enjoy perpetual health of mind and body, and by the glorious intercession of Blessed Mary, ever Virgin, may we be freed from present sorrow, and rejoice in eternal happiness. Through Christ our Lord. Amen.

APPENDIX E:
THE ANGELUS

The Angelus is prayed in the morning, at noon and in the evening.

V. The angel of the Lord declared unto Mary,
R. And she conceived by the Holy Spirit.

Hail Mary...

V. Behold the handmaid of the Lord,
R. Be it done unto me according to Thy word.
Hail Mary...

V. And the Word was made flesh,
R. And dwelt among us.
Hail Mary...

V. Pray for us, O Holy Mother of God,
R. *That we may be made worthy of the promises of Christ.*

Let us pray:

Pour forth, we beseech thee, O Lord, Thy grace into our hearts; that we, to whom the Incarnation of Christ, Thy Son, was made known by the message of an angel, may by his Passion and Cross be brought to the glory of his Resurrection. Through the same Christ, our Lord. Amen.

Three Glory Be's are prayed in honor of the Most Holy Trinity:

Glory be to the Father, and to the Son, and to the Holy Spirit. As it was in the beginning, is now, and ever shall be world without end. Amen.

Likewise, a *requiem* is prayed for the holy souls in purgatory:

V. May the souls of the faithful departed,
R. Through the mercy of God rest in peace.

During the Easter Season, instead of the **Angelus** we pray the **Regina Caeli** while standing.

V. Queen of Heaven, rejoice, alleluia.
R. The Son whom you merited to bear, alleluia,

V. Has risen as he said, alleluia.
R. Pray for us to God, alleluia.

V. Rejoice and be glad, O Virgin Mary, alleluia!
R. For the Lord has truly risen, alleluia.

Let us pray:

O God, who through the resurrection of your Son, our Lord Jesus Christ, did vouchsafe to give joy to the world; grant, we beseech you, that through his Mother, the Virgin Mary, we may obtain the joys of everlasting life. Through the same Christ our Lord. Amen.

IVE Press

New York – 2008